BEST Y.

MW01108293

OF

THE EARLY LIFE AND TIMES

OF

SMOKY MOUNTAIN PEOPLE

An Anecdotal Encyclopedia
of
Smoky Mountain Lore

Mountain Wit, Wisdom, and Hogwash....
Absolutely the most comprehensive coverage
ever undertaken, including medical remedies
that saved our lives and hundreds of dollars!

By

Bonnie Trentham Myers

C O M M E N T S:

A Preacher's Wife Wrote That?....

My Favorite ....

Best Yet...

Warm and Witty...........................

Couldn't Put It Down...................

Reading That's Fun......................

Chocked Full of Amusing

Anecdotes.............................

Down To Earth, Wit and Wisdom

Legendary and Laughful..............

Great Human Interest Stories.......

›

DEDICATION

To my three Children:

Lynda Myers Boyer,

Glenn Leland Myers,

and Donald Trent Myers (1942 -1998),

twin grandsons Aaron and Eric Myers,

Lillian Lancaster and John Mason

for your patience and computer skills, without which

this book would never have been written!

SMOKY MOUNTAIN LORE

LATCH STRINGS AND LEATHER BRITCHES
BED BOARDS AND BIRTHING STOOLS
LEECHES AND LIGHTENING BUGS
TOMATO BEER AND TUMBLE BUGS

CRAPPED CABBAGE AND CAT HOLE
LETTER EDGED IN BLACK
SUGAR TIT AND SPIT BALLS
FEED SACKS AND FOOT WARMERS

COBWEBS AND COW TEA
SAUCERED AND BLOWED
BALL HOOTIN' AND BUCKEYES
GOOBER FARM AND GRITTED BREAD

RAMPS AND RED EYE GRAVY
DOG TROT AND DOWSING
PACK SADDLES AND PANTHERS
TROUSER WORMS AND TOOTH PULLERS

TALE HOLDERS AND TATER HOLES
ASAFETIDA AND APPLE PICKING MULES
CROWN OF FEATHERS AND CHARMING WARTS
HOG KILLING AND HORSE THIEVES

BODY SNATCHERS AND BOARS
CAMP MEETINGS AND CORN SHUCKING
GUM STAND AND GOOSE GAP
J-HOOKS AND JOURNEY PROUD

FOXFIRE AND FITIFIED SPRINGS
BEARS AND BEAR MEAT AUCTIONS
SNAKES AND SALT LICKS
STRANGERS ND SUPERSTITIONS

PROLOGUE

During the past 60 years or so I have collected more than a bushel basket full of notes and scraps of paper- sometimes containing just one word or a sentence reminding me of something funny, helpful, or tragic. My children have urged me to write down my old medical remedies as well as their father's sayings, which amused and mystified us.

A few years ago I was traveling by plane from Montreal to Boston. Because a tornado had struck in Boston, I was forced to continue to Atlanta. On that flight I sat by a man who said his name was Carl Sagan. He gave no indication of who he was or how well-known. He asked me many questions and soon had me talking like a radio. I told him how I was born in what is now the Great Smoky Mountains National Park, and I began to recount some incidents I remembered. He appeared to be fascinated by my stories and asked if I had ever heard of Alex Haley. I told him I had enjoyed seeing his miniseries, Roots. Carl Sagan told me that Alex Haley was writing a book about our area, and he believed Alex had sold movie rights to the book. He indicated Mr. Haley would be very interested in my stories. Mr. Sagan took my name, address, and phone number. Perhaps two months later Alex Haley left a message on my answering machine saying he would keep calling until he found me home.

Soon afterwards, Alex Haley and his wife, Myron, flew from California to meet me to hear some of my stories for the book he was writing on the Smoky Mountain people. I enjoyed meeting them very much and happily prepared and sent him a one- hour tape filled with mountain lore. He and Myron played the tape the night he received it. He called me the following day and said, "Bonnie, you sure can run your mouth!" I had the opportunity to talk with him and his wife a few more times before his untimely death. I do not know if he wrote those stories or if he finished his project. However, his comment that the death of an old person is like the burning of a library remained with me.

Not until someone phoned me from The University of Tennessee asking for an interview regarding my Smoky Mountain tales did I begin sifting through my notes in earnest. The caller reminded me that with the passing of my generation, the stories we have to tell will regrettably be lost forever.

I certainly would not want to claim that writing this book is to take up where Alex Haley left off. But I hope that in telling some of the stories Alex would have told, I am helping to further the project he began.

BEST YET STORIES

OF

SMOKEY MOUNTAIN

PEOPLE

Pull up a chair while I tell you my version of the early life and times of Smoky Mountain people. I will provide stories and bits of philosophy I have picked up along the way. If you are looking for a gen-u-in cornfed hillbilly, look no farther. I was born December 1, 1921 in the Fighting Creek Gap area two miles south of Gatlinburg, Tennessee. This area is now part of The Great Smoky Mountain National Park. My background certainly qualifies me as an old-timer, who can authentically review a people whose spirit lives on.

When we reach way back in time to examine life in these mountains, we find that it was rough and hard. The people were poor but content. They lived in an area that was extremely isolated from big city ways. Families relied upon each other. The most read book - maybe the only book in some homes - was the old family Bible. The preacher's mule at the back porch was generally a welcomed sight.

The hard day's work was done with primitive tools and aching muscles. Unquestioning faith made them strong. That strength no doubt kept them alive. At night the family gathered around the fireside and sang the old hymns by the light of the kerosene lamp. What our vocal technique lacked in quality, we made up for with volume and enthusiasm. I cherish the memories of my father singing bass to the old hymns: "When the Roll Is Called Up Yonder," "Amazing Grace," "There's Power in The Blood," and "The Old Time Religion."

I should be telling you how good it was in the "Good Ole Days," but by my calculations it was not always so good. Truth is, just about the only good thing about it was that we were young. We had no electricity, no telephones, and no central heat or air. That was before the days of television, frozen foods, ball point pens, dishwashers, clothes washers, dryers, and computers. In fact it was before almost everything we enjoy today. But we had no utility bills! We never saw a man wearing a pony tail or ear ring. Our "grass" was mowed. "Pot" was something we cooked in, and "aids" were people who worked in the principal's office. One nickel mailed a first-class letter and bought two postal cards.

I was six or seven years old before I ever saw a radio. I was visiting a cousin near Knoxville. Her family had a Delco power-generating system. On their kitchen table sat a little shiny black box with knobs and a dial. My cousin looked in the newspaper to see what channel to dial for an interesting program. Instead of listening to the program, I tried to figure out how that newspaper "KNEW" what was in that little black box. Then my cousin flipped a button on the wall and the whole room lit up. For the life of me I could not figure that out. She started playing with the knobs and dial. The sound began to become intelligible. I could actually hear some voices and music accompanying the grating static that filled the room. Later, members of the family took a bun and put a wiener in it and called it a hotdog. It sure did not look like any dog I had ever seen.

Today's generation can hardly conceive of a world so different and so disadvantaged. Yet differences and disadvantages do not always correlate with strangeness or peculiarity. Magazine and newspaper writers have come here seeking the very worst among us, trying to portray us as a strange and peculiar people. They have exploited an image of Appalachia to turn the simple life of the mountaineer into grist for the literary mill. I've searched from "holler to hill" and cannot find a single fellow named "Jed" or "Snuffy Smith."

A few writers have capitalized on the very poor and uneducated who met their preconceived ideas of what the people were like. They used the few to unjustly stereotype the entire region. We Southerners resent being stereotyped by Peyton Place, Tobacco Road, The Beverly Hillbillies, and Christy. Honest and fair treatment of a culture requires that we report the unpleasant things we would like to forget as well as the pleasant and fun things that should not be lost.

It would do those writers well to spend some more time among the Southern Appalachian people to learn that the old stereotypes are myths mixed with a tiny bit of truth. With our silence our grandchildren and great-grandchildren will not know their ancestors as the very strong people who lived worthy lives of substance and meaning.

Southern Appalachia, like any region in the United States, has its cultural mix. Some may erroneously conclude that every cabin has bed bugs and that children have no books in the homes. A few years ago a nice "flatlander" family loaded their car with books and knocked on the door of a friend of mine. They introduced themselves saying, "We understand the children of this area do not have books in the home." After a tour of the home, they quickly excused themselves saying, "You have more books than we do!"

Last week I heard a "comer" mention that the Beverly Hillbillies struck oil here in Tennessee before moving to California as millionaires. This idea makes me wonder if other people do not realize that particular television series was nothing but highly exaggerated fiction and that finding oil in Tennessee is highly unlikely. Tourists continue to ask to see some "natives," assuming that all of us are "big and barefooted." It is interesting, too, that so many flatlanders who have moved here say they feel safer here than anywhere on earth.

Some imply that we are lazy and shiftless. If the mountain people were too lazy to grow their food, how were they able to feed their families? The very few early stores were stocked only with items needed to help the people be self-sufficient such as salt, sugar, coffee, coal-oil, and horse shoes etc.

We have lived close to nature, far from the complexities of the big cities. The simplicity has allowed us to live a free and peaceful life. The irony is that this peaceful life is coveted by millions of tourists who come to the Smokies every year. When they arrive, they find that peace disturbed by the other nine- to fifteen- million people who visit us each year.

I have traveled in Canada, Mexico, Hawaii, and approximately forty other U.S. states and have found that Smoky Mountain people are just like people elsewhere: honest, kindhearted, loyal to friends, and quick to help someone in distress. A smile or a friendly hello to a stranger is expected. Recently a small boy was critically injured by an automobile. He was close to death for two days. When he began to improve, his mother put an article in our local paper saying that her family had moved here from a northern state. She said few there would have even noticed their tragedy. She was overwhelmed with how local people had responded in so many ways.

Like any other region, we have our share of eccentrics, but we also boast of renowned artists, influential writers, esteemed professors, and other nationally recognized professionals. Like other people we enjoy doing dumb things just for laughs. Like the Cajun cook on TV who comically capitalizes on his local Louisiana culture, I tell people I am a hillbilly so I can act corny and play with the language. I hope you will appreciate my picturesque manner of speaking. I sometimes exaggerate a little, as it is difficult to talk without using expressions which are unconsciously part of our colorful heritage. In fact to do so would be going back on my raisin'. This is in no way intended as an intellectual or historical discourse. It is simply an "Old-Timer" telling it like it "wuz!"

I've given myself permission to tell you who I am. I will take you back to many corners of my past-- looking through misty windows to see the lives of early Smoky Mountain people. This is an untidy sprawl of remembered events and a lifetime collection of interesting tidbits. The medical remedies served two valuable purposes: (1) they were instrumental in saving our lives, and (2) their use probably saved us hundreds of dollars.

I start with a warning that while I'm running off at the mouth, my train of thought sometimes gets derailed. Some family members may not appreciate some of the "bare" facts, but I'm betting my great-great grandchildren will appreciate knowing what life was really like for this old gal.

Because of the diverse nature of the information, I have arranged it in encyclopedia format--home remedies, family stories, local lore, and information about how we lived our lives are mixed together in one compendium.

It's fun thinking back years ago,
I should like being back there, although
I don't mind admitting
I don't miss sitting
Out back when it's fifteen below!
                    --Author unknown

A

ALARM CLOCKS - Long before alarm clocks were available, the old rooster crowed loud and clear at the crack of dawn. Better still, my father could decide on any hour to awaken, and his internal alarm clock never failed.

ALCOHOL - alcohol was kept on hand for medicinal purposes. It was often said we church folks did not drink because we wanted to know if we were having a good time. We never had alcoholics in the mountains, just drunks. If a man drank at all, he drank too much. We seemed to have only "teetotalers or drunks." Since alcohol was considered evil, those who drank sometimes made up excuses. They might say to one another, "I'll hold a gun on you so you can drink some, if'n you'll do the same fer me." (2) While weaving his way home, one of our "drunks," fell into a newly dug grave. When he awakened the next morning and saw he was in a cemetery, he yelled, "Hallelujah! It's resurrection morning and I'm the first one up!" (3) I overheard a drunk describing why he quit. He said that snakes would hang down from the ceiling with their heads right in his face. He was hallucinating, of course. (4) Eat cabbage leaves before plans to drink alcohol. (5) Eat crackers, pretzels, or bread with alcoholic drinks.

ALLERGIES - Eat one teaspoon of local honey daily beginning six weeks before spring flowers or ragweed season.

ALMANAC- Every family purchased a farmer's almanac each year to determine when to plant various types of plants and to learn basic household hints. One important part of the almanac was the section telling the signs of the moon. I do not know why we could not look at the sky to determine if the moon was in the knees or heart, but for some reason the people who wrote the almanac were the only people who knew that information.

ALUM CAVE - A mountain-sized rock, located in The Great Smoky Mountains National Park. Alum Cave was known for the alum and saltpeter gathered in and around it. The alum was used for tanning tan leather and medicinal purposes. The saltpeter was mixed with ashes from chestnut wood to make gun powder for muzzle-loading guns. It was also used for laxatives and to set dye coloring.

When we were youngsters in the mountains, it was a treat to climb the very steep trail to this huge overhanging rock and to realize how important it had been to earlier settlers. The chance that we might meet head-on with a bear, panther, or a rattlesnake was always foremost in our minds.

AMPLIFIERS - Homemade: As naughty or nosey children we held one end of an opened empty metal can against a door to amplify sounds or voices in the next room. Perhaps the following couple could have tried the metal can. An old woman was looking through the key hole watching a couple in the next room trying to close their overstuffed suitcase. Her husband became suspicious that she was watching something more intimate. He overheard the couple next door say, "Let's both get on top." He shoved his wife aside and said, "This I've got to see." We were somewhat more discreet than they.

ANATOMY - A young mountain boy's essay on anatomy. "Your head is kind of round and hard and your brains are in it. Your hair is on it. Your face is the front of your head where you eat and make faces. Your neck is what keeps your head out of your collar. Your shoulders are sort of shelves where you hook your suspenders. Your stomach is something that if you don't eat often enough, it hurts, and spinach don't help none. Your spine is a long bone in your back that keeps you from folding up. Your back is always behind you no matter how quick you turn around. Your arms you got to have to pitch with, and so you can reach for the butter. Your fingers stick out of your hands so you can throw a curve and add up arithmetic. Your legs is what if you have not got two of you cannot get to first base. Neither can your sister. Your feet are what you run on. Your toes are what always get stubbed. And that's all there is of you except what is inside and I never saw it."

ANEMIA - Remedies: 1) Drink ginseng tea. 2) Eat raw spinach.

ANGER - Mountain wisdom: Look to The Earth to Release Anger. Walk barefoot on the ground as often as possible. Listen to the sounds of rushing waters, singing birds, or wind rustling through the leaves.

Once I worked for a company that paid large sales commissions. The company managers allowed sales people to undercut and steal clients from one another. My first day on the job an older man said, "You will sometimes get so angry on this job you will want to kill!" Since I had never worked in that atmosphere before, I thought that was impossible. Several months later I was ready to explode because another salesman took a customer whose transaction I was ready to close. Another salesman saw my emotional state and said, "Come with me. I guarantee to help you recover from this anger within 30 minutes!"

Naturally I did not believe one word of it. He took me outside and instructed me to "Look to The Earth" as he called it. We looked at the freshly mowed lawn, and we hunted for a four-leaf clover. We did anything to keep me "looking to the earth." On and on we walked. I discovered some very dainty flowers I had never seen before. Then I found a four-leaf clover. Suddenly he stopped. Looking me in the eye, he asked "Where is your anger?" I was amazed and dumbfounded. I had totally released all that anger!

All the years that Ray T. Myers, my late husband, and I made a garden, he insisted every day that we walk to our garden and look it over. This visit he called "managing the garden." He has been gone since 1976. Every day, rain or shine, I continue to "manage my garden."

I've heard that we should talk to our plants, for it will make them grow.

But who's been talking to my weeds, Is what I'd like to know?

ANIMALS - Our animals are not generally given credit for knowing when storms are coming. When our old Tom cat turned his tail to the fire we knew to expect cold weather, usually snow. Horses determine who leads. Chickens have a pecking order. Dogs decide who rules a given territory by urinating on the corners. Birds stake out a territory of about an acre and fight off intruders. Wild animals are believed to dislike fire, so that hunters always built a campfire for protection while they slept. Wild animals such as bobcats or panthers were known to crawl over the roof of the early homes at night.

ANKLE SPRAIN'S - Dip a brown paper bag in apple cider vinegar and wrap around the ankle. Use an ice pack for the first 24 hours. Use heat afterwards.

ANT EATERS - Anteaters are better known by mountain folk as "doodlebugs." Finding their funnel-shaped homes in the ground, we sang over and over "Doodlebugs, doodlebug, come get a grain of corn." Soon we would see him coming out of his home.

ANT LOVING CRICKETS - These crickets live in ant nests and feed upon secretions from the ants.

ANTS -To deter - Cucumber peels. (2) Ants will not cross a chalk line. Rub chalk on the threshold of the door. I tried it, and it works. Ants go crazy, run in circles trying to avoid it. (3) To rid- Place red or black pepper, ground cloves, lemon juice or white vinegar in their path. (4) Mix equal parts powdered sugar and borax with water to make a paste. When ants eat this, they die. When ants eat their fallen comrades, they also die. Eventually the whole colony is killed. (5) Traps- Make a paste from one-third cup molasses, six tablespoons sugar, six tablespoons dry yeast. Put on cardboard. (6) In the early days most foods were canned at home. Sugar was purchased in fifty pound sacks. My Mother and Grandmother Ogle had a very interesting experience with ants. Preparing to do some canning, they discovered hundreds of ants had invaded their sack of sugar. In those days sugar was too precious to discard. Since it was lunch time, Mother said she would put a kettle of water on to boil while they ate lunch. Afterwards they planned to pick the ants out of the sugar one by one and drop them into the boiling water. When lunch was over, and the water was boiling, not ONE ant could be found. Your guess is as good as mine. Did those ants understand the threat? Did they have ESP?

APHIDS - Crush 8 or 10 tomato leaves, mix with water, and apply to the ground. End of Aphids.

APPENDICITIS - Today, see a doctor immediately. Mountain people applied caster oil packs to the abdomen without heat for six hours.

APPLE-PICKING MULES - Old Beck, our most spirited mule, would pull down limbs from the apple tree with his teeth! Somehow he managed to kick with his back feet to shake the apples off. Some gumption! Old Jack, the other mule, was not so inclined, but he shared the loot. It was great fun to watch.

ARROWHEADS - Many arrowheads have been found throughout this region. We found many on our farm located in what is now The Great Smoky Mountain National Park. It is believed there were Indian and white encounters in almost every path, every farm, and nearly every home during the very early days.

ART - Deep cave art, unlike anything else in America, has been found in seven caves in this area. Carvings are believed to have been made by native Americans more than 450 years ago. No one has yet been able to decipher them.

ARTERIES - HARDENING - Fill a quart jar half full of white raisins. Add one pint of any kind of gin. Shake two or three times daily for three days. Take one teaspoon before breakfast. Do not use if you are on medication. Many claim great results. (2) Eat a raw potato three times daily. (3) Take one teaspoon apple cider vinegar in one cup hot water, morning, noon, and night.

ARTHRITIS - Soak coarse brown paper in apple cider vinegar and wrap affected joints for 45 minutes three times a day for three weeks. (2) Drink tea made of alfalfa leaves or seeds. (3) Spend 30 minutes each day pulling on an imaginary rope in all directions. (4) Carry a buckeye. (5) Edgar Cayce said to rub on peanut oil for a cure.

ASAFETIDA - Also known as "Devils Dung." While I never saw it or smelled it, mountain folk in the very early days wore it around their necks. Its odor or presence was supposed to ward off illness. Perhaps just keeping others at a distance was its chief benefit. (2) Our family enjoyed telling the story of the old farmer who wore asafetida during a trip to the grocery. Rain fell on him; then the sun came out. This change apparently activated his asafetida. His children ran to meet him and to receive the candy he had promised to bring them. The children were so repelled by the odor, they ran back to their mother, holding their noses. One of the children exclaimed, "Ma, Paw's dead and don't know it!"

ASTHMA - Mountain folk cut a sourwood tree branch of a length equal to the height of an asthmatic child. This branch was stored in the attic. When the child's height exceeded the length of the stick, his asthma was supposed to be cured. (2) Another common treatment was to stand the child beside a fruit-bearing tree and measure his height. At this spot a hole was bored into the tree. A lock of the child's hair was placed in the hole which was then plugged. The patient was supposed to have only one more bad attack before being cured. Two members of my family received this latter treatment. My Sister Lillie Watson's hair was put into a chestnut tree. Grandmother Ida Myers followed this procedure with my son Don when he was at her home on the old Mack Myers home-place in Wears Valley. She cut his hair and placed it in a cherry tree. Following this outlandish procedure, Don had one really bad attack. Afterwards he had no more asthma attacks. He suffered from allergies all his life. I've often wondered if their "cure" was simply the power of suggestion. (3) Take one teaspoon corn oil. (4) Chew honeycomb every day. (5) Eat a raw potato daily. 6) Drink buttermilk daily. (7) Keep a Chihuahua dog in the house. (8) Put powdered ginseng leaves in a pan. Place a hot coal on top of the ginseng. Inhale the smoke. (9) Breathe the smoke of mullein leaves.

ATHLETE'S FOOT - Tie a wool string around the affected toe. (2) A more recent remedy for widespread athletes' foot is to mix sugar with Betadine and bind it on the affected area overnight. Repeat if necessary. This remedy is said to work well.

AUCTIONS - After the Civil War, residents in Cades Cove agreed that land prices should remain fixed. When the extensive holdings of a Mr. Fonte were to be auctioned off, the community organized against the auction. They refused to bid against one another. As a result, 160 acres went to Dan B. Lawson for just $10.00. Another 80 acres sold for $16.00.

AUTOMOBILES - Also known as "Tin Lizzies" and "Skunk buggies." Henry Ford unveiled this "car for the millions" for $850 in 1908. In view of today's high-tech cars it is very difficult to describe my Father's first car, a Model T Ford, bought during the 1920's. He had no choice of colors, only black. The throttle or gas lever was on the right under the steering wheel. The driver turned on the ignition and gave it a bit of gas by pushing the throttle forward. He ran to the front of the car to insert a hand crank just under the radiator. He then cranked with all his might. If it coughed, the driver ran back and gave it more gas. It had a clutch and a brake pedal on the floorboard, but it had no gas pedal. Sometimes when a car would not start, drivers jacked up the rear wheels to start it. I have no idea why they did this unless it was to send gasoline to the motor.

Everyone carried a repair kit which included pliers, hay-bailing wire, a jack, air pump, patches, and glue. Flat tires were repaired on the spot. Tires had rubber inner tubes which were scratched to roughen the surface around the hole. Glue was placed on the tube and then the patch was applied. It was necessary to wait about twenty minutes for the patch to dry. The tube was then put back in the tire before it was filled with air and replaced on the axle.

I recall riding from Jefferson City to Gatlinburg one Sunday night when we had six flat tires. It grew dark and we had no flashlight. One of the boys wore a white shirt, so he stood in front of the car to reflect light back to the rear so the rear tire could be repaired. A real nightmare!

When riding down a hill, drivers often turned off the ignition and coasted to save gasoline. This practice was later outlawed. If gasoline was so low that one could not go up a steep grade, drivers turned the car around and backed it up the hill to keep going.

Reactions to the sight of the first cars were very interesting. Jacob S. Dunn was said to be riding in the first car ever to enter the Gatlinburg entrance into what is now The Great Smoky Mountain National Park. My half-brother, Wesley, went out into the road and smelled the tracks of that first car.

Some people in Wears Valley who had never seen or heard a car actually became hysterical when the first car lights came into their valley late one night. They said they thought the end of time had come.

B _____

BABIES - Light years before ultrasound (and ultrasound expense) mountain folk had interesting methods of determining the sex of an unborn baby. An individual would slip a ring on a 20-inch string. Holding both ends of the string, he or she would allow it to swing over the expectant mother's abdomen. If the ring swung in a straight line, it was a boy. If it swung in a circle, it was a girl. (Note the symbol to determine if it was a boy or girl.) (2) Another method was to drop some of the expectant mother's urine from the first urine specimen in the morning into some Drano. If it turned brown or golden, it was a girl. If it turned green, it was a boy.

During early days the new mother was kept perfectly quiet in bed for at least ten days after the birth of a baby. This practice was supposed to allow the organs to "knit back." I was a victim of that treatment with my first baby. On the tenth day, I was so weak I had to be turned over in bed. With the other two babies I was up walking very shortly with no such problem.

For whatever reason, the first command when a baby was to be born was to "boil some water!" Until forceps became available there were no utensils to sterilize. The midwife could, of course, use warm water to wash her hands and to have warm bath water in which to bathe the new baby.

BABY FOOD - Long before baby-foods were available here, and before the baby cut any teeth, mothers practiced a custom we find quite disgusting to feed babies. The mother chewed the food and transferred it to the infant's mouth. If the infant was extremely hungry, the mother passed her index finger back and forth across her mouth to show the crying infant that she was chewing as fast as possible. Oddly enough that gesture seemed to pacify the baby. I am thankful baby foods became available in the stores before I needed them.

BABY POWDER - A good substitute for baby powder is cornstarch.

BABY SITTERS - Long before this term was coined, mountain women who had to go outside found a way to keep their babies out of trouble. When leaving the little one alone in the house with no way to confine them, mothers sometimes raised the bed leg and set it on the baby's dress tail. This helps to account for the custom that baby boys back then wore dresses for several months.

BACON - According to our hog-killing superstitions, if your bacon curled while frying, the hog was killed at the wrong time of the moon.

BALDNESS - Many remedies were applied to the scalp to cure baldness. Some of them follow: Mix one teaspoon rubbing alcohol and one teaspoon Vaseline. Apply to scalp twice per week. Leave on overnight. (2) Mix two tablespoons vodka and one-half teaspoon cayenne pepper. Rub on the scalp. (3) Rub tea made of peach leaves onto the scalp. (4) Break sections of grape vine, set in a glass, and let the juice drain out. Massage into scalp for 30 days. (5) Mix caster oil with enough alcohol to dilute. Rub on the scalp. (6) Add five drops of iodine to one pint water and two teaspoons of baking soda. Massage well three times per day for three weeks. Wash with mild soap. (7) Add six drops of iodine and one teaspoon of honey to one pint of apple cider vinegar. Apply every day for fourteen days. Use mild soap. (8) Massage aloe twice per day.

BALDS - The treeless areas atop these old mountains we call balds have long baffled old timers. Trees grow on other mountain tops, and there is no tree line. Botanists have their own theories. Old-timers wondered if the Indians kept them cleared or had some unexplained natural circumstance created them? If the Indians kept them cleared, would they not have grown back long ago? Cherokee Indians in the area believed these balds were cleared after a great monster with spreading wings and sharp claws hid among the trees and swept down to destroy their villages. This belief does not explain why the trees never grew back.

BALL HOOTIN' - HILLSIDE LOGGING - J-HOOKS & J-HOLES. When a single horse pulled a log down a mountain side, it was called "Ball Hootin." J-Hooks were used to fasten the horse to the log. When the log began moving downhill too fast for the horse, it jumped aside and the open link, known as the J-Hook, easily slipped off. The log could then roll by while the horse jumped safely into a specially prepared opening, called a J-Hole. I do not know how the horse learned to do this. Perhaps when the log overtook him and hit his heels, he learned quickly.

On today's narrow country roads, where it is impossible for two vehicles to pass, clearings also called J-holes are created. These clearings are made large enough for one vehicle to pull aside allowing the other to pass.

BALLS - The nearest thing to a basketball or kickball we mountain children had in very early days was a hog's bladder, cleaned, blown up, and dried. Also, when this ball was blown to full capacity and was put in the fire the resulting explosion sounded like a shotgun blast.

BAPTIST PALLETS - The name given a bed roll, used on the floor when there are too many guests and not enough beds. These pallets were necessary in many early homes.

BATHING - A local television personality recently asked me to do some filming on the subject of death and bereavement among mountain people.

When we were introduced, he looked me straight in the eye and asked, "Did your mother bathe?" I was so shocked that I thought I must have misunderstood the question. In total amazement, I asked him to repeat the question. I replied jokingly, "Of course. She took a bath every Saturday night in that number 2 wash tub!"

The Saturday night bath was a standing joke at our house. We bathed regularly, not only on Saturday night, but whenever the need arose.

To even hint that my mother might not have bathed was really a shock to me. As far as I knew, everyone in every home bathed.

We based our Saturday night bath joke on an incident in which one of the mountain girls went to work as a housekeeper for a family in the city. She wrote a letter home describing the beautiful home she was now living in and the huge bath tub. She said that she could hardly wait until Saturday night so she could take a bath.

BATTLING STICK - One of the tools, we used for our Monday wash-day was a battling stick. This four-foot long paddle was used to keep clothes moving in the boiling wash pot or to hold a soiled garment when it was placed on a rock in the creek. Beating clothing with the paddle removed some of the dirt.

BEARS- Bears were often topics for tall tales and friendly advice. I am not aware of bears ever coming on our property when we lived in what is now the park. We had to drive toward Clingman's Dome or Newfound Gap to see one. (1) Catching a bear- Mountain folks mixed a quart of honey with a quart of moonshine (whiskey). After the bear drank this mixture, he quickly went to sleep. Then one could easily chain him, shoot him, or hit him in the head with a sledge hammer. (2) Selling bear meat- When the very early settlers sold bear meat they had to leave the left front paw attached to prove it was bear meat. I have tasted bear meat, but can hardly recommend it. (3) Protections from bears- Since it is virtually impossible to outrun a bear, mountain people filled a tin can with rocks to rattle very loudly. A loud noise will usually scare a bear away. I heard only one man who claimed to have outrun a bear. He swore that he zigzagged every few feet so that by turning often the bear couldn't catch him. Despite protests from others that this simply would not prevent a bear from catching him, he explained why it worked was because he said he was the only one traveling on dry ground! We were told to make no aggressive move toward a bear. We were also told to lie down and pretend to be dead. It was believed a bear would leave us be. However, I feel that if I had experienced such a confrontation, I would not have to pretend to be dead. I recently heard on TV that a woman indeed pretended to be dead, and the bear walked away. (It is commonly believed that neither bears nor panthers will eat anything already dead.) If you shoot a bear and only wound him, he will chase you. If two people are together, there is no way to outrun the bear. Your only alternative is to outrun the other guy.

(4) Protecting bears- Some 600-700 bears live in the 800 square miles of The Great Smoky Mountain National Park. Thoughtless tourists who feed them are causing great problems for us natives, and they are doing the bears a great disservice. Once bears get people-food they come back for more. Officials use darts and food traps to catch the most troublesome bears. As of this writing, it is legal to kill a bear in downtown Gatlinburg, since so many are causing real problems. Some home owners are concerned about the dangers of gunshots. Bears sometimes have to be euthanized if they refuse to stay in the wild. "Honey Bear 75" was one better-known nuisance bear. After eating people-food, he no longer feared people. After he was stamped with the number "75" inside his lip, he was taken to distant wildlife refuges ten times. Each time he returned, crossing highways, rivers, and mountains to get back to Cades Cove. It was estimated he traveled more than 1500 miles to return home.

(5) Legal problems- Our good friend and distant cousin, Lucinda Oakley Ogle, of Gatlinburg, recently had a legal problem regarding a bear that hounded her for months. While visiting with Lucinda I saw the bars on her windows and doors. I heard her harrowing stories of how the bear came seeking food. Lucinda never knew if he might be able to break in. After pleading for help for several months, a man came and shot the bear for her. If he shot it on her property, it went a few yards onto the park boundary before it died. I do not recall the huge amount of the fine and/or perhaps a prison term that this crime entailed. But the people of this area were up in arms that her life had been in danger every day for months, and then such a penalty was involved. It was a tremendous relief to many of us when the matter was finally resolved in her favor.

(6) Bears as companions Once my family had spread our picnic lunch at one of the overlook sites near New Found Gap, when a bear came to join us. We gladly moved aside and let him eat our food. He put his foot in a glass jar of pickles, beat it on the ground until he broke the jar, then ate the pickles. I have often wondered how he knew to break the jar. Another time during our Trentham family reunion a bear insisted on joining some one hundred or more of us for lunch. Since the bear was not exactly welcome, the men gathered clubs and stood guard while the women and children ate. A newspaper reporter happened to be in attendance. A picture of the bear, my sister, and I appeared in the paper along with the title, "Look who came to dinner." I remarked that it may have been one of the relatives.

BEAR MEAT AUCTION - Mountain men worked out their own ingenious system when several men hunted bears together. If only one man shot and killed a bear, he did not take all the meat. The hide which made a great rug was auctioned off, and the proceeds were divided equally among the men. The meat was then cut into the number of pieces equal to the number of hunters. One man hid behind a tree where he could not see which portion the auctioneer was touching. The man who was hiding called out the name of another hunter. This hunter received that piece of meat. This system insured that the meat would be divided fairly.

BEAR TALE - Two men killed a bear in the hills of south Blount County. The bear was so heavy they could not carry him to their truck. The hunters went home, got a mule and sled, and returned to the site. Approximately 500 yards before reaching the bear, the mule froze, started shaking with fear, and refused to take another step. One of the hunters pulled off his shirt and tied it over the mule's head to blindfold him. The hunters then led the mule to the site and loaded the bear onto the sled.

When it came time to remove the shirt and let the mule drag the sled back to their truck, the mule took one look at the bear, started braying, and with one big lunge broke loose from the sled. They finally caught the mule 15 miles away in Madisonville, TN.

BEAZELL, BUSH - In the 1930's while making his coffin, Bush Beazell got the bright idea of holding his own funeral. He organized mourners, sermon, and all. This unusual funeral attracted one of the largest crowds ever in Tennessee at that time.. Twelve women fainted; one man had a stroke. I did not attend.

BED BOARDS (BELIEVE IT OR NOT) - Homes in the mountains were typically rather small. As a result, bedrooms and beds were in short supply. Mountain hospitality often meant bedding down visitors, as hotels and motels were scarce as hens' teeth. My parents told of families who dealt with this problem using bed boards. When a guest stayed for the night, a wide wooden board was placed lengthwise in the bed so a stranger could sleep fully separated from their daughter in the same bed. Such a situation spawned the only comment I ever heard regarding the use of a bed-board. The stranger and the daughter were attempting to climb a fence the day after they had been separated only by a bed board. The daughter remarked that if the stranger couldn't climb over a bed board, he surely couldn't climb that fence.

BED WETTING - Take one teaspoon of honey every night before bed. (2) Drink tea of corn silks. (3) Drink no fluids after 5:00 P.M.. (4) Chew cinnamon bark.

BEE MITES - Mountain people used pennyroyal to drive away bee mites. They placed some of this plant in and around the bee hive. The pennyroyal plant, from which insect repellent is now extracted, was also used in the chicken house and dog pen.

BEES, HONEY - Almost every family had honey bees. I am sure my father had a special rapport with his bees. I do not recall that he was ever stung when he robbed the bee hives. He used what we called a "bee-face" for protection. This was a hat surrounded with wire and cloth. The see through wire and cloth were attached to the hat. The cloth fell over the shoulders and chest. He wore extra long gloves and used a "smoker." With the smoker, he pumped air that blew smoke from burning rags onto the bees.

One time about one hundred bees were on my father's back. He asked me to take my hand and wipe them off. Not me! Those bees always watched for me. If I even started into the orchard where they lived, they met me at the front gate and swooped down at me. We just did not understand each other.

While robbing their bees, some mountain men filled their mouths with honey and water. Then they spit it high into the air immediately above themselves, letting it fall onto their clothing. If the bees got on their clothing, they would be getting the honey rather than stinging the beekeeper.

Honey bees are said to be the hardest workers of all the insect world. One crew hauls the pollen, another hauls the water, and another brings the nectar. They travel as far as three miles to gather nectar for honey. The honey takes on the flavor of flowers, such as clover, goldenrod etc. My preference is sourwood. Sorry to say, some commercial honey is mixed with corn syrup.

The plastering putty-wax, known as propolis, which the bees use for the foundation of the honeycomb and seals the crack and crevices in the hive should, in my opinion, be declared today one of the greatest healers of all time. But then no one could make their millions of dollars from such a product. Ice cold toes with no feeling ready to be amputated have been healed after honey or propolis was applied. When you see what it has done for burns, tonsillitis, Fever, diphtheria, stomatis, Salmonella, herpes, rhinitis, acne, gastric or duodenal ulcers, influenza A, staphylococci even cancer, a great antibiotic effective against inflammation, bacteria and infection, when lots of present day medicines fail to be any longer effective, don't say that I didn't tell you that propolis sometimes mixed with honey or royal jelly could be the medicine of the future.

BEES, BEES, BEES -
The bee is such a busy soul,
He has no time for birth control.
So, that is why in times like these,
There are so many sons of bees.
(author unknown)

BEE STINGS - First remove the stinger being careful not to squeeze it. Pour salt in the palm of the hand. Moisten the salt with spit, and rub the site of the sting vigorously. (2) Rub the skin with the inside of a banana peel.

BEE TREE - A bee tree is a tree in which a swarm of bees live unclaimed in the wild. Mountain men had a unique system for finding a bee tree. A man would find a honey bee on a flower. Then he rubbed honey in the palm of his hand to lure and capture the bee. He then closed his hand to protect the bee. After a while the bee ate the honey in the man's hand and was released to fly back to its tree and tell the other bees. The captured honey bee would return to get more honey with many more bees. The man would watch the direction they returned to the bee tree. Each trip for honey helped the mountain man get closer and closer until the tree was found.
When someone found an unclaimed swarm of bees in the wild, he put three hack marks on the tree. That told others of his claim on the bees. This unwritten law was duly honored by our people.

BEES, SWARMING - When the bees "swarm," the queen bee flies up in the air and one of the stronger male bees mates with her. He then dies. She leads half of the hive to follow her to find a new home, leaving the other half in the original hive. I have no idea how it is determined who goes and who stays.
I hated this bee-swarming ordeal when I was a child. We children had to beat loudly on pots and pans to persuade the new group to settle down close to our hives. If the new swarm was allowed to fly away to someone else's property, that hive would be lost. That land owner then owned our bees.

Twenty or more families dwelt in close proximity to our bee hives when we moved to Pigeon Forge. When a hive swarmed, I felt none of those people understood the reason for that "gosh awful" noise we children had to make as we attempted to settle the bees down.

I was quite embarrassed. I would much rather lose that hive than have to make all that silly noise. The logic of our noise was that the queen bee emits a high-pitched tone that the group follows. Our loud noise prevented the bees from hearing the queen, forcing them to settle on the nearest tree or bush. Our noise-making had to continue until every last bee was scooped up. What a relief!

BEHAVIOR - Grandma's recipe for changing children's behavior: "If you want your ice cream, you must eat your spinach." If you ate sweets before meals, it would "ruin" your meal.

BEN - Ben was known in the community as "the village idiot." Reportedly, as a child, he was extremely ill with a very high fever. In those days the patients were "starved" (allowed nothing to eat). It was widely believed that old saying applied in Ben's case - "Feed a cold and starve a fever." Ben was extremely hungry and slipped out to the orchard at night to eat his fill of green apples. We believed that eating all those green apples complicated his physical and mental condition. He was in good mental health until this episode. Thereafter, he roamed the neighborhood, exhibiting some very unusual behavior. This included drinking milk from neighborhood spring houses.

Once confronted regarding some missing milk, he replied, "Well, if I did drink your milk, I didn't have any cornbread to go with it." Ben believed that if he pulled his hat down over his eyes, no one could see him. That would make his toilet stops along the public roads private. Once my father was quite aggravated with Ben. He wanted to scare him a bit. My father told him, "I'll go in the house to get my gun and shoot you." Much later, forgetting about Ben, he found him waiting where they last met. Ben called out, "You'd better shoot me if you are going to, or I'm going to leave."

BET - I once heard a story I thought was indicative of mountain ingenuity. A man bet he could eat a bale of hay. When someone covered his bet, he burned the hay and ate the ashes. He apparently won the bet.

BIBLE - The Bible, known as "The Good Book," occupied an honored place in most mountain homes. All family records of importance were kept in the Bible.

BIRTH CONTROL - COITUS INTERRUPTUS - Mountain people attempted "planned parenthood" in many ways. They had a very picturesque description for coitus interruptus -- "Pulling the dash before the butter comes."

Some of the earlier natives had a method that beat the pill. An incision was made through the penis into the urethra, near its junction with the scrotum. This wound was about an inch in length and was made with a flint knife. The edges of the wound were burned with a stone, and the wound was subsequently kept open by the introduction of a small piece of wood. When the wound healed, this left a permanent opening. During intercourse the seminal discharge flew backward through this opening creating a seemingly effective check on further procreation. I wonder if doctors ever took notice of this method.

Another method of birth control was to ingest a few drops of turpentine to abort. (Much castor oil had to be taken along with the turpentine since it caused great constipation.) Slippery Elm was also used to abort, but I never learned how it was used. Many women believed that allowing a baby to continue nursing prevented another pregnancy. Young children ages 4, 5, or even 6 were known to ask mothers to meet them behind the door for a feeding. I knew first hand of one such case. It appeared the child was extremely shy or perhaps retarded. I wondered if such behavior affected the child's self-esteem and development.

BIRTHING, IT'S TIME TO "SNIFF" HER - Some very early midwives used an unusual method to assist in the delivery of a baby. Some powdered "snuff" was placed on a plate. When the baby was nearly ready for birth, someone would say, "It's time to sniff her." At that time, someone blew the snuff into the expectant mother's face. Because she was dealing with another, more unpleasant, situation her reaction to having the snuff blown into her face would be so violent as to bring forth the baby. It also took her mind off the most painful part of the birthing process.

BIRTHING STOOL - The old-fashioned birthing stool was used by primitive women whose natural wisdom we could emulate today. The birthing stool and the method of use appear to have enabled women to bear many children with less fuss and pain than the more modern methods.

BIRTHMARKS - Native Americans believed God puts his "mark" on certain individuals to signify they were somehow special. I heard one Indian say that any person who has a birthmark is a healer. Then he raised his pant leg to show me his birthmark saying that he was known as a healer.
I wondered if the birthmark on my left leg, about the size of a dime, explains my life long interest in healing.

BIRTHS - Child mortality rates were high during the early part of the century. Many mountain women saw rows of graves dug for their children. There is a row of six small graves in our Trentham family cemetery, located on what was our property, located in The Great Smoky Mountain National Park.

BLACK DROUGHT - A well known laxative, Black Drought, was used extensively in early days. My father gave an acquaintance instructions regarding how much of the loosely powdered black drought to take. He said to take as much as would lay on a dime. When Dad saw the man a few days later, he asked if the black drought was OK. The man very shyly reported that he did not have a dime but he had two nickels. "Well? How was it?" "I got my money's worth" he explained.

BLACKSMITH SHOP - My father, Noah Trentham, had a blacksmith shop on our property in the Park. There he made shoes for our mules and tires for the wagon and buggy. He made and repaired many of the farm tools and implements. I pumped the bellows many times keeping the coals and metal hot for him. It was a joy to see him bend the red-hot iron as he twisted, turned, then beat it with his hammer into the desired shape on the anvil. Then he dropped it into a container of water. I enjoyed hearing it sizzle as he dropped it into a container of water. It was immediately done.

BLADDER INFECTION - Eat raw or roasted pumpkin seeds. Make pumpkin seed tea. (See pumpkin.)

BLANKET MOUNTAIN - Two stories exist as to how Blanket Mountain got its name. One story claims the Indians signaled with a blanket from that location. The other story is that surveyors found the mountain too steep and rugged to follow the line to the top. They hung a colored blanket for the surveyor to sight. When that corner was established, the area was thereafter known as Blanket Mountain.

BLEEDING - Cover an open wound with cobwebs and brown sugar pressed together like lint. (2) For many years old-timers have invoked the Bible verse found in Ezekiel 16:6 to stop bleeding. They substitute the victim's name in place of the word "thee." "And when I passed by thee, and saw thee polluted in thine own blood, I said unto thee when thou wast in thy blood, Live: yea, I said unto thee when thou was in thy blood, Live."[King James version]

My first experience using scripture to stop uncontrolled bleeding was for a patient at Blount Memorial Hospital. Doctors could offer no further help. When my phone rang, the caller said a family member was dying from loss of blood. They had called every minister in the local telephone directory down to our name, Myers, to learn where the verse was found in the Bible that stops bleeding. I took the patient's name, the caller' name and phone number and told her I would look it up in my Young's Analytical Concordance. I knew that particular scripture is the only verse in the Bible having the word "blood" in it three times. When I returned the call, the person who took the message immediately hung up. Then I started to worry. If they were depending upon ME to do this, the patient was as good as dead. I watched the newspaper for days, and the patient's name never appeared in the obituary column. (3) An amazing instance in which this scripture was used occurred recently in Maryville, Tennessee. A very large man had an epileptic seizure and fell backward onto a showcase. He shattered the glass with his head and suffered severe cuts on both his forehead and the back of his head. While the ambulance was en route, someone asked for a Bible and read Ezekiel 16:6. While the reader did not use the man's name instead of the word "thee," the blood flow, nevertheless, had almost stopped by the time the ambulance arrived at the hospital.

BLIND TIGER - was not a live one. It was the name of a place in very early days in Sevierville where bootleg or moonshine could be purchased. Another similar establishment in Gatlinburg during my high school days was called "The Bloody Bucket."

BLOOD CLEANSER - (See Spring Tonic)

BLOOD POISONING - Before the days of tetanus shots, a woman came to our home in the mountains with blood poisoning in her badly swollen arm. My father mixed equal parts of sulfur, gunpowder, and alum. She took orally what would lay on a dime. Then my father added vinegar to the mixture and applied a poultice with this mixture to her arm. Much improved, she went home within three days.

BLOOD SOUP - As nauseating as it may sound, I have talked with two people who have eaten it, and both insisted it was very good. To obtain blood for the soup, a chicken or duck's neck is cut and hung by its feet to allow the blood to drain out. I do not know the recipe for the blood soup, but it is said to contain vinegar.

BOAR/RAZOR-BACK HOGS - I have been unable to distinguish between the Wild Boar (Russian Boar) and the Razor-Back hog, one of which remains in the Smoky Mountains. So I will give what applies to one or both.

Hundreds of wild hogs roamed these mountains many years ago. They picked their own living, and required no attention from man. Therefore, they became the cheapest source of meat and the source of much mountain lore. The boar's weight gain was a hundred and fifty percent during the first eight months of its life. Because the boar was wild, its meat was leaner. Mountain folk began to prefer wild boar to the domestic hog. Cornbread and sow belly was a favorite menu item for many mountaineers.

The razorback or boar was a great favorite except for its destructiveness. According to mountain lore, it could burrow, uproot, and overturn much like a bulldozer. It could run like a deer and climb like a goat. It was said a wild boar was also mean as a snake. Like an elephant it held a grudge forever and most always got even. It appeared to understand human language and understood if "cursed" in more than one language.

Some said it had a medical degree, because it would strike a man's femoral artery and seemed to know that would kill faster than ripping at any other place. Some men said they would prefer fighting John Dillinger (the outlaw) than to tangle with a boar.

If it was rooting or sleeping, it was studying some devilment. It could read your mind. Next to the dog and the crow it had the greatest ESP. Any smart dog who knows a boar will not go after it without wearing a very special wide thick collar. This collar is used to prevent the boar from targeting the jugular vein. With just one swipe by the boar the dog would be dead.

Perhaps the boar should be feared more than any other local animal because it is so smart. Fortunately it is hardly every seen by hikers, but it can smell food cooking from at least two miles away. Feeding a wild boar red pepper helps to keep it away, but the only sure cure is to shoot it.

"BODY SNATCHERS" to "BODY FARM?"- Approximately 100 years ago farmers living in the counties adjoining Knox County needed to take their produce to Knoxville, but they heard horrible stories about disappearances. It was said that a tow sack might be pulled over a farmer's head, and he would never be heard from again. Many farmers refused to travel alone. If they traveled alone, they never slept a wink. They sometimes brought many family members, so that one could stand guard while others slept.

Of course, the Knoxville law enforcement made sport of those stupid hillbillies who made such claims. However, a newspaper article in 1903 suggested an inordinate increase in pauper burials causing 310 coffins to be exhumed and examined. Eighty-seven graves contained bodies, and 227 contained wood or sawdust. Some burials had been paid for twice by Knox County government. The names of some well-to-do people were forged on burial certificates. Mountain folk knew all along it was not safe.

This story made me wonder about the possibility that imagining something could make it happen. Those mountaineers imagined or knew this was happening. They pictured with great fear, this awful scenario of dead bodies in Knoxville, Tennessee. Almost 100 years later comes the BODY FARM. Over 1500 bodies are housed in the laboratory for the University of Tennessee's Anthropology Department. This is possibly the strangest classroom in the whole world. At this site, researchers study decomposition rates of bodies in every imaginable state or time element. This research is being shared world-wide. This information is supposed to help police become more accurate as to time and condition in murder cases.

I wondered if "thought/imagination" by many people, picturing something acts like a magnet bringing that into being?

BOILS - OR CARBUNCLES - To stop boils, apply turpentine. I used this remedy successfully many times when I detected a boil beginning to develop. (2) Apply a bandage of bacon fat until the boil ruptures. (3) A better remedy is the use of a paste made of slippery elm bark bound on the boil until it ruptures. (4) Apply a black salve, known as Ichthammol. This product is so old-fashioned a pharmacist must special order it today. It costs less than two dollars and has great drawing power. Our family has used it for more than 50 years. (5) Apply a scrapped raw potato to the boil.

BOUND - Foster children. Orphans and wards of the state were known as "bound" in very early days. Children would say, "I am bound for six years." They often remained "bound" until they became adults.

BREAD - Some of the Native Americans had a curious manner in which to bake bread. On a hearth stone about the size of a dish, 12-14" in diameter, they built a hot fire When the stone had reached baking temperature, they swept the fire coals off, laid the dough on the rock, and covered it with a deep dish. The stone provided the heat and the dish provided an environment like an oven. The bread was said to taste great.

BREAD ROUNDS - When a man was known to steal bread, he was given the nickname "Bread Rounds." Everyone in his community was instructed to address him openly as "Bread Rounds", followed by his full name each time he was seen. This soon drove him from the area. If he repeated the theft, the new community did the same until he learned his lesson.

BRIDAL SHOWERS - A favorite homemade bridal gift of long ago was made for the kitchen. Mountain women bought and sewed two identical dish cloths together so that the end product looked similar to an old-fashioned pair of "bloomers," or pantaloons. Accompanying the gift was the following poem:
Now don't get excited
And don't be misled.
These are not for you
But your dishes instead.
Just pull out the ribbons
And rip out the stitches.
You'll now have two dish cloths
But you sure lost your britches.

BROOMS, SCRUB - Because wet mops were not yet available, we mountain folk used what we called a "scrub broom." A board about

6 inches wide and fourteen inches long was used to make them. Numerous holes were drilled in the board. The core end of the cornshuck, which was attached to the ear of corn was placed on top of the board, while the shucks were pulled into the holes, forming a very useful mop to scrub the floors.

Grass-covered lawns covered with grass, as we know them today were uncommon back then. Yards often had no grass. Since bare ground was the only surface for walking, dirt and mud were often brought into the house, soiling the floors. In such instances the scrub brooms were needed almost daily. We mowed our grass with a push roller type lawn mower and which was no fun to use.

BRUISES - A football coach in North Carolina, just across the mountain, said the following words over his team members who suffered injuries. At first the boys made great sport of this ceremony and called the coach a "crackpot." After experiencing the results, they later came to him and requested it. These were the words:

"Bruise thou shall not heat,
Bruise thou shall not sweat,
Bruise thou shall not run
any more than the Virgin Mary
shall bring forth another son,"
While crossing himself with the sign of the cross he said:
"In the name of God the Father,
In the name of God the Son,
In the name of God the Holy Ghost. Amen."

BUCKEYE - Carry one in your pocket to ward off arthritis. It was said that coal miners would not enter the mines unless they had a buckeye in their pockets.

BULL TONGUE PLOW - A large wooden plow used to break up virgin land, usually pulled by oxen.

BULLETS, HOME MADE - I have melted lead and poured it into molds to make bullets. Since cartridges became available in the stores I do not recall Dad ever using any of our molded bullets. As children we cut them in half and used them as sinkers on our fishing lines. My father also had a powder horn, but I do not recall ever seeing him use it.

BUMS - Before hotels were available, travelers and bums would knock on our door late in the afternoon and ask to stay the night at our home. We usually fed them the evening meal and breakfast . I do not recall my parents ever charging anyone anything for this favor.

We had a big house and kept many people. The bums had codes they put on fence posts or gate posts to tell the next guy if you were O.K. They put a cross if you were religious, a plus sign if you were OK, or a pound sign if you were in law enforcement.

One such traveler, who had stopped many times at our home, was en route during winter time to his Primitive Baptist foot-washing. As was the routine, everyone left his shoes by the fireside overnight so they would be warm the following morning. My father and his first wife seized this opportunity to play a practical joke. They filled his shoes with soot, which would filter through his socks onto his feet and cause them to look as if they had not been washed in weeks.

One can hardly imagine his surprise the following day at the church when he pulled his shoes off for the foot-washing. Needless to say he never came again for a free nights lodging at the Trentham home.

BURMA SHAVE - In the 1940's and 1950's, we had Burma Shave signs along our Tennessee highways as were found around the country. Each sign had one line of the series. Some of my favorites:

Slow down, Pa
Sakes alive
Ma missed signs
Four and five.

If you

Don't know
Whose signs
These are
You can't have
Driven very far.

Every shaver
Now can snore
Six more minutes
Than before
By using
Burma Shave.

Don't lose your head
To gain a minute
You need your head
Your brains are in it.

Within this vale
Of toil and sin
Your head grows bald
But not your chin.

Missed a curve
Just a whizzin'
The fault was her'n
The funeral his'n.

My electric razor
Shaves my chin
Bring back the jingles
And I'll turn it in.

All of the jingles were signed..........Burma Shave.

BURNS- (1) Hill folk did what was called "blowing the fire out of burns." This entailed blowing ones breath on a burn. I tried this remedy one day. While stirring apple butter, two big blobs popped out on my right hand. I quickly washed off the apple butter and decided to blow the worst and biggest spot and leave the one that was burned less. For perhaps thirty minutes I blew my breath continually on the larger spot. I have the scar to show today where the lesser burn was located, while there is no scar at all where I blew on the worse or larger spot. Perhaps it was the oxygen being applied that helped.

(2) The mountain ceremony used for burns: Slowly pass the hands, palms down and open, gently over the burns 3 times. Blow the breath gently following the hand each time. Repeat silently or simultaneously say: "There came an angel from the east. Bring frost and fire. In Frost, out fire. In the name of the father, the son, and the Holy Ghost. (Say word for word, make no mistake.) Place the head over burns, but turn so that the breath follows the hand away from the victims body and away from the healer. Blow gently on the burn. Do not bind with any dressing. Put only talcum powder or baby powder on the burn. Do not let water touch it. (I do not remember if it was necessary for the healer to be present for this ceremony.) The patient must exercise so scar tissue will not develop. If tendons are involved, exercise is essential!!! Healers were known to work for two weeks on a badly burned person.

C

CABBAGE - To preserve during winter time. A deep hole was dug where the ground sloped and had good drainage. The hole was lined with straw. Cabbage heads were stacked neatly in place below the frost line and covered with more straw then dirt.. A large piece of metal was place over the hole to divert the rain. Some families buried just one cabbage head in a hole and left the root-end sticking out of the ground. My family never used either method, but the families who did, claimed to have enjoyed some mighty good eating.

CABBAGE - CRAPPED - Thrift was one secret of survival on some of the small mountain farms. The lower leaves on the cabbage plants were removed without hindering the development of the cabbage head. The leaves were cut into strips and cooked. This dish was called "CRAPPED Cabbage." Our family never ate this dish, said to be very good.

CABINS, LOG - While many of the homes were simple log cabins, some homes consisted of two separate units with a narrow hallway joining them together. This hallway was called a "dog-trot." I cannot claim the distinction of being born in a log cabin. We had a weather boarded two story white house with four bedrooms, kitchen, dining room, and large front and back porches. A stone fire-place supplied the heat.

CAMP MEETINGS - After the crops were "laid-by (harvested and stored), a brush-arbor was built for a church revival meeting. Entire families came by wagon or buggies and camped for a week of religious renewal. Bringing food supplies for the one- to two-week camp meeting afforded a great opportunity for families who seldom saw each other to get together for fun and fellowship. It was said this type revival was popular because many people would not attend services in the churches but would attend outdoor services.

CAMPBELL, TOM, AND SOPHIE - Mountain women learned many useful crafts. Sophie, our neighbor in the Great Smoky Mountain National Park, made, sold, and smoked long-stemmed clay pipes, which she cured by baking in the fireplace under the ashes. Some of her pipes are still in existence today in the hands of her relatives.

Mountain men were known to be rugged individualists, depending upon their own wills and strengths for their existence. Tom Campbell was such a man. To put a floor in Tom and Sophie's cabin, Tom had to carry 1600 board-feet of lumber perhaps a mile up a very steep mountain trail. 1600 board-feet is equivalent to 200 boards of lumber, 8 feet long by 12 inches wide, by 1 inch thick. Needless to say, it took many trips to bring up that much lumber. (There was no Home Depot to deliver.)

CANCER - (old time cure) Drinking a tea of red clover blooms three times a day, or propolis mixed with brandy was said to cure stomach cancer. (2) Inhale apple-brandy for lungs. (3) Eat at least three almonds every day. (4) Poke root mixed with zinc chloricum removed skin cancers. (More recent cancer information.) Luella Pemberton's mother, suffering with cancer, and weighing just 60 pounds was sent home from the hospital to die. Luella's mother had washed clothes on a washboard and sent her to college. Luella was so distraught that she prayed day and night for a cure. She began to see dogwood blooms with her eyes open and shut. She felt she was being given this as a sign for a cure, but she had never heard of anyone using dogwood tea. She did not know if Dogwood tea was poisonous. However, she found a book in the Oak Ridge Library describing an Indian princess who was cured with dogwood tea. Her mother drank the tea and recovered.

Luella wrote about her experiences in the Knoxville newspaper. I have her personal letter describing the details.

When I became afraid that my malignancy from breast cancer had returned, I would cut a young dogwood tree into small pieces so that the interior of the wood was exposed. I cooked it in a stainless steel container for about 6 hours. I drank one-half cup four times per day diluting it to taste. That would be the end of my discomfort.

In 1958 doctors at a cancer conference stated that wood cement might contain a cure. The statement has been made that if a simple cure for cancer is found it would bankrupt the United States.

CAST FOR BROKEN BONES - (Home-made) Mix red clay with water. Put splints on each side of the broken bone, and plaster with the clay. When the clay dries put the arm in a sling.

CATALOG - (see MAIL ORDER CATALOG)

CATARACTS - Put brown sugar in the eyes each day for 5 days. A hospital administrator told me about a woman sent home to wait for cataract surgery. When she returned, the cataracts were gone. At first she refused to tell what she had done. After much urging in the interest of medical science, she confessed that an old mountain woman told her to put brown sugar in her eyes. The hospital administrator added that the drops given after cataract surgery contain brown sugar in solution!

CATS: (1) Our beautiful cat, Tom, had four white feet, a white face and chest, and a curly tail that laid forward across his back. He always went with me to milk the cows. He was huge and loved warm milk. I squirted milk in his direction and he never missed a drop. When we were forced to move out of the park, we took Tom to Pigeon Forge. Unhappy with city life he went back home. Again, we took him to Pigeon Forge, and he went back home. One night Mother made him go outside. He gave her a definite look of displeasure, but she made him go out anyway. He went back home to the park for the third time, so we let him stay. It almost broke my heart to let him stay at the old home place unattended, but I was homesick twice in my life and believe me there is no cure except to go home! Later reports of a "wild-cat" fitting his description were reported in that area of the park. (2) Leaving when someone dies - Cats are known to leave home never to return when a family member is known to be terminally ill. Such was said to be the case with Sir Winston Churchill's cat, named Ginger Tom. (3) Smothering babies- Experts who dispute that cats smother babies should have been with me when I found our Siamese cat with his mouth completely covering my infant daughters' mouth. She was no longer resisting when I happened to find her. I'd rather not say what happened to the cat. (4) We later raised Siamese cats, which we enjoyed very much. Our neighbors reported that when we left home, our two Siamese circled around and around the house meowing or wailing in different pitches. One of them climbed upon the chest of drawers in our bedroom and jumped from there onto our bed each morning at exactly 6:00 AM. I often wondered how he could tell time. (5) Speaking of cats, did anyone ever see a cats carcass up in a tree? Sometimes we go to great lengths to get a cat down, such as calling the fire department, etc. Before they starve to death, they seem to determine that they have to come down backwards as their claws are all wrong to come down head first.

CAT HOLE - Many mountain homes, including ours, had a "cat-hole." Usually a 6" x 6" hole cut somewhere at the base of some interior wall to allow the cat to come and go as he chose. One of my brothers, who walked in his sleep, got up one night and crammed his shirt in the cat hole. I've often wondered with all the many snakes, why none ever found the cat hole and came inside our home.

CAT NIP - Our cats rolled and frolicked on the catnip plants that grew in our garden. It was said if a person chewed the catnip leaves they became fierce and quarrelsome.

CAVES IN TENNESSEE - Tennessee has 6800 registered caves with 170 in our adjoining Knox County.

CEILINGS - High ceilings in early homes made heating quite difficult, but fuel was cheap. Therefore, it was practical to use fuel in the winter and enjoy the benefits of the coolness provided by high ceilings, in the summer.

CEMETERIES - The cemeteries located in The Great Smoky Mountain National Park are to be maintained in good condition by the park service. Anyone born in the park or their descendants can be buried there as long a space is available. A relative must make application, showing that it was the wish of the deceased.

Just now confirmed with Glenn Cardwell, former Park employee, that descendants are definitely eligible. He also added how shocked he was when someone told him that they wished that he would break his leg. Why? so you will be stopped long enough to write down all the stories that you need to write about the park. I urged him to get busy writing.

Many of the early graves were not marked or were made of mountain stone. Sometimes graves are dug in cemeteries only to find a body already there. To avoid that situation, a dowser often checks the site to determine that the chosen plot is clear (see Dowsing.) (I wonder why the police today do not use this method rather than do all that digging when searching for bodies. It works every time. The rods close for the length of the body, then open)

CEMETERY - PET - We had a pet cemetery where we buried all the family pets with great ceremony. Every year around "Decoration Day" we put the grounds in tip-top condition and decorated the graves with flowers. My pet chicken had a very special place.

CENSUS TAKERS - Early census takers wrote exactly what they saw. Such listings as: "dejected wives", "helpless widows", "idiots", "in the poor house or jails" were comments found on census forms. Many names were misspelled, which may account for several different spellings of the same name. I am aware of one rare case in which a family member at odds with his siblings, changed the spelling of his surname, and moved to another town.

CHAIRS - The seats of many early chairs were made of corn shucks twisted into a rope. Beautiful designs and very durable. The frames were, of course, made of wood.

CHARMING WARTS - (see **WARTS**.)

CHESTNUT TREES - The mighty chestnut tree - immortalized in Longfellow's Village Blacksmith -- was known in our area as the "Big Tree." During the 1920's and 1930's, a terrible blight decimated the chestnut population and robbed the Smokies of a valuable resource. The chestnut trunk, which reached nine or ten feet in diameter, was regarded as the best hardwood because of its straight grain and the ease with which the wood could be worked. I remember well these huge trees that adorned our mountain side. Seeing all of them die was a tremendous loss. We enjoyed the great chestnuts as did all the wild animals. There is hope they may be brought back.

CHICKENS - (1) Many of our chickens roosted high up in trees at night safe from animals such as foxes and possums who raided the chicken houses. (2) Sassafras poles were used to build chicken roosts because the wood was said to deter chicken mites. Mites were never a problem for those who roosted in the chicken house. So it must work. (3) As soon as they are hatched, chicks will peck feverishly and will run for cover if a bird flies overhead making a shadow. There appears to be a built-in fear of hawks, since it has not experienced this with the mother hen. (4) You can feed green tobacco worms to chickens and they will become so "drunk" on the nicotine they will flop from side to side and will become addicted. (5) Scattering tobacco leaves or pennyroyal in the chicken roost also helps to rid of chicken mites if present. (6) Since chickens do not sweat, mist them during hot weather to avoid chicken heat stroke. (7) I have heard that a chicken adopts as a parent the first person or animal it sees after being hatched. I once had what I thought was just a "pet" chicken. I picked him out of the shell when he was being hatched. This could account for the fact that he followed at my heels everywhere I went just like a little puppy. However, I accidentally stepped backward and killed the little guy. But for that tragic accident, I might have been able to explain that strange phenomenon.

CHIGGERS - We rubbed pennyroyal weed on our wrists and ankles before picking berries to avoid getting chiggers. Also putting kerosene on the cuff of pants or soles of the shoes was a deterrent. A quick bath or a swim in the old swimming hole after picking berries generally washed chiggers off. Once imbedded, however, painting with nail polish takes care of the little rascals. Before nail polish became available, we smeared imbedded chiggers with lard mixed with lots of salt to kill them.

CHILDREN - During our day, children were seen and not heard. When guests came, we said hello, then usually vanished. Respecting your elders was the rule. We were never allowed to interrupt.

CHIMNEY TOPS - A person can sit astride the very top peak of the Chimney Tops in the Great Smoky Mountain National Park and throw a rock 1000 feet down either side of the mountain. However, I became so frightened trying to get off those rocks I promised the Good Lord if he would help me to get off there safely I would never go back again. That's one promise I've been able to keep. (2) It was believed no one owned the land surrounding the Chimney Tops when that property was being acquired for the park. In such cases, a cabin, called a possession cabin, was built. Someone lived in it the required seven years to meet the homestead requirements then, he deeded the land to the park. I understand more than one possession cabin was needed to obtain all the land for the park.

CHRISTMAS - Christmas time today brings to mind shopping 'til you drop and how much you can spend. Early Christmas had very little commercialism. In our mountain home we took the bed down in the guest room, which we called the upper room, and replaced it with a huge tree whose top reached the ceiling. The tree was hemlock, white pine, or cedar. Very early decorations commonly consisted of colored paper cutouts, popcorn on a string, holly berries, and sweet gum balls dipped in soap suds and left to dry. There were no decorations in the early stores.

The Yule Log -- a huge "back-stick" used in the fireplace was soaked in water for several days before Christmas, a tradition observed in some homes.. As long as that log burned during the Christmas season the men were exempt from doing any farm chores. (I suppose the women had to feed the farm animals and milk the cows.) A piece of the Yule log was kept to begin the celebration the following season.

We had lots of mistletoe and holly with the beautiful red berries. I later learned mistletoe was believed to be sacred, offered protection from evil, assured fertility, and was credited with mysterious powers. Any young girl not kissed under the mistletoe would remain single the following year.

I never once believed that Santa Claus came down your chimney and delivered toys to the entire world in one night, because my mother was too honest to have us believe that. I think her reasoning was that when we learned the true facts about Santa Claus, we might believe Jesus was a myth also. The appearance of Santa Claus was filled with great anticipation akin to the Second Coming of Christ. Somehow I wish the Santa Claus myth was really true so that little children the world over could receive wonderful gifts.

We always hung our stockings next to the chimney. They were filled with oranges, apples, nuts, and candies. All other gifts were put under the tree. If you had been particularly bad through the past year, a knot was supposed to be tied in your stocking which bore no gifts. However, I never saw a knot in any of our stockings. Cookies, sparklers, firecrackers, whistles, and hand carved toys were some of the gifts. Can anyone imagine a child today being happy to find any of the above-mentioned items in his/her stocking? I once asked for a car as my gift one Christmas. Weeks before Christmas there appeared a large box under the tree with my name on it. My sister had taken potatoes, cut out wheels, the steering wheel and fashioned a beautiful car. But, alas, by Christmas the potatoes had shriveled rendering it the funniest car you ever saw.

There were lots of noise makers such as horns, whistles, and drums. The men heated hickory coals red hot, poured water on them, then hit them with a hammer. This created sounds like a firecracker. Another noise maker was an inflated hog's bladder. This was tossed in the fire for an impressive blast. Families were serenaded at Christmas time with cow bells, plow points, and anything that made a noise. If the family to be serenaded heard the noise makers first and let it be known by making their own noise, they did not have to treat the incoming group with food or drink. One old mountain man tied a string to the trigger of his shotgun, then stretched the string across the road, causing the crowd unknowingly to trigger the shot. He did not have to treat the group.

Neighbors, separated by some distance, communicated with one another on Christmas day by shooting rifles. Those who could afford the ammunition answered with another shot. The mistletoe, holly, firecrackers, and, of course, the Christmas tree are still very much in evidence today.

My late husband, Ray T. Myers, was a minister. I always enjoyed his Christmas messages. I enjoyed hearing that when the baby Jesus was born, the shepherds endured the heat, or the cold, rain or shine, day and night to protect their sheep from the wolves. When the shepherd rounded them up each evening, he held out his rod over which each sheep must jump. If the sheep was sick or needed attention it would not jump over, so the shepherd knew it needed attention. Also, at this time the shepherd counted each sheep. If one was missing, he did not sleep until he found it. But even more interesting was that each shepherd had a distinct whistle. His sheep recognized and heeded only his voice or whistle.

Ray's Christmas message went on to remind that the baby born there in the manger grew into the one known today as our good shepherd. He also has a distinctive call. No matter how far away we may have strayed, he still seeks us.

CHRISTMAS PUDDING - A Christmas favorite was rice pudding with an almond hidden in it.The single girl who found the almond would be the first to marry.

CHURCHES - In our early churches the men sat on the right side of the church; women sat on the left. The young people sat in the center pews, but boys and girls rarely sat together. The boys sat near the back or hung around outside waiting for the services to end so they could ask to walk a girl home.

Early churches had very little money, but we did not really need very much. The collections, or offerings, were taken in up in a man's hat. The preachers came only once per month, preached an hour or more, and then went home with a member of the congregation for lunch.

Some of the early preachers expounded on the fiery furnaces of hell and scared you so badly you'd vow to be good. Then they hollered and made ugly faces until you were not sure if you really wanted to go to heaven and spend more time with them.

Members caught hell right here on earth if they so much as danced to a jingle or used a curse word. Church members duly noted the lifestyle of the weaker members. Missionary Baptists especially frowned on card playing, drinking moonshine, and dancing. An offender was brought before the church elders and given the opportunity to apologize to the church and confess his failures or sins with the promise to reform.

If a member of the congregation committed any one of those "forbidden sins" while failing to apologize or confess his sin, he or she was "churched" or "turned out", meaning that fellowship or membership was withdrawn. That person became an "outcast" for life - quite a disgrace. If a church member attended services at another church, it was at one time considered grounds for dismissal. But in my early days the Methodist and Baptist held joint revivals.

Local church records indicate that churches dealt with members who beat a slave or drank alcohol. One member played cards on Sunday, gambled, and was banished for life. Other records of early church activities included discussions about such issues as noisy children, the selection of song books, the appointment of a begging committee, the attendance of visitors and deadbeats, wearing the usual badge of mourning for three months, and knife-trading in the church. This is in sharp contrast to activities of today.

For many early preachers, the King James Bible was the pillar and rock. Hell was a place burning with fire and brimstone, while heaven was a rather vague but pleasant place. As found in Genesis, the world was created in exactly six days, and all of man's troubles were caused by the first woman, Eve, when she ate the apple. Hard-shell preachers probably received their title because their preaching was so harsh. Then there was "Regular", "Bedrock", "Freewill", and "Primitive Baptists." One small group was called "Two Seed in the Spirit Baptists." They allowed no violins and no dancing. Other titles depended upon the amount of water used for baptisms. For example, "Half-pint Baptists" sprinkled only the head. If the body became thoroughly wet, members were called "Five-Gallon Baptists." But Baptists who practiced total immersion were known as "Forty-Gallon Baptists." We Baptists have been called very narrow-minded and have been accused of believing only Baptists will go to heaven. But I'm more narrow minded than that - some of our gang may not get there.

Because church life was so important to everyone, many stories were told about events surrounding churches. For example, our church services were usually much more spirited than today. Some of the preachers encouraged people to express their joy by shouting. In one little mountain church, the preacher had preached for some time when he stopped suddenly and asked, "Why doesn't someone shout?" At that exact moment a goat stuck his head in the door, going "baa,baa." The goat continued until some men put him outside.

Toward the end of the service in our little church, known as Evans Chapel, someone would comment on the sermon. They usually quoted the text or general outline. On one occasion the text had been "Cry Loud and Spare Not." A man got up and made many favorable comments on the sermon and ended by saying, "And, by all means, don't forget the text: Crawl around and widen out!"

One man prayed in church saying only the alphabet. When questioned about this, he said, "God doesn't speak English. It's not the words, but the intent. " So he said he let God put those ABC's in order. At one funeral the minister was trying very hard to find something good to say about the deceased. He said, "This corpse has been a member for the past 25 years."

My family told of a preacher, who was not good at reading. He had a friend read his scriptures for him as he preached. The reader read a sentence and the preacher would then make comments on it. At one point the preacher had his finger over the next line. The reader, unable to see the words, stated, " You have your finger on the line." The preacher, thinking that was part of the scripture, took those words and made some great points about them in his sermon.

As I was growing up, I promised myself I would never marry a minister. However, my late husband, Ray T. Myers, became a minister and preached in Oregon, Texas, Florida, Georgia, Kentucky, and Tennessee. He held tent revivals mainly in East Tennessee. As I look back over my life as the wife of a minister, quite a few incidents stand out. Some were very rewarding and some were otherwise.

Ray & I organized and built Madison Avenue Baptist Church in Maryville, Tennessee. I had the distinct privilege of making every motion that made it become a church. I named it because I liked the name Madison Avenue. We had lived on Kickapoo Street in Texas just prior to that. How fortunate it was I did not like the name of that street?

A very limited number of churches in the area practice snake handling. For that reason, Ray kept a good eye out for snake handlers. He always told me if there was no back door in a building when a snake was brought in, he wouldn't bother to inquire where did they want one. Some rambunctious revival preachers, led members of the congregation to become "unhinged," but within a week or so they regained their senses.

Our ministry had a few embarrassing moments. Once our number one son went into a church member's kitchen, looked it over and observed: "Your stove is just like my mother's 'cept hers is not dirty." We did not realize that as a small child Don did not know when we were joking or when we were serious. On his first day in school the teacher decided to have the children tell Bible stories. Among the little hands that went up was the eager hand of the minister's son. Don told the following "Bible story": "Three bears were sitting on a block of ice. Papa bear said, "I have a tale to tell." Momma bear said, "I have a tale to tell. " Baby bear said, "my (tails) told (cold)."

Once in a department store a young female member of our congregation saw Ray T. from many yards away. She ran toward him with both arms stretched wide open to hug him. She never gave me even a slight nudge. I did not mind when I was with him. We finally got a live-in housekeeper so I could go with him after a very serious incident happened to a fellow pastor.

It appears that the lives of ministers today are about one thousand times easier than for us and our children. Our number one son once had a fist fight. You should have heard the good ladies of the church exclaiming, "How awful! The minister's son had a fight." He had good reasons to defend himself. We could not take our children to the public swimming pool. Instead, we had to sneak off to the back cove of the lake to allow them to swim. Only I and one little 82 year old woman on our street could not wear walking shorts.

One of the most spectacular events in our ministry involved a very serious problem that arose in the church. We were so distressed that I gathered together about 18 ladies of the church. I told them how serious the problem was and that it could tear our church apart. We had a special prayer regarding the matter. The next afternoon, one of the deacons involved dropped dead. That scared the pants right off us. We never prayed another prayer in this group. Strangely enough, that problem was never mentioned again.

My faith has been very important to me. Each night Ray and I held each others hand and prayed together just before we went to sleep. When we were traveling and church time came we often stopped at the nearest church and visited their services. The one I enjoyed most was visiting with the Cherokees in a little church in Cherokee, N. C.

I have sometimes wondered if each of us had to preach our own funeral, if we could find anything really good to say about ourselves? I once stopped and honestly reflected upon what I could possibly find to say about myself. I decided I would have to say I made lots of mistakes and did a few good things. I did not ask for the many unusual psychic things that happened during my lifetime. When I was criticized for my far-out thinking, I was deeply crushed. However, I believe I have had an understanding of some of the deep mysteries of life. I had to realize that not everyone is at the same level of understanding. Therefore there was no need to try to explain. I also believe many good Baptists will be very surprised when they enter the next dimension. "Eye hath not seen, ear hath not heard, neither has it entered into the heart of man what God has in store for those who love HIM."

Who builds a church within his heart
And takes it with him everywhere
Is holier far than he whose church
Is but a one day house of prayer. -- Author unknown.

CIGARETTES - Our childish out-behind-the barn home-made cigarettes were made of corn silks or rabbit tobacco. We used strips of brown-paper bags to form a roll-your-own cigarette. We were also careful to keep a sharp watch-out for Dad or Mom and not to catch the barn on fire.

CISTERN - Our cistern was partially underground much like a well. It was used to store a water supply for doing the laundry. Gutters were installed on the barn, and rain water was channeled into this holding tank. Kerosene was sometimes put on the top of the water to prevent mosquitoes or wiggle tails.

We used a pitcher pump that had to be primed with water before it could bring up water from the well. Therefore, it was important that whoever used the pump drew enough water for the next person to be able to prime the pump. The pump was made of iron. In the winter, extra care had to be taken when drawing water. If your hand happened to be wet during freezing weather, it adhered to the metal pump handle. You were stuck there until someone brought warm water and removed you from this predicament. I know from experience. Outside, in freezing cold, I was glued to the pump while I screamed for help!

CITY BOY - A young boy came up from Knoxville to spend the night on the farm where the chores started at 4:00 A.M. He surmised that "It doesn't take long to spend the night around here."

CIVIL WAR - East Tennessee officially remained part of the Union, but Rebel territory surrounded it. However, residents fought on both sides. In Cades Cove, 21 men joined the Union, 12 men joined the Confederates or rebels. Confederates considered residents traitors, unleashing warfare on the civilian population. In one unfortunate instance two local brothers fought against each other. Both were killed and buried side by side. The father was quoted as saying, "One was right and one was wrong, but God will decide!"

Many mountain people lost their last bite of food, their livestock, their clothing, and even their shoes and boots. It was the worst kind of situation - neighbor against neighbor, vengeance, harassment, flogging, robbery, murder, rape, and starvation. Tales abound about the horrors of the war. These horrors included ambushes on the trails, shoots fired from forest cabins, attacks under cover of darkness, and setting fire to everything that would burn. Families were shot as they fled the flames of their burning cabins. I heard of one family in which the father was called outside and shot, then the house was burned with his wife and children barricaded inside.

When Union soldiers came through here it was said they went through the country robbing widows and orphans. They sometimes paid them with greenbacks if they were on the Union side but nothing "atal" if they were democrats. They poured boiling water in the bee gums to drown the bees and kill the queen bee. Then they laughed about it.

If a Yankee was buried in a family graveyard, Rebel soldiers dug him up and buried him in a sinkhole. (One soldier was not buried deep enough. A hog rooted up the grave and carried off the head.) When they shot at the Yankees, Rebel soldiers were to aim the shot "betwixt the gallowses."

Sentinels were stationed at the top of ridges to blow horns to alert the people that the rebels were coming. Some men slept in the bushes every night for two years, living in constant fear of being killed. At dark, they went to the woods for a nights rest. Guns, seeds, and clothing were hidden in hollow logs. The best clothing was put on the children, as the children's clothing usually was not removed from them. One family hid their money in the cook stove. They forgot about the money, built a fire, and lost all their savings. With their menfolk killed or taken away, women were left to till the land, raise the children, plow, plant, and harvest the crops. Traps were baited with corn which was used to catch squirrels, rabbits, bears, and wild turkeys for food. Opossums and weasels were trapped because they were a great threat to chickens, ducks, and geese. Weasels only sucked the blood from the chickens but opossums ate them. When a woman had raised, butchered, and salted her hog, the hated enemy swooped down and carried it away. In my genealogy research of the Trentham family, I found a situation in which soldiers forced a Trentham woman to kill and prepare her pet pig for their dinner. In retaliation, she put so much pepper in it they could not eat it.

The rampaging soldiers took everything they could find. In one case they took everything except a blind mule. The people buried their seed corn in special built holes in the ground so that when the Rebels came through, they could not find and confiscate their corn. When the people resisted them, they burned and destroyed everything they did not confiscate.

At the close of the Civil War, food was very scarce. Soda and salt were non-existent. Mountain women placed lye in wood ashes in what was called an "Ash hopper" to obtain a soda substitute. The ash hopper was a wooden trough with spring water running through it. But there was no substitute for salt, which at that time cost $1 per pound. Women were known to walk five miles just to buy one pound of salt.

Families who would never lie developed ways to tell the truth and still avoid helping the enemy. When Cades Cove was being raided almost nightly for fire arms and other items, the Frederic Emert family had a gun buried in the ground. When they were questioned regarding a gun, the reply was "We don't have a gun on the top side of God's green earth." (Which was true.) A family in Townsend named a room "Greene County." When soldiers asked them where a family member was, they truthfully told them he had gone to "Greene County."

Bitterness and hatred lasted for many years after the war. Many confederates moved away because of the hostility.

CIVIL WAR SONG:
I'd rather be a union man
and carry a union gun
than be a Gormly man
and steal a cow and run.
(Author unknown)

CIVILIAN CONSERVATION CORPS - The Civilian Conservation Corps came to the Sugarlands in 1933 where interesting incidents reflected the conflicts of cultures. One of the young corps members shot a pig one night and shouted that he had shot a bear. When the CCC boys started dating our local girls, fires were deliberately set to keep the CCC boys busy on weekends and away from the girls. One of the CCC boys dated my older sister. My late father-in-law also joined the Corps to support his young family.

CLANNISH - Mountain folk were considered clannish, but we preferred to call it loyalty. If strangers came asking questions, we could pretend to be dumb, dumber or dumbest until we learned who they were and exactly what they wanted. Any information was generally hard to come by. Incorrect directions or misinformation was often deliberate. (2) While this is a bit more unusual, it is fact. A friend's family moved to a fairly remote area of east Tennessee. Her husband was soon advised by some of the town folk, "We don't care what you know about the people and activities of our town, but if you tell it, we'll put your little shoes away." Unsolved murders seemed to bear out this policy.

CLEARING NEW GROUND - Grounds in these mountains were said to be cleared twice: once to cut the timber, and second to remove the rocks. Fences were made from rocks. Our own rock fence was perhaps 3500 feet in length and 5-8 feet high. It made a wonderful home for snakes.

CLOCK OF LIFE, THE -
The clock of life is wound but once,
And no man has the power
To tell just when the hands will stop,
At late or early hour.

Now is the only time we own,
Love, live, toil and a will.
Do no wait until tomorrow
For the clock may then be still.
(Dave Rufinoft received a watch from Will Rogers with the above engraved on it.)

CLOCKS - My father wound the old clock every night with a key. He placed the key in holes on either side of the center of the clock face. Housed in a wooden frame, the clock stood on the mantle and would strike once for each hour of the day or night. (2) Alarm clocks were all metal and spring wound with a bell that could "wake the dead." My father never once set an alarm clock as he set his "mental" clock and could awaken at any hour he chose. None of his children has that ability or tried to develop it. (3) In the very early days before clocks were readily available, marks were made on the porches of some homes to use the sun's rays to tell the time of day. I used some of that sundial method to tell the time of day when I worked the 3-11 shift at the local hospital. I worked in my garden until 2:00, got my bath and got to work by 3:00 P.M. With my back to the east, when I could step on the shadow of my head, I knew it was high noon. From that point on, I learned just a certain angle for 2:00 P.M. (4) To tell time at night, fox hunters held up four fingers high over their head to mark the hour. Holding their hand as far away as they could reach, locating first the Big Dipper and North Star, then measuring by hand the amount of space between the earth and the star, they could determine the time of night. (5) When asked the time of day, a young boy who resided in one of the homes using the sundial, replied that it was a puncheon and a half before noon. My half brother overheard that reply, and teased him unmercifully so that they had hand to hand combat for years to come.

CLOTHING - Early materials for clothing consisted of leather breeches and leggings, shirts of linsey-woolsey, and coon skin caps. Women's clothing consisted of linsey-woolsey dresses and petticoats, heavy knit stockings, and coarse shoes. Factory made supplies were available when I came along so that we always started the school year with a new pair of shoes and new clothing. When we had a few good dresses, a good coat or two, and those new shoes, we were as proud as a pig with two tails.

COBWEBS - Cobwebs were spread over open wounds to stop bleeding. Trained medical personnel in most cases fail to appreciate this remedy, but it seemed to work. Some unscientific forecasters have used cobwebs to predict weather. Presumably, if the web is wet, they predict rain.

COFFEE - Early settlers used dried and ground dandelion and chicory roots for coffee. (2) A medical directive received from The Food and Drug Administration while I was working at a local hospital said that if coffee were not already on the market it would be classified as a poison. As result, before I could give a coronary patient a cup of coffee I had to check the patient's chart to learn if his attending doctor had given written permission for coffee. I do not believe the public was given this information. I also learned that one should not smoke and drink coffee at the same time because the blood pressure shoots to highest level for more than two hours.

COLDS - Drink a tea of one teaspoon ginger and a bit of sugar mixed in one cup of water. (2) Swing both arms in circles to warm the body. (3) Take a hot bath. (4) Eat chicken soup. (4) A cure I collected many years ago came from a very old newspaper article. I do not know the source: It says: `The common cold has plagued man from time immemorial. That an ear-nose-and-throat specialist, had been able to cure most of his patients colds by an amazingly simple therapy of having the patient immerse his forearms in a basin of hot water, 40-45 degrees centigrade (104-113 degrees Fahrenheit), for 30 to 60 minutes. That soaking the forearms increases the blood circulation and temperatures in the walls of the nasal passages, which in turn wards off new cold-causing micro-organisms. He claimed a cure rate of 75% for his grandmother's remedy, which for centuries has been used in many of Europe's rural areas.

COLD SORES - And herpes lesions - Drink and apply red wine. This is said to work remarkably well. (2) Take grape seed extract

COLIC - Give an infant weak dill or fennel tea. (2) Give a VERY SMALL AMOUNT of paregoric .

CONSTIPATION - Drink tea made from peach tree leaves three times per day. (2) Drink a cup of hot water before breakfast. (3)

Take the very old remedy - syrup of Black draft or drought. (4) Eat an apple at bedtime.

CONTRACTS - Early contracts were not drawn by lawyers, who dotted every "I" and crossed every "t." Your word was your bond: You simply promised to pay, sealed it with a handshake and that was all that was necessary.

'COONS - (See RACCOONS)

COPYRIGHT - Poor man's copyright: Place the information to be copyrighted in an envelope or tightly sealed package for mailing. Ask the postal worker to stamp all seams with a cancellation stamp, showing the date on every seam. Do not open. Place the material in a safe place for future reference. If needed it can be opened. That date shows you had the work in question at that earlier date.

CORN SHUCKING OR HUSKING - Party Time: My family did not drink moonshine or dance. However, some families had corn shucking parties. Instead of putting the corn in a crib, it was piled high in the barnyard with a half gallon of moonshine buried underneath. Two opposing teams shucked until late night or until they found the moonshine. The team who won was allowed to pass around the jug of whiskey among themselves. With fiddles playing they drank and danced the rest of the night. Any man who found a red ear of corn (which was very rare) was allowed to kiss any girl he chose. When the corn was all shucked, the host was ridden on a rail to his house. There he danced a little jig, and pretended to comb lice out of his hair while stomping them on the floor. The women folk cooked ham, pork, beef, vegetables, and desserts for a great feast. Everyone in the community was invited to the corn-shucking. They spent the entire night. (2) Only one grain of red corn was said to be so hard it could stop a mill grinding rock.

CORNFIELDS ON HILLSIDES - When we say corn was grown on hillsides so steep that people fell out of them, it is no joke. My family was hoeing corn on such a hillside when a traveling salesman climbed up to talk. My mother was ready to flog him when he stated that anyone who would hoe corn in such a place would "steal." He very quickly qualified that by adding that you had to "steal" dirt to dress the corn. My father once remarked to my sister, who was attempting to work above the corn row, "You can't hoe corn with your rump up the hill!"

COUGH SYRUP - No cough syrups in drug stores today compare with the wonderful old red clover tea that my mother made after I had coughed for several months. It tasted so good and stopped the coughing immediately! (2) Sip a mixture of 3 tablespoons lemon juice, 1 cup honey, 1/4 cup hot water, and 2 tablespoons whiskey (possibly moonshine).

COURTING - What we call flirting today was called "casting sheep eyes" in earlier days. When a boy cast sheep eyes at a girl that he liked, she either gave him a favorable or a sour look. It was all over if the look was sour. If she was not interested, she might also kick him in the shins. Among the young men this act was called "Breaking your leg." (2) If we began dating a young man of whom our parents did not approve, my Mother would say, "He looks like a poor pattern!" This comment was meant to discourage further interest. I presumed this meant she was looking forward to having handsome grandchildren and that he would make a poor example. If a girl married beneath her social status, she had driven her ducks to a poor pond according to my mother. She told of the most beautiful girl among her childhood friends who apparently married beneath her social status. Mother described that situation by saying, "She flew all around the pretty flowers and lit on a chicken turd." (3) Long before my time it was said that a young man considered himself financially stable enough to go looking for a wife if he owned a gun, a dog, a lantern, salt, a frying pan, and some sour dough starter. With only the horse and buggy or wagon for transportation, and with the rugged, gutted, muddy almost impassable roads, it is little wonder the young men had to do most of their courting close to home. With neighboring communities perhaps 15 or 20 miles away, a young man could scarcely walk such distances. My brother, Orlie, told of going to a neighboring community to see one of his young ladies. The boys of that community threw rocks at him as he started home that night. This "rocking" as it was called served to tell him to stay away and leave their young ladies for the men of that community.

Due to those conditions is little wonder there was much marrying of cousins. It is said if there is a genetic disorder when relatives marry relatives, it compounds that disorder many times over. My mother and dad were said to be fifth cousins but it didn't affect me, affect me, affect me!

COW, HARLIE RINDSTAFF'S - A close friend was washing up all the dirty pots and pans I had used to cook our meal, when he remarked, "You are just like Harlie Rindstaff's cow. She could eat more hay, drink more water, give less milk, and sh-t on more ax handles!"

COW TEA - Beside any plant you
wish to give special fertilizer, bury a large bucket with its top level with the ground. Twist a large rag to make a rope. Drop one end of the rag rope in the bottom of the bucket and circle the other end around the plant. Fill the bucket with cow manure. Keep it covered with water at all times. Add a lid to prevent flies, and see your plant grow. My brother-in-law used this method with one cucumber plant and harvested an unbelievable crop of cucumbers.

COWS - To prevent a cow from kicking us while we milked, we placed the handle of a garden hoe in front of the opposite hind leg and in front of the leg nearest us. We then put the other end of the hoe well up under our left arm while we milked. One week of this usually cured a cow from kicking. (2) When cows are pregnant, add at least two ounces of apple cider vinegar to their feed each day to keep them healthy. (3) When a calf is born, if you immediately cup your hands around its face, and blow your breath in its face, it will be your buddy forever. (4) If calves chew on wood, mix one ounce of apple cider vinegar to one gallon of water to drink. (5) Cows and young calves will pretend to be dead so that crows will come and pick the vermin from their ears and eyes. (6) Each farmer had a "brand" signifying ownership. This was usually a notch or a nick in the ear. (7) Among the cows there was always a lead cow, the only one to wear a bell. I have no idea how this position was determined, whether among the herd or by the owners. Once you heard the bell you knew where to find the herd. Sometimes when my brother and I were supposed to bring the cows in for the night, we could not hear the cow bells. We put our ears to the ground to determine the direction to go looking for them. On our 363 acres, we had three main sections where they might be. (8) A shy young boy came driving his family's cow one day, knocked on our door and inquired if we had a "female" (fee male?). My older sister, seeing the situation knew what he meant. Without embarrassing him, she directed him to the barn lot and the bull.

CRICKETS - (see WEATHER)

"CROWNS" OF FEATHERS IN PILLOWS OF DECEASED
- A prominent part of mountain folklore regards the feather crown, angel wreath, or heavenly crown. Years ago when someone died, a relative immediately split their feather pillow open searching for a woven mass of feathers resembling a bun. It was soft to the touch but quite heavy. It was fascinating how the feathers were sometimes woven into a perfect circle. Many believed that a crown of feathers in a pillow was proof that the deceased was going to an eternal reward in heaven. If they found a "crown," everyone rejoiced. If they did not find one, I don't know what happened, but I can imagine. The answer to the mystery of these crowns is unknown. With fewer feather pillows used today, it will perhaps never be known. My theory is that pillows were used for many months or years and the feathers naturally matted in a circle from usage. I believe it had nothing to do with the eternal abode of the person who happened to be using it when that final hour came.

The scarcity of finding feather crowns today was best explained by one Old-Timer as "There just' ain't as many people that's deservin' em these days."

CUSS WORDS - Yes, I know it is spelled curse, but "cuss" should be more appropriate. Not one time in my entire life did I ever hear my mother or father use one "curse" word. My mother used the words "Oh Pshaw" which I surmised could be a corruption of a word not so nice. We children were not allowed to say such slang as "gosh" or "darn." We watched our words very closely because we were warned that using the wrong word would result in our mouths being washed out with soap.

D

DAISY - Our most rambunctious milk cow, Daisy, got choked on apples almost every summer. We kept a broom handle with a rag tied on the end to push those apples on down to save Daisy's life. She never learned, so we were always prepared for another episode. Jerze, the other milk cow, ate the same apples but never any problem. (2) When a cow was purchased from a neighbor, it was considered routine to rename the new cow the name of that neighbor's wife. When one of the deacons in our church gave us two dogs, we followed that tradition without so much as a thought. We named the dogs after the man and his wife, Charlie and Johnnie. We felt this was a compliment. They were highly offended. We were utterly shocked. Our explanation about the naming of the cows might have helped us a bit, but we should have consulted with them before naming the dogs. We renamed the dogs, however.

DANDELION - During my early days, young maidens blew three times on a dandelion flower. If just one fuzzy seed remained, it was an omen that her sweetheart was thinking of her.

DANDRUFF - Apply apple cider vinegar, and leave one hour. Shampoo three times per week. (2) Apply one tablespoon of witch hazel mixed with one teaspoon lemon juice. Rinse after one hour.

DAY - TYPICAL DAY IN THE LIFE OF A MOUNTAIN WOMAN

1. Uncover fire coals in the hearth and build a fire. Carry out ashes.
2. Build a fire in the cook stove.
3. Feed, water, and milk the cows.
4. Carry water from the spring house to the kitchen for cooking.
5. Make breakfast: Make coffee, fry ham, bacon or sausage, make biscuits, fry eggs, make gravy, set table, add jelly, butter. Awaken family.

6. Wash dishes, sweep floors, make beds.
7. Dress children for school.
8. Chase chickens out of the garden. Hoe the garden. Pick and string beans.
9. Wash clothes on the scrub board. Build a fire under the wash kettle to boil white clothes.
10. Wind bobbins on the spinning wheel. Spin thread. Weave linens on the loom.
11. Protect infants or young children from snakes, spiders, lizards, etc.
12. Churn milk to make butter.
13. Make lye soap.
14. Darn and patch family's clothing.
15. Rob bee hive.
16. Watch for bees to swarm, beat on pan, lids or bells to stop bees from leaving premises.
17. Dose sick children with caster oil or olive oil for earache.
18. Cook two more meals on wood stove, wash dishes
19. Fall in bed ...dead tired.

DEATH IN THE FAMILY - When someone died in the mountains, the church bell was "tolled" once for each year of the person's life. The tolling was not the usual ding-dong done for church services. It was instead one strong tap and then a long pause. Most everyone in the community stopped what they were doing to count the number of times the bell was tolled. With no telephone service, tolling of the bell was our only means of communication. If someone was known to be critically ill whose age corresponded with the number of times the bell tolled, it was a safe bet as to who had died. Someone always went to the home or grave site to confirm it, however.

Everyone in the community cooked food and visited the bereaved. At night members of the family "sat up with" the deceased. I never really understood that custom. It was later suggested that it may have been to prevent rats from eating on the bodies. Perish the thought. Another story suggests Irish immigrants brought the practice from Ireland. There it was believed evil spirits entered the house if someone was not there to keep them away.

My favorite story, somewhat embellished, regarding sitting up with the dead, goes like this: We actually had a neighbor woman whose backbone was bent at a 90-degree angle. When she walked past our house she had to turn her head side-ways in an effort to look at me. I can still see her smile.

When she died, the funeral attendants would lay her head down in the casket and her feet came up. When they laid her feet down, her head came up. After much frustration, they went to the hardware store and bought some rubber straps with hooks on each end. They were finally able to complete the job. The body was brought back home, and the coffin was left open. But we knew nothing about that strap that was holding her in place.

I, along with my father, my brother Harmon, and one distant relative were commissioned to sit up that night with the body. About nine o'clock my father looking us over, said, "We have been sitting up with this sick lady. If you folks are going to sit up, I believe I will go to bed."

With that he left.

By ten o'clock this relative, said, "If you two are going to sit up, I believe I will go to bed. " And he left.

Soon a really bad storm came up with much lightening and thunder. My brother Harmon said "Bonnie, if you are going to sit up I believe I'll got to bed." And he left.

That storm got worse by the minute. Finally a crack of thunder came and knocked out every light. That rubber strap came loose, and Aunt Donnie came rising up out of that coffin. I rose up out of that funeral home chair. I threw down that hand held fan, I rushed over to that coffin, and said, "Aunt Donnie, if you are going to sit up, I believe I'll go to bed.

DEATH SIGNS OR SUPERSTITIONS - Many mountain people believed very strongly that if a bird got into the house, it was a sign that a family member would die within 3 days, 3 weeks, or 3 months. My family had a neighbor upon whose head a bird lit. He fell from a bridge and was killed within three days. (Perhaps he had no aura) Many people I know today still believe that omen, but I had given it little thought until the night of February 9, 1998 when I dreamed I was seeing a red bird up in the corner of my bedroom. He looked worn and exhausted. Naturally I viewed this dream with some alarm. But I told myself it was only a dream, since no bird was actually in the house. I dismissed it as just another one of my unusual dreams. A phone call that afternoon told me my oldest son, Don, had been admitted to St. Mary's Hospital with kidney failure. He was later diagnosed with Multiple Myeloma (a type of cancer). Only someone who has experienced this can realize just how paralyzed I was with fear. I was afraid to breathe, afraid to move. This cannot be true! It wasn't a live bird! Everyone I spoke with who had ever heard of multiple myeloma added "and they died." But three days passed, three weeks passed, and I begun to have some hope....Don died on May 28, 1998.

DECORATION DAY- Before cemeteries established interest-bearing bank accounts to maintain them, each family and church congregation was responsible for upkeep of the cemetery- usually found located next to the church. Decoration day was held on one Sunday in the spring to bring all the families together. Arrangements were made to mow and clear weeds around the monuments, a church service was held, and flowers were placed on the graves of family members. Often, singing and "dinner on the ground" were part of the day's events.

DEER - Deer meat was one of the most important food sources for our early settlers. It could be preserved by salt for long periods of time so there was little waste. Many deer can still be seen in Cades Cove, where we recently counted more than one hundred.

DENTISTRY - Unlike today we never had dentists. If you lived in the very early days and needed a tooth pulled, imagine, if you can, lying on the floor with a knee held against your chest. Your mouth propped open with a stick. A knife being used to cut about a quarter inch deep around the tooth, sometimes the wrong tooth. Tooth pullers sometimes slipped off the offending tooth, causing excruciating pain. When the tooth finally came out, your mouth was filled with salt. Thankfully, my father did none of the above. But his tooth- pullers, taken from the old family trunk, smelling of moth balls was bad enough. Some children came up with a much better plan for extraction of their baby teeth. They tied one end of a string around the offending tooth and the other end to a door knob. Then they waited for someone to open the door.

DENTURES - (see SLIPPERY ELM POWDER)

DEODORANTS- Early on packaged deodorants were not available in our stores. Wet baking soda or vinegar was used to prevent underarm odors.

DIABETES - There was no insulin or oranase available for our diabetics. We knew little about diet to aid in its control until recent years. I recall my brother-in-law used honey in an attempt to control his diabetes. (2) Jerusalem artichokes, raw white potatoes, or flax seed oil combined with cottage cheese was believed to be most effective. (3) 1/8 tsp. cinnamon is said to triple the effects of insulin. (4) 1/8 to 1/4 teaspoon ground cinnamon with each meal is said to help control blood sugar.
Recent: Mix 1 part bilberry tincture to 1 part bearberry tincture. Add 10 to 20 drops to glass of water between meals to control blood sugar naturally.

DIARRHEA - Drink blackberry juice. (2) Pour high-proof whiskey in a cup and set on fire. Mix the residue with water and drink. (3) We also drank tea made from peach leaves every 4 hours. (4) We drank a mixture of burnt toast, scraped into a cup of hot water. (5) Black pepper in boiled milk was also used. (6) If all else fails, and it is a severe case, put two or three drops of turpentine on a teaspoon of sugar. One drop might be sufficient. (My family used to say that this remedy would bind you over until next court.) (7) Dr. Newburn, a local doctor, said that eating the biggest steak you can afford is the best remedy for diarrhea. He said that meat gave the worms something to eat on instead of eating your intestines.

DIDDLE - "Diddle" George Harrison Kerley, a 1936 graduate of Pi Beta Phi High School, Gatlinburg, Tennessee, now lives in Sacramento, CA. He phoned me on May 3, 1998 regarding our upcoming class reunion on each third Saturday of September. I asked how he got the nickname of Diddle. He said when he lived in the Pi Beta Phi school dormitory whoever had the largest foot was always given that nickname. He wore size 11 while Clark Franklin who had just graduated reportedly wore a size 14. He told how Bruce Stinnett had once asked in class if four and three "are seven, or is seven." Stella Huff, the teacher, said, "If you had one little thought in that empty head of yours, you would be intelligent."

DIDY - Short for diaper was the name used by early settlers. It was still in use when I was young. So, yes, I wore a didy. (Accent on the "I.")

DINNER BELL - Instead of a dinner bell, we used a huge sea shell with the tip cut off. We first poured water through it to enhance the sound. We then blew it like a bugle to call the family to dinner. It could be heard for at least a mile and certainly over most of our 363-acre farm. We used this shell to call the family from the cornfield for lunch. Of course, at that time we had breakfast, dinner, and supper. These terms are hardly acceptable in today's society.

DIPHTHERIA - The only folk remedy early people had for this dreaded disease was to dip a clean white cloth in pure kerosene oil, and swab out the patient's throat. Adults swallowed as much as a tablespoon of the oil. This caused one to vomit the deadly mucus and was credited with saving lives.

DISCIPLINE - My parents never raised us by the books, as there were no books available. They sometimes took us out to the woodshed and applied psychology to the seat of learning. When we were too rambunctious all my Father had to do was look out over the top of his glasses at us! That said it all. We knew we had gone as far as Dad would allow, and we always heeded that simple command. Mother and Dad knew the best way to "straighten-out" us youngsters was to bend us over the knee. They never told us WHAT to do; they just made us WISH THAT WE HAD!

My Mother did most of the corrections, but my father gave me one slight spanking when he found me enjoying with the chickens a half bushel of shelled corn I had poured in a lob-lolly of mud. He missed several opportunities, however. Usually, when Mother started to whip us, she would preface it with, "Now this is going to hurt me more than you!" But we dared not say, "Don't do it. We wouldn't want you to hurt yourself."

Mother once took my brother, Sam, and me for a "switching" in the chimney corner. While I was getting mine Sam would peer around the corner of the house sticking his tongue out at me. This hurt worse than the switch. The switch was a long slender limb cut from a tree. It was used instead of a paddle, and it hurt like the dickens. To get even with Sam I returned the favor. Mother never caught us at this or the correction would no doubt have been worse.

DIVORCE - The word divorce was never in our vocabulary when I was married in 1941. Our parents told us if we made a blister we would sit on it, or if we made a hard bed we would lie in it. We knew to work out our problems, never to allow even a thought of divorce as a solution. That's what we did. In fact I do not recall ever hearing of a divorce until around the 1960's. Some men or women were known to "run-away" thereby leaving a spouse and children to fend for themselves.

DOAK, SAMUEL - Of interest was the prayer the Reverend Doak prayed just before the soldiers were to do battle with the British at Kings Mountain. He prayed: "O Lord, have consideration for the British, for thou knowest we intend to bring them to thy bosom."

DOG DAYS - Begin on July 28 in the south and extend six weeks. If it rains the first day of dog days it will generally rain every day of dog days. Our parents cautioned us that the dew was poisonous during those days. If we had a sore on our foot, we were very careful not to allow any dew to touch it. Contact with the dew was thought to cause blood poisoning and even death. I'll never forget hearing Dr. Ralph Shilling, a doctor in Gatlinburg, giving our nurses "what for" because we were having so many unusual infections among our patients during dog days. The nurses were pleading that they were as careful as ever. He was not impressed.
I interrupted saying: "Dr. Shilling. Don't you know that it's dog days!"
With that he just turned and walked away. The nurses appreciated that I had stepped in. I am not sure he was.

DOGS - We were never allowed to feed homemade flour biscuits to our dog. Biscuits were said to cause them to have "fits." Old timers believed that during a storm a dog in the house drew lightening so that the dog would be put outside. The way some dogs tremble during storms may be a clue.

DOORS LOCKED - During the early days, life was simple, and people were perhaps more honest. Hardly anyone locked their doors, because they trusted each other. If anyone had a key, they told the neighbors where they kept it in case someone needed to get into the house. We could go to the hardware and buy a "skeleton" key that unlocked practically every building in town except the bank. I can't recall using a key to lock our doors until the 1960's. Ray T. always contended that a locked door only told an honest man that you were not home.

DOW, REV. LORENZO - While doing research on my Trentham family tree, I came across the name of Rev. Lorenzo Dow, an extremely colorful preacher who held services in this area. The article said that "Martin Trentham was the devil raised by Lorenzo Dow from a pile of tow sacks. I found articles showing that Dow went to great lengths to get his point across. (2) During one sermon he preached that at any moment Gabriel might blow his trumpet to signal that the end of time on earth had come. He gave an impassioned description of the great horrors that the unsaved would suffer in a burning hell. He had a young black boy named Gabriel stationed with a horn in a nearby tree. After Dow covered the subject quite thoroughly, Gabriel blew his horn. The sound sent many folks into hysterics. When the crowd learned the truth, Dow had to plead for the boy's life. The crowd was going to lynch him. (3) On another occasion, to find a thief, Dow told the people that if everyone in the community came to the next service, he would point out the thief. He brought a good sized rock to the service and told the crowd that when he turned around three times he would throw the rock and hit the thief. Instead of throwing the rock, he watched to see who "ducked." He then pointed him out as the thief. (4) To catch another thief, he told the people that if everyone in the community would come that night, he would point out the thief. (Naturally the thief had to go rather than being suspected.) This time Dow ceremoniously set a wash kettle and an old dominecker rooster before them. He said that everyone was to march around and touch the kettle. When the guilty person touched the kettle the rooster would crow. When all had passed around and touched the soot-blackened kettle, the rooster had not crowed. At this point he checked all the hands of those present. The one who had NO soot on his hand was pointed out as the thief.

While visiting in this area, Dow learned about the "Jerks" a very strange unexplained phenomena that was happening to many people scattered throughout the area (see JERKS.)

DOWSING - also called water witching, is a process Mountain Folk have used for generations to search for water, minerals, oil, long lost cabins, grave sites, and missing objects. Water witching was most often discussed behind closed doors until someone needed a dowser's services to locate a much-needed well for water. We cannot explain a scientific principle at work, but we have no choice but to admit there is very convincing evidence that dowsing works. Perhaps it results from a sensitivity to radiation or perhaps rays not yet identified. It seems that a special sensitivity is necessary, since some people cannot do it. (2) Process- The dowser walks about randomly loosely holding in his or her hands a dowsing stick or rods. The location of the mineral, water, or object is indicated by movement of the rods. When I was a child, a flexible tree limb, shaped like a "Y" was most often used. This limb was about 24 inches long and was usually taken from a fruit-bearing tree. Sometimes the dowser held two smaller L-shaped sticks in each hand. We later began using a section of coat hangers bent in the shape of an "L." The shorter ends, approximately 6 inches, are held in each hand. The longer ends, about 15 inches long, are held parallel to the ground and point forward. When something is located the wires will swing across each other. (3) When locating water, the sticks or limb will turn in ones hands and point downward. Upon finding water, some dowsers will hold one end of the stick in their mouth and turn in a circle, allowing the branch to point to the direction the water was flowing. While using a limb from a fruit bearing tree, I located a site to dig a well for a new house we were building for sale. I was able to estimate the depth of the well by holding one end of the limb over the site. I counted the number of times it swung up and down before becoming completely still. Then I multiplied that number by two. When the well was dug, I had miscalculated by two feet! (4) Locating graves- When tombstones are missing, the evidence of a previous burial can be found by dowsing the site. This action saves digging a second grave. Dowsing rods will cross every time the dowser comes to a grave site. They will open again at the end of the grave. Located in our Trentham family cemetery is a headstone that was set long after the funeral. This tombstone was slightly misplaced so that a body does not show up in the correct place. A dowser at the site found the location of the body with no problem. At another site, the dowser was told that a body was there, but he went round and round in a circle. He finally scratched his head and admitted that the only sign of a body was directly under the headstone, but it was much too small for a body. The family finally told him that the body was cremated and the ashes were placed under the headstone. (5) Locating other sites- Pete Prince not only located the exact location of the house where I was born, but he proceeded to stake out every corner, every door, and every window. He even located the fireplace and height of the mantel of our home in the Smokies. My sister and I watched in amazement as he completed this perfect floor plan of a house removed many years before that he had never seen. (6) Locating objects- Once we moved to another city midway through the school year. Our children had already received their report cards, which were misplaced during the move. The children would not be allowed to enter school the following Monday if they did not have the report cards. I was frantic and ready to resort to anything to find them. When my dowsing rods pointed to a filing cabinet, I went through all four drawers piece by piece, but I did not find those cards. Time and time again the rods indicated that they were there. Finally, I jerked the top drawer all the way out. There behind the drawer lay those cards! (7) Recent update- On October 17, 1967 The New York Times carried an article describing how Marine Corps Engineers were using improvised divining rods to detect tunnels, mines, and booby traps both in training and in combat. Major Nelson Hardacker of the Fifth Marine Division stated that the devices would not work for some men but that they were in the minority. The article went on to state that this divining had been practiced all over the world for more than two thousand years to find water, oil, and minerals. The article also indicated that certain successful dowsers started their experiments with maps without going to the location in person. They used a pendulum instead of a divining rod to locate lost mines, walls, and even ancient sewers on maps. If this is the case, it cannot be magnetism or any other physical energy, because it works at a distance and responds to thought. It must be a form of psychic energy.

E

EARS- (1) Earache- Warm a small amount of olive oil, also known as sweet oil. Control the temperature so that a drop will be comfortable on the inside of the wrist. Put two or three drops in the aching ear. (2) Fill a cotton sock with rice and tie the sock closed. Apply to the ear. (3) Blow smoke into the ear. (4) (More recent remedy) Pour one drop of warm melaleuca oil, also known as tea tree oil, into the ear. (5) Parents who smoke around infants can expect many trips to the hospital with childhood earaches. I know one baby who went to the hospital 26 times. The mother smoked constantly. (6) Ear ringing may result from too much aspirin. (7) Ear wax- hard to remove. Soften with hydrogen peroxide; syringe out once the wax is soft.

EASTMAN KODAK - Mountaineer ingenuity is credited with helping this fine company to locate in Kingsport, Tennessee. With information that George Eastman was looking for a southern location, J. Fred Johnson, and other businessmen reportedly arranged to meet him in Bristol to show him around. A-Model and T-Model cars were not very dependable. The very narrow muddy roads made travel even worse. The businessmen used two cars to assure dependable transportation for him. When Mr. Eastman's car broke down the second car had gone far ahead so that he was stranded for a time. The men knew about his great love for hunting. They stocked a field with lots of quail and brought them lots of food. They secretly stationed sharp-shooters to make sure his every shot brought down a quail. Exuberant that this was the greatest hunt he had ever been on, he closed the deal. Bristol is proud to have Eastman Kodak today.

ECHINACEA - was used by the Cherokees as a snakebite remedy and a general cure all for infections. (2) Recent: Echinacea is one of the most-prescribed herbs. Doctors have used it to treat fevers, cholera, boils, abscesses, chronic ulcers, poison ivy and oak, acne, nervous headache, meningitis, gangrenous wounds, tonsillitis, respiratory infections, bronchitis, measles, chicken pox, scarlet fever, eczema, appendicitis, gonorrhea and syphilis. It is one of the most researched herbal medicines in the world. When taking it for colds, flu, boils, cuts, respiratory infections, kidney or vaginal infections, it is best taken at the first sign of distress. Take 500 milligrams every hour for two or three hours. If conditions persist, take 500 mg four times per day up to ten days. Take a break for four days. This schedule can be repeated for up to eight weeks. Discontinue after eight weeks. Echinacea should be used only under observation of a physician for lupus, HIV infections, multiple sclerosis, Graves disease, diabetes, or other auto-immune diseases. Do not take Echinacea during pregnancy. Echinacea is listed among what is believed to be the twelve most powerful herbs. **(see HERBS.)**

ECHO, LITTLE SIR - At some point on our farm in what is now the Great Smoky Mountains National Park, we could yell and the mountains repeated very distinctly every word we said. This made me wonder if there is a spot anywhere in this area now where echoes can be heard. Some fifty years after we moved away, I went back to the old home place and could not get the echo. Tall trees now grow over the entire area, which no doubt was the reason it will not echo. Can anyone today tell me where to find such a echo? If so, please phone 865-970-2815.

ECLIPSE OF SUN - The chickens went to roost and the cows came home during an eclipse of the sun. I understand that some people killed themselves in fear during an eclipse before it was determined that the eclipse was a natural phenomenon.

EDUCATION, SALVATION, DAMNATION - In very early days, the one and only community building at Elkmont was used as a school, a church, and a theater. Silent black and white movies were shown to enthusiastic locals. The building became known for Education, Salvation, and Damnation.

ELECTRICITY - During my generation the Tennessee Valley Authority came over the hills and through the woods to bring us electricity. My family's first access to electricity was in 1933 when we moved to Pigeon Forge, and we got our first electric-powered radio. Battery radio's had been available earlier. All other available appliances at that time soon followed. Our Stewart Warner refrigerator ran for 31 years without any problem. It is said that refrigerators now are built to last only ten years so that company employees will have a job. When electricity finally came some of our locals were afraid to eat corn bread baked in an oven heated by electricity for fear it would poison them. Now we can certainly laugh at such fears, but I am fearful some day we may have proof that the electromagnetic waves from power lines may be extremely dangerous to health. I am especially concerned about the health of young children living near transformers. Twenty seven members of a family that lived within a mile of my home have died of cancer. Their home was directly under a major power line. Our government is, of course, denying any danger at present. It is understandably because of the cost. However, I hope that soon this question is honestly researched.

EMBARRASSING MOMENTS, ONE OF MY WORST- About 1930, a group from a Knoxville radio station came to the Fighting Creek school in our neighborhood, where my two sisters, two brothers, and I attended school.
Well into the program the jokes became too risque for my dear mother. She stood up near the rear of the building and said loudly enough for all to hear, "Come on children, let's go home." The five of us stood up and trooped out of the building behind her. If the earth could have swallowed me up, I would have felt better. I can hardly describe even today the extreme embarrassment I felt at that moment. I'm sure that was a great source of amusement to the performers and perhaps to the crowd that we left behind. But that was our mother.

ENTERTAINMENT - All the farm work kept us quite busy, but there was always time for play and recreation. With no television or radio, we made our own entertainment. Dad made a wonderful bulgur wagon for us to ride. We had a train that ran around the mountain side on a track. We often swam in the old swimming hole in the summer. We enjoyed the wonderful sled runs in the snow in winter. During the evening play time, we enjoyed such activities as kick-the-can, ante-over, and blind man's bluff. We also created fun at the expense of family members and boarders. The family was often divided into two factions, with each playing pranks on the other. My Mother aided and abetted both groups. She once ordered a huge spider with tingling legs which we put in the school teachers bed. When her feet touched the spider she landed on her pillow. Among the many dares from my brothers was to suck a raw egg or bite a redworm in two pieces. I'm not telling which dare I took.

All the family sitting around the fireside at night was a great time for "haint" tales, especially when we had all the boarders. The true snake tales had me afraid to put my feet on the floor while listening.

My very religious mother would not allow a deck of cards in our house. We were not allowed to attend the movies. This was during the era when the Westerns were the popular movies of the day. The cowboy kissed the horse instead of the girl. When my big brother, Orlie, came in from Denver, Colorado, where he lived for many years, we were finally allowed to go with him to see our first movie, "Steamboat Around the Bend." Mother also would not allow me to play basketball on our school team because of the uniforms. She said they were too revealing. She should see me today at age 81.

We enjoyed riding Beck, our most spirited mule, who once ran with me into his stable and bent me back over the saddle with apparently no ill effects. I did have one tragic encounter---all my fault. As mother was leaving one Sunday afternoon she cautioned us not to ride the mules. I am sure if she had not mentioned them we would never have thought of it. We watched until she was out of sight, then ran to harness Jack, the more gentle mule. My sister and brother had ridden quite a ways, while I walked. Threatening to run the mule if they did not let me ride, they allowed me to climb on. In the saddle was Gladys, holding Sam in front of her, while I tried to hold on to the back of the saddle behind her. We had gone perhaps no more than ten feet when I fell off, breaking my right arm above and below the elbow and fracturing the socket. This allowed the fluid to escape. Since I was only six or seven years old, my arm grew out of line. Bone specialists later said they could break it and swing it back in line, but I would have to choose between having it stay bent 90 degrees at the elbow or to stay straight all the time. I decided I could use it very well as it was. It has indeed been some hindrance while playing the piano or typing, but I went on to become champion volley ball server in my county during grade school, to hit a mean baseball and have a decent typing speed on this computer.

EPILEPSY - While I doubt the Food and Drug Administration would approve this remedy today, mountain folk drank a tea made from the root of the male peony plant. The tea was steeped (cooked slowly) for twenty-four hours, strained, then consumed for several days for epilepsy. To cure young children, the peony root was merely hung around the neck of the child. (2) Another mountain remedy was made from the root, seed, and leaves of parsley mixed with anise and caraway. These ingredients were steeped in white wine until one-third of the liquid had evaporated. Patients drank 4 ounces morning and evening. They were supposed to refrain from drinking any other beverage for three hours afterward.

ETIQUETTE - Our parent tried to teach us good etiquette such as holding something over our mouth when we sneezed. All the while, I thought that was only to keep ones dentures from flying out. Seriously though, we have failed to emphasize some of the basic table manners. Some of the manners our mother taught are listed below: (1) Come promptly to the table when the hostess calls you as food tastes better when it is hot. (2) Sit straight in your chair with both feet flat on the floor in front of you. Sit quietly with your hands in your lap until after the blessing or until the hostess starts passing the food. Keep your elbows off the table.

(3) Wait for the food to be passed to you. Take some and pass it on. Never leave it beside your plate. Wait until all the food is offered before you begin to eat. We jokingly said that any food we could reach at the dinner table without the body leaving the seat was considered acceptable. If one's seat left his chair, however, it was considered "Ill-Manners." When eating we extended our little finger to show how refined we were. To crook it at a 90-degree angle meant we were super-refined.

(4) Never butter your bread directly from the butter dish. Put the butter on your plate or bread plate. Break the bread apart, and spread it with butter.(5) Keep the conversation pleasant. Never talk with your mouth full. Do not make biological noises or blow your nose at the table. Do not use your finger to push food onto a utensil. Never wave silverware around while eating. Do not lick fingers or wipe hands on the tablecloth. My father dealt with too much laughter at the table by conspicuously peering over the top of his glasses --that silent shout said "that's enough!" (6) Early on it was considered good manners to leave some food on your plate and never to take the very last helping from the serving dish. Later came the pressure to clean our plates. When we finished eating, if someone offered us more food we made the following announcement: "No, thanks, I have eaten an eloquent sufficiency, if I should eat any more, would be redundancy. My collateral qualities are quite "cu-dil-I-fied." (I have never been able to find that word in the dictionary.) (7) Allow your hostess plenty of time to finish her meal before serving dessert. Help clear the table before dessert is served leaving water glasses, cups, and saucers. Never pick up a dessert dish and hold it in your hand while eating. Remain at the table until your hostess suggests going elsewhere. Children must ask to be excused. (8) Offer to help with the dishes except in a formal atmosphere, but do not insist if the hostess does not want help. Always thank the hostess for the invitation. If you can honestly do so, compliment her on the cooking. Never eat and run. Also, if someone brought you a dish, pie or whatever of food that was totally unedible so that you had to chunk it, but that you need to be gracious, you could truthfully say as a compliment "that it didn't last long around here."

EVANS, REV. RICHARD - The Evans Chapel Church was named for Rev. Richard Evans. When he first came as pastor, he introduced himself to the congregation. He said, "My name is Richard Evans. Since I was a young boy, I have been called Dick, and that same old dick has been hanging to me ever since." It appeared he might as well have dismissed the service at that point. (2) He and his wife had eleven daughters. He said the devil owed him a debt and paid him off in sons-in-laws. (3) He once spent the night where a group of young people was having a dance. One of the girls asked him to dance with her. He said, "Hold it a minute, and let's have a word of prayer." He prayed so long that the girl collapsed and the crowd became so embarrassed that no one wanted to dance any longer. This incident began a revival meeting during which 200 souls were converted. (4) Rev. Evans told a story about a woman riding a steer that refused to ford the river. Rev. Evans came along and saw her situation and asked where she was going. She replied she was going to hear a Rev. Dick Evans preach if only she could get this &%$###%%%^&@$ steer across the river. Rev. Evans helped her to get across the river, but he did not introduce himself. One can imagine her surprise when she arrived at the church to learn that he was Rev. Dick Evans. (5) Two miles south of Gatlinburg in the Great Smoky Mountains National Park is the Sugarlands Visitor Center. Several hundred feet to the rear of the Visitor's Center is the cemetery that was located to the right of the Evans

Chapel Church. The highest tombstone marks the grave of Rev. Evans. Alongside is Mrs. Evans. This was the church I first attended.

EXPRESSIONS - OF TENNESSEE HILLBILLIES.

A fixin' to...................... planning to
A whoop and a hollar..... a considerable distance
Afeared........................... afraid
Aim............................... plan to
Aingern........................... onion
Air................................. are
Allow............................. thought

Ary................................ none
Ast.... ....to ask
Atter.................................after
Awful poorly.................. very ill
Bad off............................ very ill
Bait................................. a good meal
Bald faced liar................ a very deliberate liar
Beat around the bush...... avoid a subject
Big dope.......................... carbonated drink
Big sight.......................... much or many
Bite off more than he can chew.........take on too much
Black gold....................... coal
Blinky............................. sour milk
Bread..............................came from a bakery
Breaking.......................... failing by age
Brung..............................brought
Carry on...........................to act foolish
Catawampas.................... out of square
Chimley.......................... chimney
Clever............................. smart
Clim or clumb................ to climb
Coal .... Black gold
Coon's age...................... a long time
Corn fed......................... husky, strong
Count your chickens before they hatched......be too eager
Crack of day.................... break of day
Dig................................. to shovel or spade
Discombobulated........... mixed up
Doin's............................. an affair
Don't set well................. doesn't please
Done nothing out of the way - did no wrong
Doodle-de-squat............. worth nothing
Dope............................... soft drink
Druther........................... prefer
Edzact............................ exact, to reason out
Et................................... eaten
Every bit and grain.......... entire

Fair to middlin'................ between good and bad
Fall off........................... lose weight
Feel gaily........................ happy
Fetch.............................. to bring
Fireboard........................ mantel
Fit.................................. fought
Flatter than a flitter......... like a pancake
Fotched.......................... brought
Frazzled.......................... very tired
Frog sticker..................... long pointed knife
Fur piece......................... long distance
Fuzz............................... lint
Gap................................ mountain pass
Gettin' hitched................ getting married
Gollywobble.................... meaning nothing
Gommed......................... mess, ruined
Goozle............................ throat, speak hoarsely
Graveyard c..................... a tubercular cough
Gully washer.................... hard rain
Gumption....................... assertiveness
Had a calf with a shuck tail.........showed great displeasure
Haint.............................. a ghost that haunts a definite place
Heared............................ past tense of hear
Hippie............................ large hips
Hit................................. it
Hogwash......................... unnecessary, unbelievable talk
Holpe............................. helped
Hoofing it....................... walking
In the family way............. pregnant
Jubus............................. dubious, doubtful
Jump the broom.............. getting married
Kiverlid.......................... bedspread
Laid up.......................... unable to work
Laid by.......................... crops cultivated for last time
Left holding the bag........ worthless
Let the tail wag the dog. pay attention to unimportant things
Liked to......................... almost

Little bitty...................... small
Made the fur fly............. worked hard (straightened someone out)
Making a scu................. a rude thing to do
Mealy mouthed............. too timid to speak
Meetin' house.............. church house
Mending fences.......... apologizing
Might nigh.................. almost
Much obleeged............ thanks
Nary........................... none
Nestes......................... nests
Notorious republican.... notary public
Once in a blue moon.... rare event
Pad............................. cushion you sit on
Painter........................ panther
Pap............................. father
Passel......................... many
Peak-ed...................... pale
Pert............................ feisty
Picking up.................. improving, gaining weight
Piddle........................ wasting time
Pizen......................... poison
Plague....................... troublesome
Play purty................. toy
Playin' possum.......... playing dead
Plike......................... play like
Plunder..................... furniture
Point blank.............. absolute
Pump Knot.............. A knot on the head from a blow
Put on...................... act smart, or put on a shirt
Ranched................ rinsed (I ranched your clothes in the creek.)
Rat now................... right now
Reckon so................. think so, perhaps
Right smart.............. considerable
Risin'.............................inflammation, a boil, carbuncle or stone
bruise
Rot gut........................... bad whiskey
Ruke............................. rake

Sang.............................. ginseng
Scout............................. elude
Scrooch up .... take less room
Shagnasty .... an ill bred person
Shed.............................. rid of
Shet.............................. shut (the door)
Shin-dig........................ dance, party
Shingle.......................... hair cut
Shore............................ sure
Sich.............................. such
Sigogglin...................... off angle
Since heck was a pup...... .a long time ago
Slaunchways................. slanted
Slop jar......................... chamber pot
Smack dab..................... on target
Sparking........................ courting
Snipe huntin'.................. duped
Sparkin' .... courting, wooing
Spring chicken................ young
Skun.............................. skinned
Skunked................... soundly defeated
Stove up......................... jabbed
Sull-up .... pout
Stub up...................... pout or sulk
Sunday meetin' dress...... Sunday best
Sunday going to meetin' dress..... Sunday dress
Take off to tall timbers... leave for greener pastures
Tall cotton..................... luxury (be in tall cotton)
Techous .... easily riled
Thunder mug.................. chamber pot
Tight.............................. stingy
Tote.............................. carry
Traipse.......................... walk needlessly
Tyin' the knot................. getting married
Twern't nothin'............... amounted to nothing (usually in response to appreciation)
Vittles........................... food

Way out........................ far away
White lightning............... moonshine
Whole lot....................... a great amount
Whup........................... to whip
Y'all............................ all of you
Yan............................. yonder (hither and yon)
Yan side........................ the farther most side
Young-uns...................... children

EXPRESSIONS OF SURPRISE

Did you ever!
Did you ever hear the likes!
For goodness sake! For heaven's sake!
For land's sake!
Good gracious alive! Goodness gracious alive!
Go on!
Great day in the morning!
Holy Mackerel!
Holy Moses!
I DO declare!
I'll be John Brown!
I'll swan!
I wish I might drop dead!
Mercy me!
My goodness!
My stars!
My stars and garters!
Now don't that jar your preserves!
Not since Heck was a pup!
Sakes Alive!
Shut your mouth!
Well, if that ain't the beat'nist.

EXPRESSION - HEALTH MATTERS-
I felt like I'd been kicked in the head by a mule.
I felt sight on this earth bad.

I had such miseries.
I ain't much stout yet, but the spells ain't common. (I'm better.)
My nerves all tore up.

EXPRESSIONS, similes and metaphors

A blind hog will pick up an acorn once in awhile. (Sometimes a person gets lucky.)
A whistling woman and a crowing hen always come to some bad end. (Granny Myers stopped my whistling with that one.)
All wool and a yard wide
Black as a stack of cats
Busy as a bee in a tar bucket
Can't cut the mustard
Can't hack it
Clean as a hounds tooth
Content as a coon in a pond full of spring lizards.
Crazy as a Bessie bug
Crooked as a barrel of fish hooks

Dead as a door nail.
Dead as a door knob
Dead as four o'clock
Don't have both oars in the water (crazy)
Drunk as a biled owl
Dumb as dirt
Fast as Snyder's pup
Fussing around like an old granny woman
Give my eye tooth for------
Go off half cocked (not prepared or understanding)
Gone off your rocker......(go crazy)
Go off his trolley ......(go crazy.....he done gone off his trolley)
Go hog wild

Had a brain storm
Happy as a pig in a mud hole
Happy as a coon
Happy as was a virgin until marriage.

Have a hitch in my get-along (have a problem.)
He reminds me of a toothache I once had
He looks as if he was weaned on a pickle
Have a burr under his/her saddle.......upset, irritated
Have his/her tail between his legs......defeated, embarrassed
Have an ax to grind..........wanting to argue an issue
Heard the wind blow before .....boasting, don't believe it
Hollered like a stuck pig.

I hear you clucking but I can't find your nest. (I don't understand.)
It would drive a wooden man crazy
It's just root hog or die......(live with it)
It's a long road that doesn't turn........(things have to get better.)
Ill as a hornet

Let the cat out of the bag (tell a secret or surprise)
Like a one-eyed dog in a meat house
Like a scalded dog (take off--run)
Lock, stock and barrel (complete)
Look like a mule eating briars
Mad as a wet hen
Mean as a snake
Off plumb (Spaced out, Flaky)
Poor as Job's turkey, too poor to gobble
Pretty as a speckled pup on a little red wagon
Pregnant: Waiting for her bee's to swarm
Pull the wool over ones eyes (confound-deliberately mislead)
Ready for the funny farm (mentally ill or unusual)
Right as rain
Rough as a corn cob (crude behavior or rough texture)
Ruffle your feathers......disturb

Scarce as hen's teeth
She caresses, smiles and purrs, proof as yet, he ain't hers.
Sleep like a log
Slick as snot on a door knob
Slick as a whistle

Slippery as elm bark
Slow as molasses.
Smart as a whip
So stingy he would skin a flea for its tallow(per Ray T.)
Sounded like a ghost in a barrel.
Straight as a martin to his gourd
Stubborn as a mule

Take off like a scalded dog
Teched in the head and nuts off the same family tree
Three sheets in the wind (drunk)
Tight as the bark on a tree (tight also meant stingy).
Tight as Dick's hat band
Tough as boiled owl
Ugly as a mud fence dabbed with tadpoles.
Weak as cat water
Went to bed with the chickens...(went to bed early)
Wild as a buck
Whole nine yards (complete)
When coming home alone at night, call out "Well here I am broke again."
Wouldn't touch him with a ten foot pole.

EXPRESSIONS- SOCIAL
Do come sit a spell
I dare not go back on my raisin'.
I plumb forgot
It scared the livin' daylights outta me!
A cow's tail whacking flies.
If you'll just stay the night, we'll (eat, talk...)
I haven't seen you since the woods burnt over.
Truth to tell.....beginning of a sentence as a transition.
Yes siree Bob tail.

To see where you are going, look at where you've been
The more people you know the better you like dogs
If you lie down with dogs, you will get fleas

His folks are like taters; the best ones underground
If a man insists he is honest, you can almost be sure he is a crook.
If a man repeats numerous times he will do a certain thing, better
watch out.

EYES - (1) Black eyes - Apply bruised peach leaves wrapped in
gauze or apply a scrapped raw potato. (2) Cinder in the eye -
Chop an onion and let the tears wash out the cinder, or wash out
with eye drops. (3) Eye cream - Castor oil. (4) Eye lashes - To
make eyelashes grow longer, apply castor oil. (5) Granulated eye
lids - Apply a weak solution of boric acid, a poultice of scrapped
potato, or castor oil packs. (6) Pink eye - Squeeze the juice of a
freshly cut tomato into the eye. Do not use canned tomato juice.
This remedy is said to be an absolute cure for pinkeye. (7) A
scrapped apple poultice is also used for pink eye. (8) A drop of
castor oil can be squeezed onto a sterile pad then applied to the
affected eye. (7) Puffy eyes or dark circles - Use chilled tea bags
or sliced chilled cucumbers applied to the closed eye lids.

F

FACIALS - MUD PACKS - Cucumber facial: To a 2" chunk of fresh seeded and pureed cucumber add 1 teaspoon lemon juice, 1 teaspoon witch hazel, 1 beaten egg white, 2 tablespoons yogurt, and 2 tablespoons non-fat powdered milk. Puree all in blender. Apply for 30 minutes. Wash with warm, mild soap. (2) Recent recipes. Add apple cider vinegar to 2 cups red clay. Beat to make a fine paste. Add one beaten egg white. Apply a generous coat and leave on 15 minutes. Remove with cool mild soap.

FACE LIFT - Mountaineer style: Tie some hairs together in the center top of the head and make them tighter every day. This technique was said to stop coughs by raising the palate and also to reduce wrinkles in the face. (2) Grimacing as a form of exercise is supposed to reduce flabbiness. (3) Pretending to have a pencil in the mouth and writing words in the air also is supposed to help the appearance of the face. (4) A friend told of his 90 year old grandmother who looks about 40 years old. Every night of her life, after going to bed she takes both hands, and pushes upward on her face. Perhaps the fact that her face may stay in that position while sleeping may be the secret. (5) Also, give your face drinks of water every chance you have. Wet both hands and rub. Hardly anyone drinks enough water.

FEED SACK DRESSES - At one time feed sacks (containing feed for cows) were printed in beautiful colors and prints. Housewives used these sacks to make dresses, curtains, and many other useful items. The thread used to sew the sacks together was considered an added bonus. A lye solution removed the brand names or slogans from the sacks if necessary. The housewife often accompanied the husband to the store to pick the prints that appealed to her. Salt and sugar sacks were of softer material and were used for handkerchiefs and dish towels. "Pillsbury's Best" was once noted on one woman's underwear when she shouted very vigorously at church. (Panties were once called bloomers and then step-ins.)

FEET BURNING - Bathe feet in fresh crushed tomatoes mixed with some water for thirty minutes or more.

FELONS - are not criminals. They are abscesses on fingers or toes, usually around the nail. My Mother had many felons on her fingers, perhaps due to putting her hands in water that was too hot. She cut a hole in the end of a lemon large enough to accommodate her finger. She wore this lemon on her finger two to three days or until the infection was gone.

FENCES - Very early fences were made of piles of rocks found in the fields or rails made from split trees. The zigzagged worm or snake fences made of poles were most common. A series of poles were laid on the ground at 90-degree angles with the ends crossing about 1- inches. Poles were alternately stacked atop the original poles to create the fence so they were able to stand without falling. Later, stakes with 4-5 holes drilled in them were placed in the ground. Poles were placed in the holes and laid horizontally to use fewer rails to cover more distance.

FIGHTING CREEK SCHOOL - Different stories were told about how the school obtained its name. My family members said two preachers fought near the creek that ran close to the school. The name of the school was derived from that incident. Another version was that two land owners fought over who would donate land for a school to determine where the school would be located. The loser of this episode wound up in the creek. (2) It was a small two-room school with the first five grades in one room and three more grades in the other room. I attended this school my first four years. During county-wide activities I was extremely embarrassed to have to say that I attended a school by the name of Fighting Creek. Any other name would have been less painful. (3) Friday afternoon spelling bees were always a delight. We stood in line until we missed a word. I was the last one left standing many times. I also won several county-wide spelling contests. In recent years I was privileged to have competed against college professors when only two of us were left standing. After passing the mike back and forth, back and forth for perhaps thirty minutes, the other contestant finally missed a word, which I spelled correctly. But the rule now days is that one more word is given to the person who spelled the word correctly. If that word is not spelled correctly, the opponent gets a second chance. Believing I had won over all the college professors, my adrenaline shot so high that I missed a very simple word, which then caused me to come in second.

FIREBOARD - The name given a mantle in the early homes. The old oil lamp, matches, snuff, and many other items sat on the fire board.

FIRE COALS - One can hardly imagine the hardships of the early people who had to keep fires burning year round, because matches were not yet available. Shooting a gun through paper sometimes started a fire. Otherwise, it was necessary to strike a flint rock with a piece of steel. This produced a spark strong enough to light some very soft fiber, called punk, which came from the heart of a decayed tree. (2) To "bank the fire" meant to cover the fire with ashes. The coals would continue to smolder under the ashes so that it was possible to restart the fire the next morning. (3) To "stoke the fire or furnace" meant to put more coal or wood on the fire. (4) Walking miles to borrow coals of fire from a neighbor was no small task. This process resulted in a much used figure of speech. If your visit was extremely short, your host would ask if you came for a coal of fire. (5) A family displaced by the Norris Dam had a fire that had not been extinguished for three generations.

FIRE-ENGINES - This is hard to imagine today, but when the first fire engines came into the mountains, they were fired by wood. They had tall tail pipes with fire shooting out the top. A very frightened mountain man was heard to say, "They are moving hell and done gone by with two loads."

FIREFLIES - At Elkmont, a small village near where I was born, is found what appears to be a very rare breed of fireflies. They flash in unison, stop for a quarter of a minute, then flash again in a mating call. This is the only firefly of this type found in this hemisphere. Until these were found, Southeast Asia was the only other site for these fireflies. Video cameras and light meters confirmed that these were flashing within three-hundredths of a second of each other. This leaves one to wonder how they can expect to be noticed during the mating call when all look alike.

FIRES - Fires were deliberately set in the mountains in very early days to help kill the snakes. When the Park was established some sixty years ago, mountainside fires were banned. I sometimes wonder to what extent the snake population has increased since we left. (2) For some reason, when I was very young I was left home alone one day while all the family worked the crops in the field. It appeared I had been sweeping up the ashes around the fireplace and caught the broom on fire. The burned broom was found underneath one of the beds, but the fire had gone out instead of burning the house down. I've known for years that my guardian angel has had to work overtime.

FISHBONE - When a fishbone lodged in the throat, we gargled with full strength lemon juice, then sipped the juice if needed. Eating a piece of bread can also dislodge a fish bone.

FITIFIED SPRING - we called local springs that gushed forth intermittently fitified springs.

FLATULENCE - OR GAS DISCOMFORT - Before Gasex or Beano we took a mixture of 1 teaspoon grated fresh ginger pulp and 1 teaspoon lime juice immediately after eating. Always eat applesauce with soup beans, but never eat applesauce with eggs. Try it, then you will know why not.

FLOUR-SACK UNDERWEAR
When I was a maiden fair

Mama made our underwear.
With little tots and pa's poor pay
How could she buy lingerie?
Monograms and fancy stitches
Were not on our floursack breeches
Pantywaists that stood the test
With gold medal on the chest.

Little pants the best of all
With a scene I still recall
Harvesters were gleaning wheat
Right across the little seat.

Tougher than a grizzly bear
Was our floursack underwear
Plain or fancy, three feet wide
Stronger than a hippo's hide.

Bedspreads, curtains, tea towels too
Tablecloths to name a few
But the best beyond compare
Was our floursack underwear. Author unknown.

FLOWER CUTTINGS - When visiting in our mountain homes almost every housewife gladly shared "cuttings" or rooted flower plants. I remember many visits which ended in the garden. A flower cutting was placed in a dampened towel or clothe until it was placed in water to root. It was strictly forbidden to say "Thank you" for your newly acquired plants. To do was to risk that the plants would not live. Mother loved her flowers. Helping her carry rich dirt from our river bottom proved to be such a task for me as a child that I stated that I would never grow a flower.

FLOWERS - A flower is worn over the left ear if a girl is "taken" or over the right ear if she is "looking." Edible flowers are marigolds, day lilies, chives, carnations, nasturtiums, pansies, roses, squash, and violets.

FLY CATCHER - Homemade, mountain style. Place raw fish in a canning jar and cover with water. Punch holes in the lid large enough to allow flies to crawl in. Once they get in, they cannot find their way out. When the jar is full or smells too "swoft," replace. (2) A second fly catcher was made by placing egg yolks, molasses and finely chopped black pepper on a discarded pie tin.

FLY POISON - I do not know the name of the plant that mountaineers used to kill flies. They chopped the plant and mixed it with sugar and milk. When the flies ate the mixture, they died. The plant had long grass-like leaves and a white cluster of tiny flowers atop a tall bloom spike. (2) Another plant similar to the ground cherry with yellow berries and an outer covering that looked like a tiny Japanese lantern was used. This may have been a member of the night shade family. (3) One recipe for a fly liquidator was to combine one pint of milk, 1/4 pound of sugar, and 2 ounces ground pepper. Simmer 8 to 10 minutes. Pour in a shallow dish. Flies love it and will soon be suffocated.

FOODS- During the very early days, the only food items the great grandparents had to buy were coffee and salt. Even during the great Depression, Mother cooked a big breakfast with bacon, sausage, ham or tenderloin, eggs, hot biscuits, gravy and jelly every morning! (Except those mornings when she was doing the job of midwife, when one of my sisters became chief cook.) We grew our crops, hunted, and raised animals for food. We had fresh milk from our cows. We kept two milk cows so that one would be available for milk all the times. If one had a calf, the other supplied our milk. Anyone in the mountains who could afford two milk cows was considered quite well off financially. We never killed our cattle for beef, however. Dad always bought beef at the store. We kept a bull that serviced the community herds, two mules, named Beck and Jack, lots of chickens, and pigs. We never had sheep or goats.

We always raised two hogs. From them we had ham, bacon, sausage, and tenderloin..We raised lots of chickens and guinea hens for eggs. We caught fish in the river and made traps for possums. We cooked the possums with sweet potatoes. We also hunted for rabbits and squirrels. Dumplings made with squirrel gravy were delicious. My family never served bear or deer meat. I ate some bear meat while in Wears Valley after Ray T. Myers and I were married but I did not like it. It was tough and had a very strong flavor.

Corn, wheat and potatoes were our largest crops. In addition, we grew cabbage, turnips, turnip greens, lettuce, peas, potatoes, pumpkins, rhubarb, beans, onions, radishes, mustard, onions, carrots, cucumbers, and beets. We had a very large apple orchard with a wide variety of apples. Some ripened very early while some lasted until after Christmas. the early June apple, the sheep nose, followed by the Rambo, which was great for applesauce, the Milan, and then the horse apple were among our favorites. Then, of course, was the winter-john, which we wrapped for winter eating. We also enjoyed peaches, plums, mulberries, possum grapes, concord grapes, blackberries, dewberries, strawberries, huckle-berries, goose-berries, raspberries, apricots, persimmons and muscadines. The wild nuts were, of course, very plentiful. They included chestnuts, walnuts, hickory nuts, and beechnuts. In September we could look forward to the paw paws getting ripe. Also known as native bananas, the odor from them is heavenly. We grew some of our spices such as sage and horseradish. We kept honey bees for honey and raised sugar cane for molasses. The sugar maples in the Sugarlands supplied sugar for the early settlers.. We raised broomcorn to make our brooms.

The Sunday dinner (lunch) always included fried chicken. Folks had the idea that one should not cook on Sunday, but we always had hot biscuits and a few other items with the reheated foods which were prepared on Saturday. We never knew who might be coming home with us from church. So Mother spent her Saturdays cooking meals for that special Sunday dinner. She always made pies and cakes.

We enjoyed biscuits and cornbread with most of our meals. Mountain dishes also included hominy, a corn dodger, collards, chitterlings, fat-back and grits, hoe cakes, and polk-salad. From all of this good food you can see why the depression never bothered us. How we managed all that food I will never know. I can see why work on the farm is never done and why mountain folks had so many kids to help with the farm work. When I was a child, I was paid one penny to pick 100 bugs off the bean plants. But a penny bought a big sack of candy in those days. Two eggs would buy more candy than you could eat. Our after-school chores included gathering the eggs, finding the cows up in the hills and bringing them home.

FOOD POISONING - Today we see a physician. Mountain families took one teaspoon of apple cider vinegar in 6 oz. water every four minutes until the mixture was used up. Then they would take one tablespoon of apple cider vinegar in 6 oz. of water every 20 minutes.

FOOT WARMER - The Indians taught that putting red pepper in ones shoes kept the feet warm. It helps.

FORT CRAIG - in Maryville, Tennessee. Governor William Blount visited this area in 1793. He found 280 men, women, and children living inside this two-acre fort which contained a spring. The log walls were twelve feet high and three feet thick. Five feet from the top of the walls were 2-feet wide walkways. These were used to watch for Indian attacks. The Indians had laid siege to the fort for almost one year. Outside the fort, homes were being burned, cattle and horses stolen. Compelled to acquire skills to survive, men became masons, smith, weavers, or woodcarvers or they took off to the tall timbers. (2) Maryville's early hospital was built at that site and named Fort Craig Hospital. Blount Memorial Hospital replaced it shortly before 1949 as my daughter, Lynda, was born there in 1949. Interesting too, her husband, Edwin M. Boyer was born at the Fort Craig Hospital. They met and married in Florida but were born only three blocks apart in Maryville, Tennessee.

FOX FIRE - As a very young child I recall seeing a small limb of wood that glowed in the dark. No doubt its name was simply a corruption of the word "phosphorous." One of our family members found this limb somewhere in the woodland and brought it home. It appeared to be a fairly common thing as I recall. Its glow in the dark was not one that lit up the room, but it had a decided glow throughout.

FROSTBITE - Soak a hornets nest in water and bathe the affected area with the water. (2) Mix turpentine with salt into a salve and apply twice daily for several days.

FUNERALS - Funeral customs varied in the early days depending on where and when one lived. The old frontier customs persisted longer in the rural communities.

Until there were hospitals people, of course, died at home. Family and friends took turns at the dying person's bedside. When death occurred, a runner went to the church and tolled the bell to the age of the deceased. People almost always knew who had died by counting the bell tolls. Neighbors came to the home and did all the chores. They cooked or brought in lots of food and comforted the grieving family, all at no expense to the family. Friends shared the digging of the grave. A homemade coffin was typically a six-sided box tapered toward the foot to save lumber. My Uncle Levi Trentham kept poplar lumber in his attic to be used for such purposes. The coffin was lined with white or black cotton and sometimes embellished with brass handles and a shiny inscribed plate for the lid. Glass was sometimes installed in the lid so that the face could to be seen without opening the lid. Unlike today, the body was prepared at home for burial. A family member or a friend of the same gender as the deceased would "lay out the dead." I can recall seeing nickels placed on the eyes of the deceased to keep them shut. The coins sometimes remained during the service but were removed before burial. A cloth was tied around the jaw to keep it closed while the body was on the "cooling board." A cloth soaked in camphor was placed over the face to help prevent it from turning dark. The wake was held in the home, where someone "sat-up" all night with the body.

Usually the funeral and burial were the day following the death. Practically everyone in the community attended. Schools were turned out, and the children marched into the church double file to attend the funerals. Almost always two or more mountain preachers delivered hours of fervent sermons to fit the lifestyle of the deceased. If he had lived a very reckless life, he was not preached into the pearly gates. A beautiful heaven with images of streets paved with gold awaited believers. Often preachers directed funeral sermons to members of the congregation whose lives were not up to their standards. Dreadful judgment and damnation was in store for the unredeemed. Hired mourners were sometimes used. "Professional fainters" were sometimes part of the event. When I became an adult and the wife of the minister, I was always armed with vials of smelling salts, which the funeral directors furnished for us to use in such cases. The vials were crushed by hand and had a very strong ammonia odor. One whiff of it usually brought the patient to quick attention. I feel sure they put a stop to the "professional fainter." My late husband conducted many funerals. We had one woman who fainted at every funeral. Finally disgusted with this exhibition, my husband grabbed the woman up from the floor, carried her outside, sat her down on the church steps without a word, yanked her dress down over her knees, and left her sitting there. He did not use the smelling salts on her.

The coffin remained open during the service or was opened after the sermons. At the end of the service, the entire congregation marched single file to view the corpse. Immediate family members were the last to view the body while the balance of the congregation sat back to view the scene. During the very early days, if the family did not weep loudly enough, it plainly showed they did not love the deceased. When my father died in 1949, I saw some people plainly watching me to see just how much I cared. They got nothing from me. Of course, we are much more sophisticated today. One hardly ever allows a tear to be shed at funerals. You do your crying on your own time at home behind closed doors. One of the most mournful sounds one will ever hear was the nailing of the lid on that wood coffin at the end of the funeral service. After the service men carried the coffin by hand or in a wagon to the cemetery **(See MOURNING.)**

G

GALLBLADDER FLUSH - Day one: Drink 1 gallon apple juice or fresh cider. Day two: Repeat, do nothing else. Day three: Upon arising drink 8 ounces of apple juice. One hour later drink 4 ounces olive oil mixed with four ounces lemon juice. (2) Better still: drink 1 cup olive oil with 1 cup fresh lemon juice. (Pour oil and lemon juice back and forth to aerate.) Eat nothing for 8 hours. A local doctor said this remedy dissolves gallstones. (3) To prevent gallstones eat pumpkin seeds.

GARGLE - For a sore throat, add 1/8 teaspoon black pepper to one cup of hot water and sip the mixture. Or, add 3 tablespoons apple cider vinegar. A favorite gargle for sore throat was a mixture of one teaspoon salt, one teaspoon soda, and a few drops of iodine. This remedy, called SSI, was one of our favorites at the hospital where I worked. I now gargle with hydrogen peroxide for sore throat.

GATLINBURG - Several stories exist as to how Gatlinburg, Tennessee, got its name. One story involved Radford Gatlin, one of the earliest settlers in the area. He opened a grocery store in what is now Gatlinburg. In exchange for his agreement that the post office for the area would be located in his building, officials agreed to call the town Gatlinburg (1855). Another story involves a property dispute Gatlin may have had with other residents over homestead claims. A rumor exists that he was told if he left the area then known as White Oak Flats, the name would change to Gatlinburg in his honor. He had a slave who died, and he was suspected of killing her. He was known to have supported the Confederacy. In fact, a vote was taken at the outbreak of the Civil War with only one vote being cast for secession. The people believed it was cast by Gatlin. The fact that he was a Democrat helped. After the election Gatlin was physically beaten. After this beating, he left the area and may have gone to Georgia. He abandoned one thousand acres of land, which he had previously homesteaded. This land is believed to be part of The Great Smoky Mountain National Park. Some historical records of Gatlinburg show Confederate Colonial William Thomas underestimated the number of Union Sympathizers and lost the battle of Gatlinburg. It was said that the Rev. Richard Evans was required to continue preaching during his Sunday services without any indication of where his sympathy lay.

It is also believed that the mother of Isaac and Caleb Trentham, Easter Ogle Bohannan, was a sister to Radford Gatlin's wife, Elizabeth. (From Huskey reunion booklet.) If this is true, that would create a family relationship to Lucinda Bugg who brought her young son, William Thomas Trentham, from North Carolina to Gatlinburg around 1794. (Lucinda Trentham Bugg was my great-great grandmother.)

GEE & HAW - Not long ago while watching the Heartland Series on TV, the driver of a team of horses on this show had yelled "Haw" to them. A New Yorker who was watching the show with me asked why the driver said "Haw." I explained that meant for the team to turn left, which they had already done. Had the driver said "Gee", that meant for them to turn to the right. The word "Whoa" meant to stop. "Giddy-up" told the horses to go forward. This individual was amazed that the horses knew the meaning of those words. This was something we hillbillies took for granted. (2) These commands remind me of the run-away team that wrecked the wagon, leaving the owner lying badly wounded in the ditch. Someone coming to his aid asked if they could go catch his horses. He replied, "Not, if they went where I told them to go!"

GENERAL STORE - All of us should lament the passing of the general store! Every kind of household item was sold. The general stores had horse collars, horse shoes and nails, hammers, shovels, check lines, saddles, barbed wire, staples, shoes, socks, long handles, straw hats, cloth, and hardly any ready-made clothing except bib overalls. There were few of the packaged goods of today, however. We bought farm supplies, nails from barrels, cheese from enormous rounds, feed for livestock, candy in glass jars, fabric to make clothing, oil lamps, flour, salt, soda, and much much more. In 1910 milk sold for 20 cents per gallon. (We paid $9 per gallon in Hawaii.) Buttermilk sold for 10 cents per gallon. Butter was 15 cents a pound. Blackberries were 10 cents per gallon while they sell for $10 today. I recall that one egg or one penny bought a small bag of candy in the 1930's. I remember one time when I was in high school, Hettie Carr went with me to the general store to buy candy. I took my paper bag which I thought contained one or two eggs, instead it happened to be my lunch. I will never forget how Hettie laughed with me. (2) The gen eral store was much more than a place to buy household needs. It was often the social center for the community. The general store was often a refuge for the menfolk who were shooed out of the house by the little woman so she could get her housework done. The men gathered around the old pot-bellied stove to whittle and "chaw and jaw!" Story telling, prevaricating, or stretching the truth was at its best in the old stores. Some regulars were said to be such liars that they had to get someone to call their hogs to come eat. The men were constantly setting up one another for jokes. Sometimes I believed some of the men were confused old crocks, but all in all it was a great time of fun and fellowship. I like to think this same group, who have long since passed to the other side are all somewhere in a circle leaning back on the hind legs of their chairs, asking: "Do you remember that time when we lived in the Smoky Mountains....." More than once I have made a list of those already gone that I would like to look up just to reminisce about the good times and the bad.

GINSENG - A locally grown herb, said by old-timers to be "good for everything that ails you." These ailments included asthma, coughs, boils, internal diseases, palsy, nervousness, and memory problems. Ginseng was also said to be an aphrodisiac. Called in the mountain vernacular "sang", it really appeared to be a cure-all. The older roots, if shaped like a human body, were highly treasured.

Ginseng grows only in a damp shaded place, requiring at least seventy-five percent shade. Responsible persons who gather this plant always plant the seeds, the red berries, for future growth. It takes eight years for a root to mature fully. It was believed to have mystical powers and to be worth its weight in gold to the Chinese. While it brought 42 cents per pound in 1881, in 1998 it was bringing $400 per pound when sold to herb dealers who shipped it to China.

GIRDING TREES - To kill a tree, without cutting it down, mountain folk take an axe or hatchet and cut rings around the entire trunk, deep enough to arrest the flow of sap. This should be done during the new moon or when the sign of the moon is in the heart.

GOAT-MAN - Many old-timers in the Smokies will recall seeing the traveling "Goat Man." His goat-drawn wagon was literally covered with pots, pans, trinkets, collectibles, and doo-dads as he traveled all over the United States. I never talked with the man, but I stood transfixed seeing such a contraption on our highways. The man, Chester McCartney, resided at the senior center in Macon, Georgia, where he died in November, 1998.. He was thought to be 97 years old. He was said to have had a sizable bank account in Colorado.

GOD-A-MIGHTY - This term was often used as an exclamation and to talk about God outside of the church. I once visited the site on Montvale Road where a farmer whom I will not name had worked very hard to stack a field of hay into stacks, or shocks as they were called. The work was all done when a violent rainstorm came and washed all the hay down the sloping ravine running through the farm. When the storm ended, the farmer stood surveying the damage. A friend was greeted with this comment: "Take God-A-Mighty up one side and down the other. He does as much damage as he does good." (2) My father helped to abstract the titles to many of the small mountain farms in this area during acquisition of the land for the park. The deed to one of the church properties in Cades Cove was deeded to Almighty-God. To find this property, one must go into Cades Cove, which has one-way traffic. Turn left at Hyatt lane, which goes to the opposite side of the cove. Turn left and go to the second house. There is a pull-off with two big rocks placed to prevent one from entering this property. The church building is no longer standing, but the cemetery is there. Many cemetery stones contain the names of Abbotts and Harmons. I questioned how they got a signature for that deed. A bit of research found it was the Daniel Bird Lawson church property. Judy Abbott Hill once held that deed in her hands, but no one seems to know where it is today. As for the signature on that deed, I am sure the Park Service handled that as in other such cases. Possession cabins were built to establish residence and then the property was turned over to the park. One such cabin was built near the Alum Cave trail that no one owned.

GOLDEN SEAL - see STOMACH TROUBLE

GOOBER FARM - During the 1920's and 1930's what is today called the Chimney Camp Ground was called the Goober Farm. We called peanuts "goobers", so it was likely that peanuts were once the primary crop grown on that property.

GOOD OLD DAYS - I would love to hear once again the newscaster, Gabriel Heater, come on the evening daily news with these words: "There is good news today, my friends......." Even if it was not so good, he always found something good to say. But for the good-old-days themselves, about the only thing we miss about them is the quiet evenings with the entire family gathered around the supper table. Then we moved near the stone fireplace for a leisurely chat with family or neighbors. It was a gentle time and place. While I know it is impossible, how wonderful it would be to have the entire family all back at that precious old home place for just one special day! The real "Good Old Days" were muddy roads, lots of sickness with no doctors and no cures, back-breaking work with primitive tools and sore muscles. It was all necessary for survival. In addition there were the "White Caps", the Civil War with father against son, the burning or ransacking of homes, and diseases such as typhoid, small-pox, or the flu that killed thousands. Can you imagine cutting poplar logs and chaining them together to make a bridge to allow a child to cross a stream to be able to attend school? Carving a community from the wilderness must have taken more stamina than we possess today.

GOOSE GAP - was named for an incident that took place a few miles west of Pigeon Forge. It was on this spot that some men stole a goose, killed, roasted, and ate him.

GOPHER WOOD- (Cladrastis Luten) is very rare and is not native to the Smokies. Gopher wood trees can be found today on what was our property in the Great Smoky Mountain National Park. One of the gopher wood trees stands directly to the right of the MCCarter Riding Stables' barn. Some of its limbs touch the barn's roof. Other gopher wood trees can be found by following the branch toward its head. These trees are within approximately 50 yards of the stream. Gopher wood is said to have been discovered in the park in February, 1796, by Andre Michaux, an experienced plants-man. This wandering Frenchman led a romantic life which included adventures in Persia, Mesopotamia, and the Trans-Caspian regions. He supposedly cured the daughter of the Shah of a mysterious malady. An icy rain was falling when he made his discovery. This rain was turning into blinding snow, and the roaring creek was rising fast. He stopped his horse somewhere in the lonely woods twelve miles from Fort Blount to examine a curious tree that he added to his long list of first discoveries of American tree species. The gopher wood tree is one of the rarest trees of eastern North America. Neither Andre Midhaux nor many other white men had ever seen the only American species of this strange genus which is best represented in the mountains of China and Japan. Noah's Ark as described in the Bible was built of gopher wood.

GOUT - Eat any kind of cherries, fresh or canned. (2) Apply hot vinegar mixed with salt four times daily.

GRAMPUS - (Hellgrammite) Around the Two-Mile Branch we could turn over a rock and find what we called a grampus coiled up neatly in his little nest. Having been away from there for 69 years I have gone back and cannot find even one. I'd give a pretty premium just to find one!

GRAVELING POTATOES - I had never heard this expression until after I married Ray T. Myers in 1941. When his mother said she was going to gravel potatoes, I sneaked along behind her watching to see what she did. Finding cracks in the ground around the new potato plants indicated a potato large enough to eat at that site. Scratching away the dirt, picking the potato, then covering the hole with dirt was what she called graveling. My family simply "dug" our potatoes.

GRAVY- Gravy was served at most meals, including breakfast, over biscuits, ham, or potatoes. After "saw-mill" gravy our second choice was "red-eye" gravy. Saw-mill gravy was made with a small amount of grease left from frying chicken or other meat. Flour was browned in the grease with salt and pepper. Milk was added after the flour was a caramel color. The mixture cooks until it thickens. "Red-eye" gravy is made with the grease left from frying country ham (salt-cured). We added one cup of water to the excess fat, along with 1 Tablespoon strong coffee. We brought this to the boiling point, then served it with the ham.

GREAT SMOKY MOUNTAIN NATIONAL PARK - a.k.a.: GSMNP - Our property, which was purchased by the Park Service, is approximately one-fourth mile north of The Sugarlands Visitors Center (two miles south of Gatlinburg, Tennessee on Hwy 441). The McCarter riding stables at the site of the Two Mile Branch stand close to where our house was situated. The park is now known for hosting thousands of tourists each year. At 800 square miles, it is approximately 70 miles long and 30 miles wide. It contains 507,869 acres. The rocks in the park are estimated to be between 500 and 600 million years old. The shore line of Scotland matches that of North Carolina. Since most of the general information regarding the establishment of the park is available elsewhere, I want to cover some of the interesting, though rarely publicized facts. (2) Of great interest was the intense rivalry between the North Carolina and Tennessee Parks Commissions for getting the "Rockefeller Money." John D. Rockefeller, Jr. gave $5 million as a memorial to his mother, Laura Spellman Rockefeller, toward the acquisition of land for the park. The method by which the Laura Spellman Rockefeller Foundation distributed that money is generally not known. As each state park commission bought up land, it made a periodic report to the Foundation. Each commission was then reimbursed for what they spent. This practice no doubt was intended to create sufficient rivalry between the two states to assure speedy acquisition of the lands for the park.

Since acreage in each state was about equal, it appeared to be an equitable arrangement. As it turned out, however, most of North Carolina's acreage was owned by a few large timber companies. North Carolina had 312 tracts to acquire while Tennessee had 1369. Those big timber companies had well-prepared maps and deeds to their holdings. Property surveys were generally very precise and accurate. Very few of the small holdings of the mountain people had ever been surveyed. Most of the deeds were "homemade" and called for natural objects that were no longer there. This made it much more difficult for the Tennessee Commission to get the same acreage. As a result, the Tennessee Commission had to hire anyone who could read a compass and drag a chain through the woods to do the surveys. As one might say today, they would hire anyone who could carry the "dumb" end of a surveyor's chain.

(3) Different local groups donated money to assist in the acquisition of the lands for the park. School children donated their nickels and dimes. Bob Hicks told of donating 10 cents to the

fund. Altogether $12 million was donated, which in the 1920's was a lot of money. I was born in 1921, but I do not recall having the privilege of donating to this fund. Many of the older people living in the region were extremely upset at having to give up their home. In fact, some believed this shortened the lives of some former residents. A sign posted at one location read: "Col. Chapman, you and host are notified. Let the Cove people alone. Get out. 40-mile limit." Another mountaineer, lamenting the meager returns of hard labor on the rocky fields and hillsides, concluded: "Well, I reckon a park is about all this land is fit for."

(4) My father, a surveyor, had surveyed more than half the little farms in our area. He knew where many of the corners were located. However, the lines move "off-degree" over the years. Unless you can figure out this variation, you are in a heap of trouble. Also, the trees or shrubs grew, making it much more difficult to recognize locations. John Morrell, a park ranger, told me after my dad died that luck was with them in many instances. John said my father had what he called a "photographic memory." Even though the trees and foliage had changed considerably, dad could still find those corners. My father worked tirelessly on these surveys and once told of finding himself on a huge flat rock on the Jake Quilliams property surrounded on every side by copperhead snakes. Everywhere he looked, he saw snakes. Knowing in advance those hazards, all of the men wore high top boots for protection.

(5) Many of the surveyors had little success in running property lines by the deeds and had to resort to having the landowners show them the boundaries they claimed. Some of the surveyors assisting in securing the deeds boarded at our house. Colonel Dave Chapman was in our home many times and should be credited for his untiring efforts toward the parks development. I recall one Andy Gregory, who was unable to remove his boot after a rock smashed his toe because his foot swelled so badly. (6) Perhaps one of the most interesting and no doubt most exasperating situation concerned the property of T. D. W. (Wilse) McMahan, an old time land speculator in Sevier County. He loaned people money, taking a mortgage on their land. When they failed to pay, he ultimately

foreclosed. He eventually acquired some 600 acres which began on a white flint rock on Copeland Creek, then ran south, then north, and finally to the beginning. Copeland Creek is noted for its white flint rocks. They can be found at 50-75 yard intervals from one end of the creek to the other. Surveyors moved that 600 acres all up and down that creek as the claim of title required. Finally, one wise or exasperated surveyor pointed to one of the many flint rocks and said: "Who can prove that it isn't this flint rock?" Seeing the logic and a solution to their hopeless dilemma, the others agreed. They made the deed based on this, and it stands today.

(7) After the surveys were completed, the survey calls were sent to Knoxville, where R.B. Newman, Jr. prepared plats and computed the acreage. These plats were farmed out to local attorneys and professional abstracters who tried to reconcile deed descriptions with the plats. They also attempted to trace the title back to an original state grant where possible. Some of the early individual land grants of 20-50 acres were originally purchased for the incredible amount of 75 cents. Preparing plats and deeds led to some really bizarre situations. R.B. Newman told of calling in two surveyors to reprimand them for the inaccuracy of their work. He showed each of the men a plat that came close to "closing,"-- getting back to the point of beginning. One said, "That's queer, it closed on the ground." The other said, "Oh, I left that opening so he could get into his property." I barely recall helping my father with the graph papers where we platted the measurements and degrees. We always took them the full 360 degrees until the plats closed. Unlike the surveyor reprimanded by Mr. Newman, my father never left an opening for the land owner to enter his land.

(8) The abstractors had the real headaches. For example, the 5000-acre state grant to A.M. Line (after which Line Springs is named) began on a stake in a laurel thicket on the headwaters of Little River. Another deed near Elkmont began with the spot "Where Robert L. Trentham's sow swam the river." (Robert L. Trentham was my grandfather.) Squire Richard McCarter, who lived on Fighting Creek, had three daughters and no sons. He divided his property between his daughters during his lifetime. The beginning

point of his home-made deed began on "a winter john apple tree in the field, thence with the meanders of a corn row to the edge of the woods....." (9) Probably the most important property corner in all of the park, certainly the most important to the Tennessee side, was the Meigs Post. This post was the beginning corner of the 76,507 acres acquired from The Little River Lumber Company and the 38,000 odd acres acquired from Champion Fiber Company. In 1797 two surveyors, Kirpatrick and Whitner, started at the mouth of The Clinch River and ran a line S76 E to what is now known as Blanket Mountain. Here they stopped, reporting that the country was impassable to horses. In 1802 Jonathan Meigs, U.S. Indian Commissioner, accompanied by Indian guides, hung a blanket on the mountain where Kirpatrick and Whitner's line ended. He then proceeded (probably through Fighting Creek Gap via West Prong of Little Pigeon to Indian Gap). He then proceeded out the state line ridge to a point where a back-sight on the S76E bearing lined up with the blanket. Here he set up Meigs Post. A common corner between the then state of Tennessee, North Carolina and the Cherokee nation. He named this point "Meig's Post Mountain" and the other Blanket Mountain.

(10) It is unfortunate that the field book containing this survey was sent to Washington. When the British burned Washington during the War of 1812, this book was so badly scorched that the last pages of notes were destroyed. There was some question as to whether the line from Blanket Mountain to the state line ridge continued on the S76E course or whether it turned almost due south. In 1893 and 1915 different law suits disputed the location of the Meigs Post. However, when the Little River Lumber Company conveyed its property to the state of Tennessee on Dec. 31, 1926, its deed read: "Beginning at Meigs Post on top of Mt. Collins and in the state line of NC." This statement finally settled the question.

(11) In 1936 Hiram C. Wilburn wrote Park Superintendent Eakin urging the replacement of Meig's Post. He pointed out that while the mound of rocks was still there, the wooden post had decayed. Not until March 1954 was this post replaced by a concrete monument set by Ranger John Morrell and George Lamon. John

Morrell, a very close friend of my Father, was in our home countless times. I was well acquainted with him and obtained from him much of the above information.

(12) It was determined that my family's property was the only propert y in all of the Great Smoky Mountain National Park that was held by the same family that homesteaded it when the park acquired the land. A news item in The Knoxville News-Sentinel on June 18, 1995 stated that officials of The Great Smoky Mountain National Park planned to ask the states of North Carolina and Tennessee for permission to charge an entrance fee to the park. This is despite the agreement that was plainly on record when this land was donated or purchased for the park that NO ENTRANCE FEE WAS EVER TO BE CHARGED. It was on that basis that we sold our 363 acres to the park. If a fee is later charged, I now go on record demanding that all my descendants be given lifetime passes to enter the park. We were given less than $34 per acre for our land. This was highway robbery!

(13) Restrictions were so great after we sold our land to the park that we were not allowed to break a twig. Should those of us who sacrificed most not be given some consideration? I think so. As far as I know an offer of lifetime family entrance passes has never been made should an entrance fee sometime be charged. Restrictions for use of the park were enormous. However, a few wealthy and influential Knoxville families were given leases to use the rustic cabins at Elkmont from 1928 to 1993. They used the cabins for sixty-five years and then complained bitterly when their leases were not renewed for a fourth time.

(14) I would like to add, however, that anytime is the right time to see the Smoky Mountains. The beauty is not confined to one season. In the spring comes the dogwood, redbud, azalea, then the rhododendron, soon followed by the iris, violets, and columbine. Summer offers soothing greenery and all the outdoor sports: swimming, hiking, tennis, horseback riding, fishing, and camping. One does not want to miss the blazing autumn colors. Then comes the unbelievable picture of winter's snow-capped mountains and hoary frost. Seeing hoar frost on the spring wildflowers is a thing of great beauty. The highways within the park are sometimes

closed due to snow. I recall a six foot snowfall in 1936. Within 24 hours the New Found Gap highway was in use. (15) I have neither the time nor vocabulary to compete with the professional writers who can go on forever about the beauty of the Smoky Mountains. However, I will quote a former director of the Park Service, Horace M. Albright, who said during his first visit to Knoxville "The whole country is a natural park." Botanist William Bartram summed it up when he said, "I looked with rapture and astonishment at a sublimely awful scene of power and magnificence, a world of mountains piled upon mountains, and it will be your own fault if you depart without being greatly benefitted in body, mind and spirit."

(16) Others say they regain spiritual balance, a refuge. History, geology, geography, legends, and historical facts and figures reveal little of the beauty, spirit, and glory that has so moved many who beheld them. World travelers come back for more and more, while we natives take all this beauty for granted. After my 80 years of sitting at the feet of these mountains, I can give the armchair tourist only a glimpse of these age old mountains. If your spirit needs an uplift or a quick get-away from the noise and bustle of big city life, I highly recommend The Wilderness Trail, a short drive that takes you deep into the quiet and peace of nature.

(17) The wild animals included the bears as well as deer, elk, wildcats, panthers, raccoons, opossums, squirrels, minks, and weasels as well as red and gray foxes. The red squirrel was also called a "boomer." Of course, the bears are one of the great attractions. Unless molested they seldom attack. Until recently we had been able to boast that no one had been attacked and killed by one of our bears until a lovely young school teacher was brutally killed. Since the bear had some cubs, the woman may have gone between the mother and her babies. We were always very careful never to get in that position. As unbelievable as it seems we hardly ever hear of one of our millions of tourist being bitten by a rattlesnake or copperhead. This fact really amazes me, since we constantly fought them while living in the park area. In fact killed thirteen copperheads the last summer we lived in the park.

(18) The park has over 600 miles of streams. My favorite is known as "Roaring Fork." Roaring Fork starts in the park area and continues in to Gatlinburg. It really roars, because its waters drop over 1000 feet in a short distance. We once lived alongside that stream. We spent many days sitting on the lanai drinking tea while listening to the roar of that stream. It was here the following sign was posted:

"He who picnics by these roaring waves,
And all the front with litter paves,
May indigestion rack his chest,
And ants invade his pants and vest!

GREENBACK - Greenback, is south of Maryville, Tennessee. (2) Many years ago a minister in this little town of Greenback prophesied for several weeks that the town would be destroyed by a cyclone due to the open sins of the people living there. On March 4, 1899, a cyclone came through at 69 miles per hour. It missed Greenback by exactly one mile. However, it blew the barn, corncrib, a horse and a cow away, and destroyed an orchard belonging to that preacher. One can well imagine all the discussion following that. Some wag said God's eye had been bad or his direction unsure or his control uncertain if he missed the whole town of Greenback and hit just a barn instead. It took away the preacher's claim to prophecy, but he continued to preach.(3) During another incident one of the good ladies in town was caught in raging flood waters. One of my relatives saw her standing in the water up to her waist holding an umbrella over herself and praying with great gusto.

GREENBRIER SCHOOL- (Also called Little Greenbrier was preserved by The Great Smoky Mountain Park and is open to the public.) The School building is located beyond Townsend near Metcalf Bottoms and the famous Walker sisters' home. The first class was held New Years Day 1882. The teacher's salary was paid by levy of $1.25 on each student. The length of term was determined by the amount collected. The first term was two months in length. Since my mother was born in 1886 near this site, I feel sure that she first attended school there.

In 1881 my great uncle, William Gilbert (Gib) Abbott, donated the land upon which the school was built. My grandfather, Ephraim Ogle, donated the huge poplar logs for the building. Some of the logs dressed out to 25 inches wide and can be seen there today. The logs were so heavy it took two teams of oxen to pull one log. My grandfather (Ephraim Ogle) was a "corner man." This meant one had to be a good carpenter who could hew the notches in the corners of the logs to fit. This fitting was called a "dove-tail." I touched all four corners to be sure to touch the one my grandfather worked on. My great-grandfather William (Buck or Billie) was considered too old to be a corner man. He was allowed to hew the puncheon floor and to split the shingle laths from straight grain oak to cover the roof. The puncheon floor was made from the flat sides of logs cut in half. His grave is found in the right corner of the cemetery facing from the front door of the school. His stone is incorrectly marked Ephraim, which was his son's name. Benches were hewn from poplar logs. They were made from a log split in half with four legs and no back rest. The third set of benches has today been replaced.

GREEN TEA - Considered among the very best general drinks, green tea is supposed to be good for nausea of pregnancy, arthritis, and indigestion.

GREETINGS - In the early days before a visitor entered someone's yard or knocked on his door, he stopped a good distance away and yelled, "Hello." In plain view he unloaded his gun where he could be seen. After being invited in, he handed his host the gun or stood it in the corner. This trust was rarely violated. One visitor was said to have gone to bed one night with a loaded gun under his pillow. The next morning its cartridges all lay on a table across the room. Not a word was spoken. The hint was enough. If a visitor failed to introduce himself immediately upon arrival, the host would say, "What did you say your name was?" (2) Some of our mountain women were the "talkingest" women you would ever hope to meet. Their gossip was somewhat like grapefruit, the juicer the better. I will never forget seeing two friends meet in the road one day. One exclaimed, "Why, I haven't seen you since the woods burnt over!"

GRIST MILL - Our water-powered grist mill ground the corn and wheat for us and our neighbors. One red grain of corn was known to be so tough as to stop the rocks from grinding. As a small child I was allowed to operate the mill. I would pour the corn into the hopper, open the water gate, and watch for the last few grains to grind. Then I closed the water gate. I recently noted that a well known local writer mentioned someone weighed their corn before it was to be ground, then again afterward and found a small discrepancy. Our customers always knew that we took out "toll" a payment for services rendered. I was surprised to think a newspaper columnist would not realize that a fee, the toll, was necessary to build and maintain a building, build a raceway for the water supply and have someone spend from one to three hours to oversee this operation.

GRITTED BREAD - Corn, which had grown too hard for frying or creaming, was grated and baked into what was called gritted bread. The grater was a kitchen utensil made from wood and a piece of tin. Many nail holes were driven into the strip of tin. This strip was then fastened in a circular or rainbow fashion to a larger piece of wood. I never tasted any, so I cannot recommend it. It sounds as if it might be a bit rough on your gizzard.

GROUND HOG - A rodent that weighs up to 35 pounds. He will eat every bean plant right down to the ground. My Aunt Sally McCarter once had a pet ground hog, who sat on his rear feet and ate his meals along with the family. He was once missing for several months and then returned. I tried to pet a groundhog once. He sunk his teeth deep into my left arm. Since we children had a saying that an animal wouldn't turn you loose until it thundered, I thought I had no choice but to choke him to death. It took some doing. He swelled up three times his size before he turned me loose. I wish I had enough smarts to have held him under water until he drowned. To say someone was "Groundhoggin it" meant that he was barely getting by financially.

GUM STAND - An area located approximately one mile north of Gatlinburg where farmers rested for the night en route to markets in Knoxville. They parked their wagons, horses, and mules filled with their apples, walnuts, corn, pumpkins, etc. Later a very small grocery store named Gum Stand store was located there. Tourists were sometimes indignant when they went in to buy gum and found none. It was difficult to explain that the area was known as Gum Stand, and not a stand or store to sell gum.

GUNS - Many old-timers named their guns such names as "Old Betsy," "Old Long Tom" or "Old Bear."

GYPSIES - When I was a very small child I recall caravans of people we called gypsies who often passed our home. Fat women wearing bright skirts, bracelets, and lots of jewelry, would say, "Cross my palm with silver." Some of them were extremely nice. I remember one woman, however, who was telling my father how he was going to make a big fortune, take a trip, etc., while she frisked every pocket. Drawing back with some metal tools, which he had in his hands, he said, "If you touch me one more time, I will hit you with these plow points!" I also recall being in a store one day, when a large group of women and children came into the store. While some members of the group caused a great commotion among themselves, the balance of the group spread out over the entire store filling bags and pockets. On the whole they were nice people you would want to know.

HAIR - As I was growing up practically every young girl wore long hair. My two older sisters had to wear long hair, which made them look older than they do today at age 85 and 88. I have no idea how I escaped, but I never had long hair. During my early years it was considered a sin for a woman to cut or "bob" her hair. It was considered immoral because it is a woman's crowning glory. Early preachers emphasized this to their congregations. Ida Headrick Myers, my husband's mother, had her hair cut when she was a young mother in the church. It caused such a great uproar in her church, First Baptist of Wears Valley, that threats were made to withdraw her church membership. Her father was the Sunday School Superintendent for 30 years in that church. Somehow the matter was resolved, and she was still a member when she passed away in 1973. I can recall one verse of a well-know song in the early 1920's and 1930's. It went like this: "Why do you bob your hair girls? You're doing might wrong, God says it is your glory and you should wear it long..." The stigma was so great that mountain girls hardly ever cut their hair until after they were married and on their own. (2) My Father really enjoyed telling of a woman who was observing a neighbor combing her hair. She remarked, "I don't see how you can stand to comb your hair every day. Why, I only comb mine once a week and it nearly kills me."

(3) Many grandmothers of that day never had gray hair because they boiled sage, rosemary, or chamomile which they used as a rinse. My grandmother, Mary Ann Ogle, combed coffee into her hair for color. Other dyes were made from onion skins, walnut hulls, and hickory bark. (4) Ideas and traditions were naturally brought from the old country. One interesting concept was that people with red hair had hot tempers and that persons with huge noses were very stubborn. Many believed that obstinacy resides in the nose, which makes it larger. Others believed that our thoughts go up through our hair, which acts like an antenna. Another belief was that a barber cutting your hair can read your mind. (5) My

brother, Sam, swears by this one. He says that hair grows slower when it is cut after the full moon and before the last quarter. He also maintains that hair grows faster in the spring and slower if cut on a Tuesday. Using this information can save on the number of haircuts required perhaps.

HAMPTON, JOHN - John Hampton and Washington Dodgen were farming land belonging to Ephraim Ogle. They went to get Ogle's mule for plowing. Ogle explained that the mule was extremely stubborn and could not be ridden under any circumstances. Hampton responded that he had never seen a mule he couldn't ride and, he proceeded to get on it. All went well until they came to the mud hole that stayed in the main road directly in front of the L.L. Maples' home. There the mule stopped, refusing to go one step farther. John kicked and coaxed and kicked some more. After one last swift kick to the ribs, the mule lowered his head, kicked his rear feet up into the air. John landed right in the middle of that mud hole.
Dodgen observing all this, said, "He threw you. Didn't he, John?" John said, "Well, he sorta did and he sorta didn't. I was aimin' to get off anyway." (This location, traveling south into Gatlinburg was just beyond the third stoplight on Main street.) (2) The next time I heard of John Hampton was when the superintendent of The Little River Lumber Company invited his father and some of his crew to go for a ride on the Elkmont train. The caboose came loose from the train and started running backward down the steep mountainside. The superintendent's father, Mr. Badgett, Pleas Myers, and Earl Dockery were killed. All the rest of the crew jumped off except John Hampton. John did not get a scratch. All the others suffered scratches and bruises. The caboose went about a mile down the mountainside, then into the center of the river. There they found Hampton still sitting in the caboose playing his fiddle. He said he knew it would stop somewhere. And, besides, he was too scared to move much less jump.

HAND SHAKE - Early on, many of our legal agreements were sealed by nothing more than a handshake and were considered ironclad. Today agreements signed and notarized are often not adequate.

HAND WARMER - MOUNTAIN STYLE - Beeswax was rubbed on the hands to close the pores. Swinging the arms around in circles also warmed the hands.

HANG-OVER - Eat two tablespoons of honey every 20 minutes for one hour. Wait three hours and repeat. Wait 6 hours and repeat again. (2) If a person is paralyzed drunk: put ice packs on wrists and back of neck.

HAY FEVER - Chew honeycomb. Mountain doctors carried honeycomb in their bags for hay fever.

HEADACHE - 2 tablespoons white vinegar mixed to taste with honey was used for headaches. (2) Swinging the arms shunts the blood flow to the head counteracting the swollen blood vessels that caused the headache. (3) Sniffing oxygen is fast becoming a headache remedy today. (Watch for food allergies)

HEALERS - Certain people in the community were known as healers. In addition to knowing herbal remedies, they knew verses or chants that were supposed to help victims of illness. One of the verses was quoted while touching the patient and saying silently, "My loaf in my lap, my penny in my purse, Thou are now the better, I am none the worse. (They would accept only a penny for their services.) Healers must walk barefoot on the dewy grass in the sunlight to renew energy. If there is no dew, walk on the earth.

HEARTBEAT - FAST - Studying the beaver we learned immersing the nose in cold water slows down the fast heart beat. From the ducks, we learned that ducking the entire head in cold water is more effective. (I wonder if an ice pack would help just as much)

HEARTBURN - Eat a raw potato for heartburn.

HEAT - Put a big green leaf in your hat while working outside in hot weather, to help reduce heat.

HEATERS -TRAVEL - Today's travel heaters contrast very much to those in my Father's early days. He would heat a big flat rock in the fireplace overnight and wrap it in heavy paper. The heated rock was placed in a gunny sack, tow sack, or burlap bag. The rock was then placed in the floor of the wagon or buggy during cold weather, and travelers placed their feet on the rock. A heavy lap robe was also used to cover everyone in the wagon.

HELL - HUGGIN'S - This mountainous section was so dense and so treacherous that few, if any, who tried to cross it came out alive. A Mr. Huggins said he would cross it or go to hell trying. Since he did not make it, that area has since been known as "Huggin's Hell."

HELL - JEFFERIES' - Located in Monroe County, near Tellico. Many stories try to explain how it got its name. One story involves Ebenezer Jefferies' prized coon dog, Bo. Bo got on the scent of a wild animal that led him into this area, which was so dense that hardly anyone was able to cross it. However, a cinder from a train set the woodland ablaze and Jefferies determined he would either find his dog or go to hell trying. Bo returned but Jefferies body was never found. (2) Another story was that two men were drinking too much "hooch." One of them, a Mr. Jefferies, took a wrong turn and was never heard from again.

HERBS - Before the days of pharmacies, mountain people used the ingredients they found around them. Over the generations, different remedies were found to work for different conditions. Certain people were knowledgeable in use of these remedies. My parents fulfilled that function in our area. The 12 most commonly used herbs are burdock, calendula, chamomile, crampbark, dandelion, echinacea, lemon balm, licorice, raspberry, ginseng, nettles, and valerian. A mountain woman kept a small container on the kitchen shelf that contained what she said was a secret herb.

She never allowed anyone to see what it was, but she always took a pinch of it and put in all the food she cooked. No one ever saw her refill it. After she died the family could hardly wait to look in that container. What they found was a note which read: "To everything you make in the kitchen add a dash of love."

HICCOUGHS - Eat one teaspoon of sugar. We mountain children "scared" the hiccups out of the victim.

HIVES - Wrap the individual with hives in a solid red blanket.

HOG KILLING - The moon signs had to be just right and the temperature had to be extremely cold for hog-killing. I hated hog-killing time. But I surely enjoyed the tenderloin, sausage, and ham. My Father would kill the hog with a gun or a sledge hammer. At the same time, the women folk kept plenty of wood on a big fire under the wash kettle to boil water to scald the hog. We canned much of the sausage and tenderloin. We seasoned the hams with salt and pepper and hung them in the smoke house. (2) Hog killing always brings to mind an incident that happened in Pigeon Forge several years ago. Some neighbor boys had obtained a book that outlined the procedure for killing hogs. That day came with the book very much in evidence. Quoting constantly from the book, the boys did each chore exactly by the book. This aroused great consternation for their much-experienced father, who had successfully done this for many years without instruction or incident. Step by step as the book directed, they reached the stage where a strong stick was passed through the hind legs just below the large tendon above the hoofs. The huge hog was now ready to be hung on the scaffold. The book said to do it one way. The father insisted that was unacceptable. He said there was no way it could work, but the boys insisted on doing it exactly by the book. The hog tilted and fell into the mess of hair and whatever muck was below. The father then asked, "Now, boys, what does the book say about that?" (3) My only personal experience after I was married was with three pet pigs we called Peter, Paul, and Mary.

Because they were our pets, the family simply could not eat them. Three pigs were wasted, so we never again raised a pig.

HOMEPLACE- What a tragedy all our buildings were torn away by the park service. Today tourists are unable to see how our family was so self-sufficient in the very early days. My father doctored the people while my mother delivered the babies. My great grandparents were required to buy only coffee and salt.

Thinking back of the old home place, no place on earth seems quite as precious. Our 363 acre farm had sixteen buildings, many acres of pasture and garden, and the molasses grinding patch,. The buildings included our home, garage, barn, corncrib, blacksmith shop, two chicken houses, wash house, the spring house, the blacksmith shop, the wood house, the dry kiln, the smoke house, the old log house where the grandparents had lived, the dark house for developing pictures, the grist mill, and of course, the "out-house" or privy. We had the "Hilton" when it came to the out-house. It was a three-holer for adults and a small size for children. It was fur- lined in the winter time. A family member said it contained a heater but I cannot recall that.

The old log house was used to store corn, pumpkins, broom corn, and popcorn. We stored dry stovewood and firewood along with axes, hoes, shovels, picks, rakes, saws and other tools in the woodhouse. The smoke house held the hams, pork shoulders, and canned goods along with Irish and sweet potatoes in the cellar. The two chicken houses with roosting poles of sassafras kept the chicken mites at bay. The dry kiln was used to sulphur apples while some apples were dried in the sun.

Honey and molasses sufficed after the sugar maples in the Sugarlands ceased to supply the sugar. The corn, wheat, vegetables, fruits and nuts along with the farm animals took care of the food. The spinning wheel and loom provided the cloth. An iron-last helped repair the shoes. A bullet mold made the bullets; a tooth-puller pulled the teeth. Steelyards were used for weighing, and a corn sheller shelled our corn. We had straw mattresses, a wash board, an ash hopper, feather beds, and wheat cradles. Stone or wooden salt-licks were in the pastures. Foot-peddled fly sweeps were used by some homes, but ours were hand held. Wooden malls or mallets, fro's, and other primitive tools filled our home and farm buildings.

It would be worthwhile to rebuild our home place today for tourist to see how we lived an almost self-sufficient life. It was located just inside the park, only two miles south of Gatlinburg on highway 441. Better known as the Noah Trentham home place. Now the McCarter riding stables at the Two Mile Branch are on the property. Restoration could be condensed so that the riding stables would not be affected. Restoration should include the original log house, which my great grand parents called home. While four of us are still living and remember all of these buildings, I believe we could get donated much of these materials and fixtures. Tourist being able to see this should help eliminate some of the traffic congestion going into Cades Cove to be able to see how we old-timers really lived.

HONEY - Was used as a sweetener instead of sugar. It was also used as a home remedy for many physical problems. Never give honey to a child less than one year old. It contains copper, iron, manganese, chlorine, silica, calcium, and magnesium. The darker honey seems to have these in greater quantity. (2) Today- In some foreign countries honey is said to be packed into surgical cavities following radical mastectomies. It is believed to kill bacteria and promote healing. Typhoid producing germs reportedly were put in pure honey and the germs were dead within 48 hours. Germs called A & B Typhus died within 24 hours while microorganism found in bowel feces died within 5 hours. Bronchi -pneumonia germs died on the third day as well as pleuritis, peritonitis and suppurative abscesses. Dysentery producing germs were dead within 10 hours. This information came from bulletin #242 from Colorado Agriculture College, Fort Collins. But do we use it today to kill germs?

HOOKED RUGS - Mother and her sister, Nancy Pickel, enjoyed making hooked rugs. They always exchanged patterns and ideas. Mother became critically ill shortly after she had written Nancy asking what colors one must combine to make orange. When the letter of reply came, I got quite a shock when I read the following: "Dear Janie, I hope you are better and when you go to die, ...use yellow and red to make orange." The spelling of "dye" as "die" with Mother so critically ill momentarily gave me quite a start. Afterwards we had a good laugh.

HORSE, HOW TO CATCH ONE - The easiest way to catch a horse in open pasture is simply to lie down on the ground (playing possum) and pretend to be dead. Horses are so curious they will come right over to inspect you. When spooked, a horse will run through a fence. A mule will not.

HORSE THIEVES - The idea of stealing horses is so outdated in today's society that for us to suggest that one could hardly trace early family trees more than three generations without finding a horse thief sounds ludicrous. We have to take into consideration that in the very early days in such a remote section, the very life of a family often depended upon having a horse. For a family to lose its only horse during those days was extremely critical. It was perhaps much more serious than losing the family car today. In those days horse stealing was a cardinal sin. Without jails the letters "H-T", for horse thief, were branded on one's cheek or the back of one's hand if he was found guilty of stealing a horse. (2) In the very early days, "take canoe" was the sentence imposed upon more serious crimes. The guilty party was given a certain number of days to build a canoe (purportedly enough time to build a canoe). After this time he was to head down the river and away from that community. With overcrowded jails and prisons today, I wonder if we should go back to some of the above ways of thinking.

HOT FLASHES - Take black cohosh as directed on the bottle. When I was a child, my mother used the wild root which grew nearby. I remember going into the woods to dig the roots to make a tea for my grandmother to drink. (2) Take one tablespoon apple cider vinegar and one tablespoon honey in six ounces water at least three times daily. (3) Eat a cucumber daily. (4) Massage the area between the thumbs and index finger in a circular motion 5 minutes. (5) Drink sage tea. (6) Today soy protein is used most effectively- either in capsule or powder mixed in juice.

HOWDY - Howdy was the usual early greeting. That was followed by, "Come in and sit a spell while I rest your hat." While I never heard the part about resting one's hat, I am told it was used. I like "Hello" much better than "Howdy."

HUNTING - For mountain folk, hunting was necessary for survival. Manual skills were taught the children, especially the boys. These skills included how to build fires, set traps, skin and preserve animal hides.

HUNTING DOGS - A good hunting dog was important to early families to obtain meat for the dinner table. Mountain children were never allowed to pet or play with hunting dogs because of risk of injury.

HYDRANGEAS - Many people enjoyed beautiful hydrangeas in their yards. To enhance their color Mother put rusty nails or Little Boy Blue bluing around the roots or in the soil. Nails produced a bright pink. Bluing produced a deep blue.

HYPOCHONDRIAC'S MOUNTAIN STYLE - A very strange malady seemed to overtake a few mountain women. For whatever reason they spent most of their lives in bed. We spoke of them as being "Hippoed." This was probably a corruption of hypochondriac. The strange thing was they were not really sick. I recall a mother and daughter who were among those afflicted coming to our house. As they came through the front door, the mother said, "I'll take the bed and you can take the couch." I recall one instance in which a family member was being buried. Someone came home unexpectedly. This unexpected visit required the "hippoed" member to jump into bed with her shoes on. Another time a family member came home unexpectedly, and this "patient" was in the back field digging potatoes. I cannot imagine why they chose to spend their lives in bed and sneaking out while no one was around. I never heard of a man being "stricken" with this strange malady. (2) This reminds of a medical history that I took for a patient in the coronary unit at the hospital. After getting the routine name, address, age, etc., I asked about her activities. When I asked if she had ever had shortness of breath, she said, "Yes." When I ask for a description, she said, " Well, I was climbing the hill to dig taters"

I

IMPOTENCE - Ginseng was used most often for impotence. Take one-fourth teaspoon ginseng twice per month. (2) Eat one-half cup unprocessed (unsalted) shelled pumpkin or sunflower seeds daily. Remedies today..(3) Take a bee pollen pill daily. (4) To soothe or generally relax tension and stimulate circulation, massage the area behind the leg in back of the ankle, about one and one-half inches higher than the shoe line of each foot.

INDIAN BLANKET COLORS - Beautiful -two rows of yellow, deep yellow, peach, orange, red, wine, dark purple, orchid or medium purple, medium dark blue or turquoise, light blue, medium dark green. Crochet hook H or international hook size #5.

INDIANS - CHEROKEE - Today we would call them Native Americans. We always called them Indians or Cherokees. Indians ate at our table occasionally. Mother became badly frightened one night while sitting by an open window when she saw an Indian looking in the window. She concluded that he meant no harm. On another occasion an Indian reached through the fence in a friendly gesture and pinched my sister. As for language, if we met an Indian and were unable to converse, we each were to hold up the right hand as a friendly signal. I recently learned from my brother, Sam, that shortly before Mother died she traced the lineage of our Indian ancestry and concluded that Sam and I are one-eighth Cherokee Indian. I had always suspected some Indian blood because her father looked like the Cherokees. (2) The Cherokee tribe was believed to have lived here since the year 1000. The Great Smoky Mountain National Park formed what was the heart of the Cherokee nation, which was part of Georgia, South Carolina, North Carolina and Tennessee. When Hernando DeSota passed through the Smoky Mountains in 1540 he wrote of the primitive conditions. He said the Cherokees appeared sedate and thoughtful, dwelling in peace, cultivated their fields and lived in prosperity and plenty. (3) The war with the Cherokees in this area blazed with death and destruction. Each side accumulated it own collection of horrors. The Indians were said to have captured Fort Loudon in 1760. Then in 1761 about 260 men destroyed the native middle towns, burned 1500 acres of corn, beans, and peas, and forced 5000 Cherokees into the forest for winter. During my early school days I never understood why the Indians scalped people until I learned that the British issued guns and offered the Indians rewards for American scalps. South Carolina was said to have offered 25 English pounds for every Indian scalp. Historians have been accused of embellishing to make these stories sound better.(4) The Cherokees did not build tepees. They lived in rather rough log structures with one door and no windows. A small hole was left in the roof for smoke to escape. The women sat in councils as equals to men but were accused of having "petticoat governments." Their rituals of planting and reaping were of interest They always dropped 7 grains of corn in each hill and never thinned the crop. The very early Indians were said never to keep any live stock, only a dog. So, they did not need any outbuildings. It was also said they never died of snake bites. Perhaps they knew the local weed that was said to cure snakebite. They had great knowledge of applying herbs and plants for even the most dangerous illnesses. Some people preferred their cures to any surgeon. (5) They used irony to correct behavior. (We call it reverse psychology today) They praised the coward for his valor, the thief for his honesty, and the liar for his veracity. They had a city of refuge like the one described in the Bible. This was a place of asylum for Indian criminals, especially murderers. This city was named Chota and was located south of Maryville, Tennessee on the Little Tennessee River. Archaeologist have done some digging in that area.

INDIAN DREAM CATCHER - Indian culture and tradition considered dreams or visions to be important. They had what was called a dream catcher. It looked somewhat like a basketball hoop with a net woven straight across from rim to rim. It was hung above their bed. A hole in the center of the net was believed to allow the evil to escape in their dreams. It was believed that dreams contain what may be happening in the future.

INDIAN LORE - The Cherokees looked upon these mountains as both sacred and dangerous. One myth tells of a race of "little people" similar to what we call fairies. The little people were both helpful and kind but could make an intruder lose his way. The myth of the tortoise and the hare is also part of Cherokee mythology. The tortoise won the race by having a look-alike stationed around the next curve, so the hare wore himself out before the race was over. (2) The early Indians believed water has healing power. They also believed if a baby's hand was placed in a spider web, the child would have exceptional artistic abilities using the hands. Another belief was that lightening would never strike a tulip tree. They searched for a tulip tree for shelter during a storm. Much of the folklore is without benefit of written word. (3) Some of the Indians had a New Years ceremony in which the fires in every home were doused and the fireplaces were cleansed. Then they went to the special place of worship to get fresh coals to rebuild their home fires. This ceremony also included forgiving all the hurts and differences of opinion during the past year. They vowed they would never mention or remember them again. What a wonderful idea for us today. Some believe that because the Indians are able to forgive the white man, they will lead America back to God. They say that revenge is like spitting in the wind. It will come back in your face.

Why praise the stranger you scarcely know
Then praise the fleeting guest,
But render many a heartless blow
To the one you love the best?   author unknown

INDIAN SUMMER - In early days, after the first frost, the Indians were most likely to attack. Ghostly war whoops and bone chilling screams were sometimes heard in the forests. These were reminders of the horrible tragedies that happened long ago. But it took a rugged people to settle such an isolated place.

INGROWN TOENAIL - If an ingrown toenail is infected, mix honey and propolis and bind on. (2) Stuffing cotton underneath the nail helps. (3) Epsom salt was often used to draw out any infection. - Recent: (4) Soak a cotton string in Betadine, Vaseline, peroxide or iodine. Gently insert it underneath the affected nail. This is to raise it while allowing it to grow over the affected part.

INSECT BITES - First scrape out the stinger, if any. If no medication is available, gather leaves of seven weeds, bruise, and rub on the sting. (2) Apply baking soda or rub with moist salt, raw onion, or tobacco. Recent: Apply Melaleuca oil (Tea Tree), meat tenderizer, aspirin, or banana peel. To prevent insect bites or stings, wear drab colors. Bright clothing, perfumes, and colognes attract insects.

IRON - Some mountain folk put rusty nails in water to obtain iron. (Before vitamins, folks.)

IRONING - I remember placing flat irons before an open fire to be heated to iron our clothes. Compared with today's electric irons, they were very crude and unhandy. One had to be very careful not to allow ashes to soil the garment being ironed. The end result was generally satisfactory, however. While my family did not practice this method, it was said that some people folded items, placed them in a chair, and then sat on them to iron wrinkles out of clothing.

IRON LAST - A piece of iron shaped like a foot. It was turned bottom side up and fastened on an iron stand approximately 14 inches high. This tool was necessary to fashion and to repair shoes. My Father used an iron last to attach new heels or to half-sole our shoes during the 1920's and 1930's. I suspect that name originated because it made the shoes "last" longer.

IRREDOLOGY - Mountain folk proposed to foretell the sex of an expected baby by looking into the eyes of the mother-to-be. If a red streak was at the 4 o'clock location the baby was said to be male. If a streak was at 8 o'clock, it was a female **(see BABIES.)**

ITCH - SCABIES - This highly contagious bug can be transferred by handling a book or any item that has come in contact with one so affected. Since scabies was so highly contagious, it was not considered a disgrace to get it, just a disgrace to keep it. Perhaps that is where the term: "seven-year" itch originated. I must confess I was once a victim. Mother greased me from head to foot with sulfur mixed with lard. Then she made me stand, as some would say: "Nekked"in front of a hot fire, that baked in the sulfur. I do not recall if this treatment was repeated, as I was very young at the time. I do recall that we had to burn all clothing and bedding that came in contact with the sulfur as that odor cannot be removed. Poke root or dog hobble killed the itch and does not smell. It was smeared head to toe and worn for 3 days.

J

JERKS - While Rev. Lorenzo Dow was in Newport, Tennessee, he heard of a phenomenon called the jerks, which first appeared among church people in Knoxville in 1803. Some people were very alarmed. Considering the report to be false, he set out for Knoxville to see for himself. While preaching there he observed several involuntary motions among his listeners. Later he preached in Maryville, where about 150 people had the jerks. A daughter in the home where he spent the night dropped a teacup and explained she had the jerks for several days and added that it was a means of awakening and converting the soul. Upon passing a camp meeting site, Dow saw that the tops of about fifty to one hundred saplings had been cut off about breast high. The ground around them looked as if horses had been stamping flies. He learned that people had jerked so violently that they held on to these stumps. He also learned that a young man from North Carolina who mimicked them was himself seized with jerks. The young man grew ashamed, and on attempting to mount his horse to get away, his foot jerked so badly he could not put it in the stirrup. Some youngsters helped him to get on his horse, but he jerked so he could not sit alone. One of them got up to hold him on the horse. The young man was then asked what he thought about the jerks. He said, "I believe God sent it on me for my wickedness, and for making light of it in others." Then he requested prayer for himself. A Doctor Nelson tried to get the jerks to try to analyze the phenomenon but was unable to do so. Dow remained unconvinced of the reality of this strange behavior for awhile. He somewhat rudely admonished a young woman for the indecency of such gestures and grunts in public. He urged her in a commanding tone to stop if she had any regard for her character. She meekly replied: " I will if I can." He took her by the hand, looked her in the face, and said, "Tell me no lies." He then realized she was doing her best to refrain from jerking. She instantly began to jerk as if she would jerk herself to pieces. He apologized to her for his abruptness and explained he did that to have an answer to those who accused the victims of hypocrisy. Rev. Dow later wrote at length regarding these strange jerks and was convinced that God was showing his power by sending the jerks to unbelieving people. He said that rich and poor, aged and young were stricken. In most cases, however, it was only lazy, half-hearted, indolent professors who were stricken. He said that the wicked feared the jerks more than smallpox or yellow fever, because they were most often subject to it, and they sometimes cursed and damned it while jerking. He said it was not painful, but was more tiring than a day's labor.(2) Records show that Tennessee Governor John Sevier attended a service in Knoxville on Feb. 19, 1804 where about 150 people had the jerks. Among this group was a circuit preacher, John Johnson, who had opposed the jerks. He had proposed to "preach the jerks out of the Methodists." But he himself was so powerfully stricken with the jerks that he would have fallen down had not the audience been so crowded that he could not fall. His circuit included Knoxville, and his name disappeared from the minutes at the end of that year.

JOURNEY PROUD - Travel in early days was very rough and time-consuming, so that many people found it very difficult to sleep the night before a major trip. Being unable to sleep was described as being "Journey Proud!"

Bonnie T. Myers birthplace, 2 miles south of Gatlinburg, TN, Hwy. 441. Where McCarter riding stable now located.

Bonnie, age 5

Ray T. Myers, Bonnie Lynn Trentham

The Noah Trentham Clan - 1933

The five children seated front row: L to R: Dowe Trentham, Ralph Trentham, Sam Trentham holding Hugh Watson, and Mary Trentham Christopher. 2nd Row seated: L to R: Eugene Trentham, Bonnie Trentham (me) Verna (Mrs. Orlie) Trentham, Lillie Trentham Watson, Mary Jane Ogle Carr Trentham, Ellis Watson and Olin Watson. 3rd Row standing: L to R: Gladys Trentham Russell, Mayme Stogner (Mrs. Olin) Watson, Ralph Trentham, Kate Trentham Stogner, Noah Trentham, Clell Watson, Munsey Trentham, Mack Trentham, Nora Oakley Trentham, Willie Trentham, Bess (Mrs. Mack) Trentham, Harmon Trentham.

Chynna Mykel Knight
Greatgrandaughter

Lynda & Glenn Myers

Eric, Glenn, Amanda and Aaron, standing
Seated: Sharon and Emily Myers

Headricks, Trenthams, Myers, Adams & Patty's

1920 - L to R: Hugh H. Myers, Bruce Myers, Hubert Myers and Ida H. Myers holding Ray T. Myers

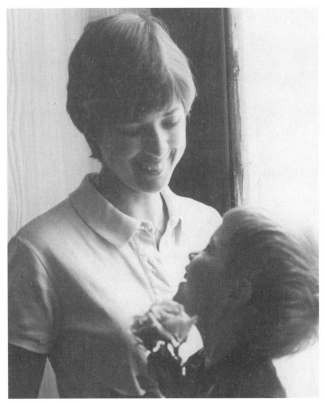

A rose from Andy on her wedding anniversary while in Europe.

Lynda Boyer and mother, Bonnie Myers

Christmas 1995 at Mimosa

32nd wedding anniversary. Ray T. & Bonnie Myers

Don, Donna Myers, Roy Ruszkowski and granddog. D.J. (Don Juan)

L to R: Bonnie Myers, Reba Carr, Glayds Russell, Kate Stogner
Seated: Roy Ruszkowski, Wesley Carr, Sam Russell, Hulett Stogner

Dr. Lynda Boyer, Edwin Boyer, Esq. and son Andy

Bonnie's 70th birthday bash. 1991

L to R Don Myers, Greg & Gabrial Qualls, Donna Myers and Jennifer Qualls.

Bonnie, Lynda, Glenn, Don

Bruce and Ida Myers Clan

Diana and Jonathan Thompson

Bonnie Myers, Alex Haley and wife Myron Haley

Mary Jane Trentham and seven of her eight children. Left to right: (standing) Kate Trentham Stogner, Ollie Carr Trentham, Mary jane Trentham, Wesley Carr, Harmon and Sam Trentham. (Seated) Bonnie Trentham Myers and Gladys Trentham Russell. (Note: In case this confuses you, I was married for 14 years to Roy Ruszkowski who died in 2001 but kept all legal papers in the Myers name while married to him.

Standing: L to R: Ralph Headrick, Bruce Myers, Hubert Myers,
Seating: Ralph Patty, Ray T. Myers.

Tommy & Hettie Headrick

Mack, Hugh and Rex Myers

Restless "Soles" Hiking Club - Everett Park Adult Center

Everett Park Adult Center, Pinochle Club

Pi Beta Phi Class reunion, Gatlinburg, TN

The Morse Code is as follows: Note all letters have no more than 4 symbols.

A •—	N —•	
B —•••	O ———	
C —•—•	P •——•	
D —••	Q ——•—	
E •	R •—•	
F ••—•	S •••	
G ——•	T —	
H ••••	U ••—	
I ••	V •••—	
J •———	W •——	
K —•—	X —••—	
L •—••	Y —•——	
M ——	Z ——••	

Morse Code numbers need no memory aid as they do have a pattern and use 5 symbols as follows:

1) •————
2) ••———
3) •••——
4) ••••—
5) •••••
6) —••••
7) ——•••
8) ———••
9) ————•
0) —————

Brief Forms:

wait •—•••
understand •••—•
don't understand —•••—•
period •—•—•—

interrogation ••——••
exclamation —•—•——
call —•—
finish •••—•—

Now you can transcribe the entire Morse Code just as I promised and in such short time as to do yourself proud! However, to receive and decipher a message is another hurdle. The following suggestions should be helpful:

E •	T —	A •—
I ••	M ——	N —•
S •••	O ———	B —•••
H ••••		J •———

If anyone has a memory aid helpful for "receiving", I would appreciate hearing from you.

Intelligent men in strategic places have spent many long hours of hard work in an effort to memorize the Morse Code as a necessary part of their job.

Now thousands of Ham Radio operators must learn it as part of their test in order to get license. A jungle of dots and dashes which have no uniformity of sequence nor pattern.

But with this simplified method anyone of average intelligence can easily **transcribe** the entire code within 45 minutes.

My first use of a coded message goes back to World War II. Since that time fellow office workers have suffered in silence while I went through the entire dictionary twice, word by word, to find the words presently used to represent each letter of the alphabet.

And before my grammar and spelling is challenged in the following memory aid story, I do know the correct usage. You will see later why this was necessary in order to be perfectly transcribed.

Step I.
Now as easy as ABC memorize the following idiotic story which helps to bring the next word or words to mind. Only the capitalized words are to be used when transcribing the code. Be sure to use their exact spelling. The first letter of each capitalized word represents that letter of the alphabet and is its **only** use. (Note alphabetical sequence.)

Step II.
Of the remaining capitalized letters omit all O's and S's. There are no exceptions to this rule.

Step III.
With the remaining capitalized letters transcribe the vowels (AEIOUY) as dots (•). All the consonants as dashes (—).
And you are on your way....

Now for the memory aid story:

the	A	IR	•—
is filled with	B	RAI$E	—•••
	C	HØICE	—•—•
	D	ØGIE	—••
	E		•
	F	AIRY	••—•
	G	NØME	——•
where a	H	U$$Y I$ A	••••
	I	$$UE	••
	J	U$T NØW	•———
at	K	ØDAK	—•—
	L	ET YØU	•—••
	M	ØØCH	——
tennessee where she	N	ØDØ$E	—•

	O	N TØP	———
of a	P	ERKY	•——•
	Q	CLUB	——•—
while	R	UDE	•—•
	S	U$IE	•••
and	T	ØM	—
as	U	$UAL	••—
are	V	I$UAL	•••—
	W	ITH	•——
	X	TAIN	—••—
who eats	Y	ØGURT	—•——
like a	Z	ØMBIE	——••

Repeat: the <u>A</u>IR is filled with <u>B</u>RAISE <u>C</u>HOICE <u>D</u>OGIE <u>E</u> <u>F</u>AIRY <u>G</u>NOME where a <u>H</u>USSY IS A <u>I</u>SSUE <u>J</u>UST NOW at <u>K</u>ODAK tennessee where she will <u>L</u>ET YOU <u>M</u>OOCH <u>N</u>ODOSE <u>O</u>N TOP of a <u>P</u>ERKY <u>Q</u>CLUB while <u>R</u>UDE <u>S</u>USIE and <u>T</u>OM as <u>U</u>SUAL are <u>V</u>ISUAL <u>W</u>ITH <u>X</u>TAIN who eats <u>Y</u>OGURT like a <u>Z</u>OMBIE. (Note alphabet underscored). For example for A you have IR, a vowel and a consonant or •—, for B you have after omitting the S the letters RAIE or a consonant, vowel, vowel, vowel or —•••, etc.

Jason Knight, Chynna Knight, Andrea Hill

Jacob and Gabrail Qualls, my greatgrandsons.

Ephraim & Mary Ann Ogle family

RAY

BONNIE

LYNDA

MAYME   M.JANE   OLLIE   SANDRA

TRENTHAM FAMILY

AARON   ERIC   AUNT "T"   AMANDA
Emily

Madison Avenue Baptist Church organized 1949 by Rev. Ray T. and
Bonnie T. Myers.

1940 Pi Beta Phi Graduates
L to R: Sanford Woodlief, Ruth Webb, Louise Montgomery,
Bonnie Myers and Harlan Reagan.

L to R: Herb Clabo, Bonnie Myers, Harvey Oakley, Tolbert and Larry
Reagan.

L to R: Hubert, Lucille, Bruce, Ida, Bonnie & Ray T. Myers

Karen & Roy
Ruszkowski

Dr. Lynda Myers Boyer

L to R: Andrew Hartung, ---?---, Rick and Erika Trager, Gerhard & Jean Hartung, Geraldine & Russ Rogers, Roy Jr. & Roy Ruszkowski, Sr. Seated L to R: ---?---, Jennifer Trager, Karen Ruszkowski and Bonnie Myers Ruszkowski.

Roy G. Ruszkowski
7-27-14 to 9-28-01

Donald Trent Myers
Born Nov. 5, 1942 son of Roy
T. & Bonnie Trentham Myers
died May 1998

The Walker sisters (in picture but maybe not in order
of the picture) were: Nancy who died in 1931, Polly
died in '45, Hettie died in '47, Martha died in '50,
Margaret died in '62, Lovisa died in '64, Carolina
died in '66.

Walker sister's living room. My mother born close by, slept in this
room.

ROBERT
TRENTHAM
Tenor

Glenn builds canoe's for sale

Trentham Hall, Trentham, England

Collecting "sweet water." See Maple Syrup page 130 and Sugarlands page 197.

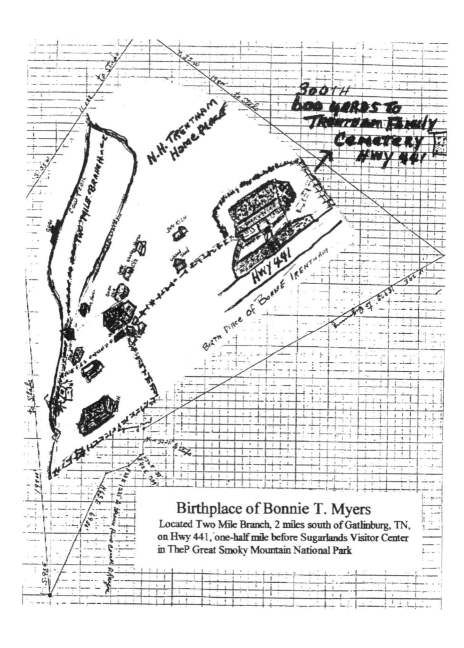

Birthplace of Bonnie T. Myers

Located Two Mile Branch, 2 miles south of Gatlinburg, TN,
on Hwy 441, one-half mile before Sugarlands Visitor Center
in TheP Great Smoky Mountain National Park

Artist sketch of Bonnie's birthplace.

Gatlinburg, Tennessee
1901

1940 Gatlinburg, TN - Pi Beta Phi High School

K

KANGAROO COURT - In early days Justices of the Peace, better known as JP's, held court on a certain Saturday of each month at their homes or in school buildings. Two people with a dispute came to the JP, where they presented their cases. The JP decided the issue if possible. If the JP failed to settle the dispute, the two people had a fist fight. The person who lost the fight, not only lost the case, but was thrown in the creek.

KEPHART, HORACE - It is said that Horace Kephart was a "boozing stupefied rapscallion" when he came here many years ago roaring drunk. He wrote about this area, depicting mountain people as being wretched backward creatures living in depravity and degradation. He mimicked the dialect. Unfortunately, many still believe his opinions correctly describe the south today. While the complete isolation of this region and the early plight of our people deserves to be told, "survival of the fittest" became part of the grim tales of a people who lived almost without roads, schools, and doctors. While I deplore the lack of early educational advantages, we have survived and now have people moving into our area by the thousands because it has twice been rated among the safest in which to live and raise a family. In the presence of the serene grandeur of the Smoky Mountains, jaded nerves find comfort away from the sights and sounds of the noisy cities and their botherations.

KEROSENE - See wounds.

KICK THE BUCKET - Many of us prefer saying, " When I kick the bucket" rather than saying "When I die." Could be that we prefer to die with our boots on, so it would not hurt our toe when we kick the bucket!

KIDNEY TROUBLE - Boil the root of Queen of the Meadow. Drink a cup full or more every four hours for two days. My father, who had prescribed and used this remedy, told my brother-in-law that one could drink it and piss over a ten-rail fence.

KISSING - Occasionally, mountain people have been criticized for not kissing each other when we meet. The chief reason for the lack of kissing was once a matter of life and death in this area. Years ago there was much tuberculosis, which was highly contagious. Caution might well have saved many of our ancestors lives. Also, being of English extraction also helps explain the very proper behavior of some of us. Loyalty to our friends and family goes much deeper than a little peck on the cheek.

KNIFE TRADING- When men met at church gatherings or in town, they enjoyed activities like horse-trading or knife-trading. In each case, many enjoyed the idea that they had "put something over on" someone else.

L

LAID-BY - When the crops had been plowed and hoed three or four times to rid the weeds, they were said to be "laid-by." That meant the only remaining chore was to harvest the crop. As soon as this was accomplished, the cross cut saw and axes echoed throughout the hills preparing wood for winter heat.

LAMENESS - Mix 1 tablespoon turpentine, 1 egg yolk, and 1 tablespoon apple cider vinegar. Rub in well. (2) Recent: I like DMSO, but when using DMSO one must be careful not to have any chemicals on the skin surface as they will be taken into the skin with the DMSO.

LAND GRANTS - Early settlers were said to receive 20 acres of land for a mere seventy-five cents.

LASSES - "Molasses." We grew sugar cane locally, but not in such abundance as to need to burn the fields. Here the leaves or blades were hand stripped from the stalks. The stalks were then fed into a machine that squeezed the juice. A long pole coming from the grinder was hooked to the harness in front of a mule or horse. This mule or horse went round and round and round all day, unless relieved by another. The juice was then boiled with the foam often skimmed from the top. The final product was some mighty good sweets, rating almost as good as honey. I was in Hawaii when the cane fields were being burned. It was a tremendous operation. Only the blades or leaves burned, leaving the stalks standing. This practice saved many hours stripping them as our family did with our small crops. In fact, with the many trees on the mountain sides, it could have been quite dangerous to even attempt such a feat here. (See Spring Tonic)

LATCH STRINGS - Before metal door knobs were available, early settlers used a latch string with which to "lock" or fasten outside doors. This cord was fastened to a moveable board that "bolted" or fastened the door on the inside. The latch string then threaded through a hole cut in the door several inches above the slot which held the moveable board. Pulling on this cord from the outside, raised this board, thereby "unlocking" the door. To "lock" it, one simply pulled the latch string or cord to the inside.. My great grandparents used this "latch string" in their old log house, and which we continued to use to enter the building.

LAUNDRY - A friend told recently of going through his closet to discard older clothing when he found an old shirt whose laundry instructions read thus: Take it to the creek, beat it over a rock, hang it on the fence to dry, and watch out for the Indians. Our laundry was not this primitive. Our barn had a tin roof. The gutter of the roof channeled rain water into a huge cistern, which collected water for our laundry. We had to pour kerosene on top of this water to kill insects that we called wiggle-tails, which could have been mosquitoes.. On washday, we built a fire outside under a huge black wash kettle filled with water. When the water was hot enough, we poured it into two large wash tubs that set on a frame or platform. We refilled the kettle with more water then boiled all our white clothes in the kettle. We washed the colored clothes on a washboard in the first tub, then ran them through a wringer perched between the two tubs. Fed through the wringer placed the clothes in the second tub to rinse. Bluing was added to this water to whiten the white clothes. We wrung them once again before hanging them on a fence or clothesline to dry.. If hung on a clothesline, we used wooden clothespin to secure them. Our washday was always on Monday.. For very heavily soiled clothing, we used a battling stick, which was somewhat less but shaped like a canoe paddle. We placed garments in the Two-Mile Branch on a rock and moved them around in the water or we agitated them in the kettle of boiling water. (2) When the first new washing machines became available, they moved so much when they were spinning, that it was necessary to bolt them to the floor to keep them from "traveling." One time my brother-in-law, Sam Russell, got on top of a washing machine to slow it down. My husband laughed heartily while watching him ride the washer across the room.

LAWS - NO FENCE LAWS - Goats, sheep, hogs, and cattle grazed these mountains in early days with brands to identify their owners. There were no fences for livestock. Fences were put around gardens and crops to safeguard them from the herds before fence laws were enacted

LEATHER BREECHES OR BRITCHES - You did not wear them; you ate them. Green beans still in the pod were strung on a string and hung out to dry to preserve them. After they dried, they were soaked in water, and then boiled to eat. I am not aware of my Mother ever preparing beans in that manner, but I do recall seeing long strings of them hanging on a porch at one back-woods home. Except for the hulls, I imagine they taste somewhat like our dried beans of today.

LEECHES - "BLOOD-SUCKERS" Yes, we had leeches. They grew wild in branches and ponds around our house. They also stuck to rocks. We had to watch for them when we wadded the Two Mile Branch that ran through our farm. Leeches adhered to our feet and legs. As a small child I can recall picking them off my legs. Or, we could remove them if we sprinkled them with salt. Leeches were worms about one-half inch long. Their bodies divided into rings or sections and they could have up to ten pair of eyes. Sight is said to be their only sense organ. They were used by early doctors who let sick people bleed to cure them. They were used especially on bruises or other poisonous skin conditions. In 1995 a friend of mine was in a well known hospital with an undiagnosed condition around his ankles. The hospital had leeches flown in from New York to do their thing. He said he felt like something out of the dark ages. My late second husband said that after using the leeches, his mother squeezed the blood out of them, and fed them to keep them alive for later use.

LEG CRAMPS - Squeeze hard on the upper lip. (2) Stand three feet from a wall with feet flat, and bend the body toward the wall. (3) Bathe the legs in apple cider vinegar. (4) Wrap legs in warm towels or spray your legs with very warm water. (5) Put your feet in cold water. (6) Recent: Calcium tablets work very well.

LETTERS EDGED IN BLACK - Before telephones were available, if a death occurred, a letter edged in black bearing news of the death was sent to family members living at a distance. To my knowledge, our family never received such a letter. I assume that jet oil or paint was used to make the black edges. When my son, Donald Trent Myers, died May 28, 1998, I sent a letter edged in black to Peter and Christine Trentham in England. They had never before heard that a letter edged in black warned that the letter held news of a death in the family.

LIAR - Want to know how old-timers detected a liar? They filled his mouth with flour. If innocent, the suspect had enough saliva to rid himself of the flour. If guilty, he would choke on it.

LICE - School children in early days had head lice. Fortunately, I never had that experience. I recently heard a man say his mother doused his head with kerosene to rid the lice. My daughter is principal of 2500 high school students. I heard her mention a few years ago that the problem of lice still exists in the schools.

LIGHTS - As children we sometimes put lightening bugs in a blue Vicks salve jar for a night light. We usually went to bed soon after it became dark. However, we used glass or brass kerosene lamps with wicks to light our houses on dark days or at night. Tennessee Valley Authority electricity did not come to the park before we moved out of it.

LOCKS - Until approximately the 1960's, we never locked the doors of our homes. Often we did not have a key. We were content and happy. If the whole world had been just like us:

freedom-loving, honest, trustworthy, generous, and brave, I believe the world would be OK.

LOST BRANCH - Was named after a man became lost and was found dead alongside this branch (mountain stream).

LYE SOAP - Lye was mixed with fat and then boiled to make soap. A feather was stirred into the mixture. If the lye destroyed the feather bristles, the mixture contained too much lye. More fat was then added slowly. When a feather no longer showed damage, the mixture was correct. It was poured into containers and cut into squares.

M

MAIL CARRIERS - In Cades Cove before mail was delivered daily to each home, it came only once per week. The carrier blew a bugle to signal the residents that he had delivered their mail to a designated spot at the top of the ridge. The people would then race to meet him to pick up their mail. Crockett Maples, Sr., one of the early mail-carriers, was atop one of the mountains when a snow storm struck. As he went down the mountain, he realized he could not make it, so he crawled into a hollow log for the night. Both feet were so badly frozen that they had to be amputated. His feet were amputated in the woodshed- without anesthesia! (Maybe Moonshine) Later, he made his own wooden feet with boots and continued to walk with two canes. His son, Crockett, Jr. carried our mail on horseback.

MAIL ORDER CATALOGS - When I was a small child, I enjoyed seeing Sears & Roebuck, Montgomery Ward, or Spiegel catalogs arrive in the mail. It was like visiting Santa Claus. While we were snowbound in the winter, browsing through the catalogs created a fairyland for us. After one year the catalogs were replaced by new copies.. The catalogs, better known as "wish-books," went to the outhouse when a new edition arrived. The slick pages were ruffled for better traction Toilet tissue was unheard of in the early days, and corn cobs were not always available nor desirable. Also, in case a spider was residing underneath the seat, a few pages from the catalog served as a glove-covering to go underneath the seat to roust it out. And, yes, a few people were bitten by spiders in the outhouse. Most often the male gender. Those circumstances sure made one appreciate indoor plumbing. However, a few snakes have been known to invade the pipes of indoor plumbing.

MANGLE - I bet few people remembers the mangle, an ironing appliance we used in the 1930's and 40's.. Clothing was spread over a 36-inch cylinder. A hot lid was then pulled down to press the cloth against the cylinder. One could sit while using it. Flat pieces such as sheets or pillow cases ironed fine, but it took so long to do a shirt or other clothing that the mangle craze lasted a very short time. I recall using it just once or twice, didn't like it.

MANNERS - (see ETIQUETTE)

MAPLE SYRUP - The Sugarlands area, known for the sugar maples trees that grew there, was the source of maple syrup and sugar for the very early settlers of our area. For several weeks in the late winter and early spring when the sun grew warm during the day, the warmth caused the sap to rise in the trees. To gather the sap, a hole was bored into the tree. A small length of an elderberry twig, which has a pithy center, was hollowed out and placed in the hole. Sometimes galvanized iron or a wooden trough was hammered into the tree to catch the flow of sap. This allowed the sap to drip into cloth-covered buckets attached to the trees. This bucket hug beneath the spout was called a "spile." After the sap was gathered, the hole was plugged to stop the sap from draining. It normally took 24 hours to fill a gallon bucket with sap. On a good day three gallons of sap would drip from one tree. Ten gallons of maple sap boiled down to produce a gallon of maple syrup.

MARGARINE - I was here before margarine. When margarine first appeared, yellow coloring was enclosed so we could color it if we chose to do so. Otherwise, it looked like lard. Today some maverick doctors are attributing so may heart attacks to the use of margarine, especially when heated, while saying there is nothing to this cholesterol scare that Americans are spending billions of dollars on high priced medications trying to lower it. They say more people are dying, having strokes and paralysis whose cholesterol is under 200 than those who are over 200. Frankly, we do not know who to believe.

MASTURBATION - As I was becoming more mature, my mother showed me pictures in an old medical book she kept. It showed very deformed children and explained that they were victims of masturbation. We were seriously told we would go blind if we engaged in that act. Many, I am sure, thought they would try it until they needed glasses.

MATCHES - My father was approximately twenty-five years old before he was able to buy matches. Until that time families kept a fire burning or used a piece of steel to strike a flint rock. The resulting sparks were allowed to fall on a substance they called "punk," Punk was the decayed heart of a tree. If it failed to ignite, one borrowed a fire coal from a neighbor (see fire).

MATTRESSES - Early mattresses were often made of fresh straw or corn shucks. Lillie Watson, my half-sister, hearing movement in her newly-filled mattress once found a copperhead snake had somehow been added with the new straw. It did not take her very long to get out of that bed. (2) The father of former University of Tennessee, Ed Boling, reportedly spent the night along with Jep Helton in Little Greenbrier. They were both ministers. While getting ready for bed, Jep asked Boling to tend the fire while he prepared the bed. This bed was equipped with a straw mattress that was worn very thin near the year's end. Helton hurriedly scrapped every remaining straw over to his side of the bed. Next morning, he asked Boling how he liked his bed. We do not know what the minister replied.

MEDICINES (distasteful) - Hold ice in your mouth before taking bad-tasting medications.

MILKING COWS BY HAND - It is funny today to think that people do not know how to milk a cow. That was an important task when I was young. Facing a cow, walk to your left- being the right side of the cow. Put your head into her flank to help prevent her from kicking when you get to work on the udders or "faucets." All the while you must try to avoid her fly-whacking tail. We never used the tail holders some families used. One of my sisters never became adept at milking. Due to the stance she assumed while milking, we teased her saying she stood outside the stable door while reaching inside to milk the cow.

MISTLETOE - The tradition of kissing under the mistletoe has changed. Earlier, when a guy kissed a girl under the mistletoe, he picked one of the berries from the cluster. When the last berry was gone, there was no more kissing. Today, we disregard that tradition. As long as someone stands under the mistletoe a kiss is in order.

MIXED BATHING- Was a very serious topic for church sermons. Mountain preachers said so much about how wrong mixed bathing was that when I first went into the pool with Jack Reynolds, Loy Pate and Hubert Myers, I fully expected an electric shock. I did not even get a tingle. Sure was disappointed.

MOON, SIGNS OF THE - Many mountain folk went strictly by signs of the moon when planting their crops, killing their hogs, and setting fence posts. I once made a derogatory remark to my father regarding his planting by moon signs, saying that it was just silly superstition. He decided to show me I did not quite know everything. First he put barn-yard fertilizer (manure) on the orchard during the light nights. It lay there almost five years before all of it was absorbed into the ground. A short time later he put manure on the ground in another location on the dark nights. It was absorbed into the ground the first year. Next he laid a walk-way of boards, like a boardwalk, during the light nights. Those boards curled up on each end almost like the rocker on a rocking chair. If one stepped on one end, the other end rose up. The boards laid on the dark nights went smoothly into the ground forming a neat walkway. Somewhat humbled by my knowledge of moon signs, I began to take notice and to keep my mouth shut. I discovered that if I dug a hole in the ground on the new moon, and filled the hole again, I would have extra dirt to throw away. If I dug a hole on the old moon, I would not have enough dirt to fill the hole again. If I set a post on the new moon, the dirt never settles-remaining loose. If I set a post during the old moon, it will set like it grew there. (2) Some mountain folk told me that immediately after midnight on the first day of the month they say "Rabbit, Rabbit, Rabbit" for prosperity. Others say this at the time of the new moon. Some ancient writing say "Watch for the new moon and glorify the Great Spirit that he may prosper you." I had made great sport of the rabbit, rabbit rabbit saying until I read that.

MOONSHINE - An art, not totally lost, but much less in evidence today. Although moonshine was produced in many parts of the United States, people in the mountains of Tennessee developed quite a reputation for making this valuable product. These shaded coves and hollers provided an excellent environment for making moonshine, sometimes known as "rot-gut" or "widow-maker." (2) One bushel of corn makes from 1- 2 gallons of 190 proof whiskey. The equipment was often hauled in one piece at a time. The copper for making the main cooking pot was very expensive. In addition, the manufacturer needed one or two thump kegs, mash barrels, and gallon jugs or oak barrels for storage of the finished product. Ingredients included corn, preferably yellow, water, and sugar. A small amount of corn was first placed in a tow-sack (burlap) and wet down. It was then put in a warm place, sometimes a manure pile, to sprout. This usually took about ten days. These sprouts were then added to the main ingredients when all was ready to boil. The main part of the corn was ground at a local mill or in a sausage grinder at home. It was then put in a barrel with water and sugar to allow it to ferment. This fermented mixture became the mash that was later boiled. The steam or vapor rose from this mixture into the coil, better known as the worm, and formed droplets of whiskey. This coil went through a thump keg that cooled the steam that became the liquid. A jar was set at the end of the coil to collect the shine. Sometimes it was collected and cooked again for a better grade before the sippin' and sellin'. (3) Transporting moonshine- Jars of moonshine were put in the bottom of bushel baskets. Then the baskets were rounded with apples. Better still- jolt wagons were loaded with 'shine and covered with hay. Then the hay was covered with manure. No law man was ever known to stick his hand in manure to catch a load of moonshine. (4) Moonshiners had signals worked out with neighbors. One or two shots from different directions in rapid succession said the revenuers were coming. Women folks sometimes "got religion" and tattled on their men folk who made moonshine. This caused strained relations at home. (5) I cannot speak with authority on moonshining, as my father was one of the revenuer. I only saw one still in operation. When I was about 10 years old, my Mother sent me to help clean a neighbor's house while the mother was sick in bed. When I knocked on their door and stated my business, they strongly insisted that no help was needed. I knew my mother expected me to clean that house before I returned home. I would not go away. When I began cleaning, I realized why they did not want me to clean house for them. In the back room, hooked into the fireplace was a "still" in operation. Quite fascinated, I watched as it came one drop at a time into the glass jar set at the end of the coil. It was very common to attach stills to fireplaces so that the tell-tale smoke from the still would go up the chimney with other smoke. (6) Once I drove through Sevierville, Tennessee, with a heavily loaded car. I later learned the "law" suspected I was loaded with "shine." Someone recognized me as being a minister's wife just before they pulled me over. The car springs needed repair.

MOTHER - The safest place on earth is when you are held in your mothers arms. I can recall sitting on my mother's lap while she warmed my shoes and socks and put them on my feet.

My mother, on a winter's day,
Milked the cows and fed them hay,
Slopped the hogs and saddled the mule
And got us children off to school.
Did the washing, then mopped the floors
Washed the windows and did more chores,
Cooked a bowl of home dried fruit,
Then pressed my Dad's Sunday suit.
Swept the kitchen, made the bed
Baked a big pan full of bread

Split some wood and carried it in
Enough to fill the kitchen bin.
Cleaned the lamps and filled with oil
Stewed more apples that might spoil
Churned the butter, baked a cake,
Just for all the children's sake,
A calf got out by the chicken pen,
She chased him right back in again.
Gathered the eggs and locked the stable,
Returned to the house to set the table,
Cooked our supper that was delicious,
Afterwards washed the dirty dishes.
Fed the cat and sprinkled the clothes,
Polished a basket full of shoes.
Then called us children around to sing,
We raised the rafters, how it did ring!
A wonderful mother, we love you so,
Just wrote these words to let you know!
Author unknown

MOUNTAIN MEN - Some of the more colorful mountain men I recall were Uncle Levi Trentham, Wiley Oakley, Isaac Bradley, Dock Cole, and Crockett Maples (whom I described under the section on mail.) Long before Gatlinburg became inundated with the millions of tourists I saw Crockett, Jr. walk down main street with his milk bucket. He and others of this group of older men gathered each day on the park benches near the Ogle's store building. They made up a funny, but untrue story, about me while Ray and I spent our two-week honeymoon at The Gatlinburg Inn. (2) Ephraim Ogle, of The Ogle Store Company, now Ogle Mall, carried his money to and from the store in a four-pound lard bucket. One day Mr. Ogle was behind his store wearing some very old clothing. A traveling salesman, seeing this poor old cold man chopping wood in the snow, asked people to take up a collection for him. The salesman learned Ogle owned the store and could very well buy him. Another salesman once handed him some money as one gives to a beggar. Ephraim took it and said, "Thanks. That will help pay my income tax." (3) Wiley Oakley, known as the roaming man of the mountains, was a tour guide and great story teller. When he was exaggerating or telling a story that was totally untrue, he would yodel at the end of the story to let the people know it was just a tale **(see LEVI TRENTHAM.)**

MOURNING - (see FUNERALS) Widows were expected to wear black and avoid social activities for up to two years. Grief therapy was unhe ard of in those days, but today, among the greatest words of comfort ever written are found in the book "During a Near-Death Experience, I Saw God." This book describes how the deceased enters the next dimension as if through a veil upon a stage. He or she announces to loved ones there, "Look everyone, I'm here, I'm home!" It describes how the glory of the resurrection of him who has gone before is as great as is the grief of the ones left behind. As a cord is wrapped many times about a heavy weight to lift it, so is the soul of our loved one surrounding you who grieve. (This book is free to the bereaved, sending a self addressed mailing label and $3.00 for postage and handling to Bonnie Myers Book, 301 Broadway Towers, Maryville, TN 37801. Be sure to address book so if the remaining 4000 supply is depleted, letters can be returned unopened.)

MUSCADINE WINE - Use one-half bushel of muscadines and 12 pounds of sugar. Crush the muscadines and put them in a large churn. Add 3 pounds of sugar. Allow to ferment approximately 7 days or until the mixture stops working. Strain out the skins, and put back into a clean churn. Add 9 pounds of sugar. Let ferment 10 days. Makes 3 to 4 gallons.

MUSH - Not the command to an Alaskan dog. It was an evening meal enjoyed by early mountain families. Cornmeal was stirred and cooked in well-seasoned boiling water. It was never routine at our house. However, occasionally after a very hard days work in the corn field, it made a delicious quick meal. My preference, however, is cornbread crumbled into sweet milk. Uumm!

MUSIC MAKER - Place wax paper over a comb. Compress the lips and blow on the paper to make some beautiful music. I am surprised how many people missed this musical experience.

MYERS TOWN - The middle section of Cades Cove was once named Myers Town because so many Myers families lived so close to one another in that area.

N

NAILS - At least once each summer one of us children stepped on a rusty nail, puncturing our foot. This occurred before tetanus shots were available. We bruised peach leaves and bound them on the site. We had no problems or fear of lock-jaw. I (2) Speaking of "nails" the word stirs up a couple of sore spots with me. The only speeding ticket I ever received was en route from buying nails for construction. Ray T. went with me before Judge Reagan in Sevierville, where Ray told the Judge that I was just a common criminal among other things. When they had all the fun at my expense the Judge said he had to charge me the court cost of $18. Case dismissed. (3) Again while a large crew of carpenters waited for some special nails they sent me into Knoxville to buy, I chanced to see a hat sale. Not aware the nails were crucial to the on-going job, I spent much time and money buying three hats. When I returned, I found the entire crew sitting and waiting for those nails-- at considerable cost to my husband. I never once wore one of those hats because I took so much razzing.

NECKTIE JUSTICE - Anyone caught stealing cattle or changing brands (cattle branding) was brought to swift justice. This was called "necktie justice."

NEIGHBORS - Barn-raisings, bean-stringings, apple-peelings, corn-huskings, and quiltings brought neighbors together. Gossip, good food, story-telling, music and square-dancing headed the list of entertainment after the work was done.

NEWSBOYS - Yelling "Read all about it" rang out on many street corners from young newsboys. I recall the sing-song tune adding some newsworthy item to provoke one's interest in purchasing a newspaper. I have not heard a news boy in many years.

NICKNAMES - So many of the mountain boys were named after their father, uncle, or cousin, that it became necessary to distinguish different people by nicknames. These included such names as Big John, Little John, Baldy, Blubber, Dubb, Lard, Fat, Porky, Shorty, Slim, Slick, Red, Midge, Blondie, Grasshopper, Weasel, Windy, Foghorn, Holy Joe, Deacon, Dink, Bear, Rocky Steve Huskey, Bugler Sam Maples, Little Ephraim Ogle, John "Bullhead" Whaley, Broom-Corn Richard, Whistling Richard, Slow-Talking Mark, Turkey Spurling, or Fishing Dick Reagan. There were so many Jim Lawsons that names included Big Jim, Red Jim, and Single-wing Jim (with one arm).

NIGHT BLINDNESS - Eat your carrots

NORRIS DAM - Before 1933, a farmer took a kerosene lantern into the barn lot to be able to watch where he stepped while doing the early morning milking and pumping water for the cattle. While Franklin D. Roosevelt was president, Senator George W. Norris was chiefly responsible for bringing TVA into existence. Congress fought the idea tooth and toe nail. They said it was too expensive, and the government should not engage in enterprise of this kind. In 1933 President Roosevelt signed the bill to build the dam. In 1936 the American flag was raised over Tennessee's first dam, named Norris Dam. It covered the property of 4000 families. A hearth fire had burned continuously in the home of one of those families for three generations. Other dams were: Chickamauga, Watts Bar, Coulter Shoals. It took 4500 men six years to build one dam. When America went to war in 1941, one of the reasons the main Atomic bomb plant was located at Oak Ridge Tennessee was because of this abundance of electric power. Another reason the site was chosen was if an accident occurred, it was hoped radiation would go up instead of out because of the surrounding mountains. Maybe they also thought if people were contaminated, it would "only" be mountain folk. Right now with so many of our fifty plus people dying of cancer in this area it is highly questioned that the chemicals loosed by Oak Ridge when these people were young children could well explain this extremely high death rate.

"NUSS" - a corruption of the word: Nurse. I haven't heard the word used in more than 50 years. As a young child, when your mother, grandmother or a favorite aunt asked you to come sit on her lap, she said, "Come, let me nuss you."

O

ODORS - Wet baking soda, apply to underarms for body odor. (2) Recent: Apply white vinegar to underarms. (3) Eat foods high in zinc: nuts, beans, peas, turkey, and liver. (4) The Billy goat takes first place, above the skunk, a dead horse, or sauerkraut, when it comes to odors. Those of you who have never lived on a farm may to be curious about the goat smell. It is the product expelled during mating that takes first prize. Hence, when something is quite odoriferous farmers say it smells like a Billy-goat.

OFF-PLUMB - Not correctly aligned. Our good friend Huey Moody of Pittsburg, Texas always described anything that was "off plumb" as "leaning toward Giles county."

OLD HARP SINGING - That title sounds as if it might to be singing accompanied by a harp, but it is not. This music, also known as Sacred Harp, was said to be centuries old by the time it arrived in America. Many old-timers liked to participate in Old Harp Singing. Today it survives only in scheduled sings that begin in early spring and go until winter time. The music is very different to other types of music. Singing the shaped notes is almost as sacred and traditional as the songs themselves. The leader gets the pitch with a tuning fork, then everyone sings first by syllables, using the shaped notes to simplify the reading. Many songs are arranged into three- and four-part harmony with the tenor as the lead. Women sing all the parts except for bass. Some of the music is mournful as it describes the sin and sorrow of the world. Some of it is upbeat and triumphant. It is quite beautiful. The songs reflect the burdens early people endured. 'Tis said that all you need to sing Old Harp is to have a voice. This means you do not have to know anything about music, singing, or notes. During the very early days someone might call for a "drone." This unusual procedure called for the entire group of singers to stand up and march around the room humming, after which they would sing as they continued to march. It is believed that the drone started shortly after the Civil War in Cades Cove when Thomas S.

Lawson was leading a singing school. While the preachers were preaching and souls were being saved, Old Harp singers were singing down the devil which was believed to keep the devil on the run.

OLD MAID - If a mountain girl was not married by her late 20's, she was called an "Old Maid", an utterly disgraceful state of affairs. One girl said she would marry the village idiot rather than to be called an old maid. I am glad that thinking has changed today.

OLIVER, JOHN AND LUCRETIA - are said to have been the first white settlers in Cades Cove. At that time there was still great fear of the Indians. Arriving in the fall with no provisions, they would probably have starved to death had not Indians brought them dried pumpkin, which saved their lives. I believe it is the John Oliver cabin that one can see to the right while driving the loop road through Cades Cove today.

ONIONS - A universal healing food that is used to treat colds, fever, earache, diarrhea, warts, lung, or liver problems. Cut onion is believed to absorb germs in a sick room. Never use a piece of onion that has been cut and left in the kitchen all day.

OPOSSUM- Mountain families often hunted 'possums for food. They came out at night and were seen in trees or on the ground when a light was flashed in their direction. Their eyes glowed when they saw the light. Once the 'possum was shot, it was brought home to clean and cook. A special board called a 'possum board was used to stretch their hide. One story was told about a great hunting dog. The owner would set out the 'possum board, and the dog would go out and find a 'possum to fit the board. One day the mother set out an ironing board. The dog hasn't been seen since.

OTHER OBSERVATIONS--picked up over a lifetime.

A rooster doesn't cackle when he is hungry.

Fat chance and slim chance mean the same thing.

Happiness is something we make inside ourselves.

Man used to call on God when he got sick; now he calls on the doctor.

How old would you be, if you didn't know how old you were?

I have enough money to last a lifetime, if I don't spend any.

I have nothing to say, and I'm only going to say it once.

Nothing improves your driving like seeing a police car following you.

The more arguments you win the fewer friends you have.

Retirement: no weekends, no holidays, never a day off.

Anyone who says you can't take it with you hasn't seen my luggage.

The only way to kick a bad habit is hard.

It was love at first sight, then I took another look.

Inquiring as to what was wrong with her car, my friend proudly replied, "He said it needed a new head on the driver!"

Sign in a junk yard: Rust in peace.

All of today's children know where babies come from, it's the birds and the bees they do not understand.

Laugh and the world laughs with you, snore and your snore alone.

I removed all cooking odors from the house. I quit cooking.

Divorce is where you pay someone not to live with you.

She's a misfortune teller.

In death, the bad forgotten, the good remembered.

In divorce the bad remembered, the good forgotten.

Who plants a seed beneath the sod and waits to see, believes in God.

OWNBY, LEM - An old-timers who refused to leave his home located in what is now The Great Smoky Mountain National Park. Blind and living alone, he refused food stamps. I recall visiting in his home and marveling how he could move around his home in his condition. He ate honey every day and had one of the most beautiful complexions I have ever seen on one who was almost 100 years old. He negotiated with the park officials, taking less for his 44-acres of property located on Jakes Creek in Elkmont so he could live there the remainder of his life. Ownby, who died in

January, 1984, was the last person to reside in the park. The last of the famous Walker sisters had died in 1964. He had famous visitors from all over the world as word spread about the honey he sold. He liked to point to a spot in the kitchen where his mother was kneeling one Sunday morning praying for the safe return of her seven brothers who fought with the Union forces in the Civil War. When all seven of them walked in the yard together, they found her on her knees praying for them.

The U.S. Sixth Circuit Court of Appeals was having its annual conference in Gatlinburg where Justices Potter Steward and Harry Blackmun were honored guests. One afternoon when no activities were scheduled, Lawyer Foster D. Arnett invited them to go to Jakes Creek to meet an old mountain man, Lem Ownby. They accepted. When Arnett knocked on Lem's door, he explained that he had two very distinguished gentlemen who wanted to meet him. He explained that they are Justices of the United States Supreme Court. Lem asked, "Are they from Washington?" Arnett said, "Yes," Lem said, "I don't want to talk to them. Let them go back to Washington." Arnett was humiliated beyond words as he pleaded with Lem.

Justices Blackmun and Stewart were doubled over with laughter. They had never been treated that way before. When Arnett returned the following week to visit, Lem asked, "Them fellers from Washington with you?" When Arnett said they were not, Lem came out of his house. During the years following, Arnett got Christmas cards from Blackmun and Stewart. They always asked him to "Tell Lem hello for them."

Lem felt that politicians could not to be trusted. He also felt that many of the folk who were forced to leave their mountain homes died of homesickness.

P

PACKSADDLE - Him, you never want to meet. This is not a saddle constructed to hold a load on a pack animal. It is a worm about an inch long that you find only in a cornfield on the blades of corn. He has a fuzzy hump on his back. A packsaddle sting is extremely painful. I don't know which end he uses to string with, but it really hurts..

PANTHERS - Also known as mountain screamers or Indian devils, it preys on deer, elk, mice and squirrels, even grasshoppers. It can see in the dark, swim, and climb trees. It can fall 50 feet and land on its feet unharmed. It can execute a 25 foot leap from a dead stop. With a running start, it can leap almost 40 feet. It has been known to clear 10 foot fences and to leap from the ground onto the back of a person on horseback. Those who try to run from him were told pull various parts of clothing off as they ran so the cat would stop to smell and shred the clothing. Turning your back and running away increases the danger. It is much like rolling a ball in front of a domestic cat; it immediately takes chase. The best solution appears to be to try to appear larger by raising your hands, throwing rocks, baring your teeth, or growling. My mother-in-law, Ida H. Myers, told this story, which was recently verified by her only surviving sister, Florence (Mrs. Ralph) Patty. After Ida attended Maryville College she began teaching school in the area known as Little Cove, between Pigeon Forge and Wears Valley. Walking home from school one afternoon, she kept hearing the patter of animal feet in the leaves. Since she was alone, she had no chance to outrun the panther, which she was sure was following her. She had but one choice. She had been told not to resist a panther--to lie down and pretend to be dead was the only chance for survival. She lay down beside the foot path. It was lucky for her that panther was not hungry; he came and covered her with leaves. One theory is that a panther or a bear will not eat anything that is already dead. However, some believe that pretending to be dead does not always work with panthers. I wouldn't have to pretend!

PAWPAWS - A locally grown papaw is our very own native banana. While much smaller than imported bananas, they ripen the second week in September. These are great to eat, and their aroma is wonderful. Our grandmothers rubbed the inside of the peel on their hair to return color to gray hair.

PEACH TREES - Our family credits this great elixir of peach tea with saving my sister's life, when even water would not stay on her stomach. I overheard my parents whispering that we were going to lose her. Medical books suggested peach tea. It worked. Peach tea is pure cyanide, so take it easy. Early in the spring, I gather the leaves, wash and boil the leaves then put it in sealed jars. I freeze the leaves for poultices, stone bruises, or boils. It is great for upset/sick stomach and diarrhea. Old timers said to scrape up on the peach tree limbs (bark) for upset stomach and to scrape down on the limbs for diarrhea. Before tetanus shots were available, we bruised peach leaves and bound them on puncture wounds such as rusty nails. I related this to Dr. Joe Henderson, our family doctor. He said, "The Good Lord was just looking over us!" **(See TETANUS.)**

PENDULUM - This is said to be useful for parents-to be, gardeners, and poultry men to determine the sex of unborn babies, plants, and animals. Slip a ring on a twenty-inch string. Hold both ends of the string to make a home made pendulum. It is said eggs can to be tested so that male or female chicks can to be hatched by choice. If the ring swings in a straight line over the egg, the chick will to be male. If it goes in a circle it will to be female. This works equally well on the American holly, which bears male flowers on one specimen and female flowers on another. A person must hold this string. Fastened to an object it will not work.

PERFUMES - In the 1920' and 1930's we had Woolworth's and Ben Franklin 5- and 10-cents stores. Not all items were that price range, however. If a boy liked a girl, he would go to one of those stores and get a gift of perfume that smelled a bit better than a skunk or a dead horse for just 10 cents.

PERSIMMONS - Only after frost has fallen on persimmons are they ready to eat. Otherwise, they pucker your mouth. You have to beat the opossums to the trees to find them. Persimmon butter is delicious.

PHONOGRAPH - Before electricity was available in our mountain region, we used a hand-cranked phonograph to play the old 78 RPM records. I played those records and sang to the top of my lungs. I enjoyed such recordings as "The wreck of the old ninety-seven," "Barbara Allen," and "John Henry" (the steel driving man). "Keep on the sunny side" was one of my favorites. "Barney Goggle" (the horse that ran the wrong way) and "On top of old Smoky" were others I enjoyed. In addition, there were many hymns. I would give a nice premium today for a record we called the "laughing" record. It was a large group of people who were laughing "fit to kill." You had to laugh with them!

PHTHISIC - Better known as asthma. All early school children could spell "phthisic" .

PICKLING - Old-timers believed that if one made pickled beans, corn, or sauerkraut when the moon sign was in the bowels, the food would be soft and slimy. Also, the same effect, if a woman doing the work was having her menstrual period.

PIG'S TAIL - Mother once hid the pigs tail wrapped in paper behind a picture frame. Just for fun she asked if any of us children had forgotten some treasure that we had hidden there. So intent was my brother, Harmon, to get that treasure that he cried for it. Always alert to find something with which to tease each other, you can to be sure that we showed him no mercy for many years teasing him about crying for the pig's tail.

PIGEON FORGE - Pigeon Forge, Tennessee, was once known as "String Town." A Mr. Lowe built an iron forge on the Pigeon River so that the name was changed to Pigeon Forge. Otherwise, we would now hear that Dollywood is located at Stringtown, Tennessee.

PIN WORMS - Mountain people believed that when the area around the mouth was whiter than the surrounding skin, the person had worms. They ate raw cabbage three times per day, while drinking tea. They did not eat other foods during this time. (2) Eating rhubarb is also said to eliminate worms.

PINE RESIN - Many early settlers ingested pine resin for the breathing tract. (2) Others used the following mixture. Simmer in an enamel pan 3-4 hours, short twigs and needles from the pine trees. Strain and mix with lots of honey. Take 1 teaspoon per day.

PINE KNOT COLLEGE - When one of our old-time preachers felt the call to preach, he could neither read nor write. Since he had a family to support, he worked in the fields by day and en route home gathered a pine knot to make a light to study his Bible at night. His wife taught him to read and write, and he became known and respected as a great Bible scholar. When asked by other ministers which seminary he attended, he replied that it was "Pine Knot College." None of the brethren had ever heard of a college by that name until he explained that what he knew was what he learned at night studying by the light of a lighted pine knot.

PINK EYE - See eyes.

PLANTAIN - Plantain is an obnoxious weed when it grows in a yard. Early on, plantain enjoyed a reputation as a cure-all for poisons such as snake bite. The bruised leaf was bound on mad-dog bites. I do not know if it worked.

PLOWS, BULL-TONGUE - A large wooden plow usually pulled by oxen and used to break up virgin land. The expression "ahead of the plow" meant that the cultivation of the crops was up to date at the moment.

PLOWS - When metal plows were first introduced, mountain people were afraid to use them. Farmers were concerned plows would poison the soil. This sounds funny to us now, but because plows were unknown, it was understandable.

PLUNDER - While I have never been able to make the connection, my Father and other old-timers, called furniture "plunder." When a family moved to another house, they moved their plunder. After I recently looked for the word in the dictionary, I found they were right! It means to remove personal belongings or household goods. Guess I don't know it all.

POEMS AND OTHER LORE - I can make no claims to being a poet but I did try my hand just once, back in 1986. Here is the result:

TENNESSEE HOMECOMING '86

Tennessee, the grandest state on earth,
Great Smoky Mountains, the place of my birth,
Memories of childhood down on the farm
Had certain beauty and Southern charm.

Apple orchards, waterfall around the bend
Cows to milk, fences to mend.
Smokehouses, corncribs filled by high noon,
Planting and slaughtering by signs of the moon.

Mountains so high as to touch the sky
Whippoorwill calls if someone should die,
Those precious memories make one's heart ache,
I'm sure God created them just for my sake.

If you just crossed to the wrong side of the tracks
With a different author or different facts,
Truth is, I wrote, rewrote and polished my best
Those twelve lines above to enter a contest.

"My Heritage" for TN Homecoming 86, I thought superb
capitalization, punctuation, every sentence had its verb

When the phone call came saying that I was the winner,
Not really surprised, since the above essay I had entered.

There was never any doubt, TN open fires...said she
Dumbfounded not once had I considered it a winner to be
Neither rewritten, nor polished... only to wordy,
Once sentence deleted and in ten minutes it was ready.

Like the winning entry, the following unvarnished truth
Comes from my pen, naturally somewhat uncouth,
The syllables are not measured nor timed,
The message is "spoke"...the last word to rhyme.

So hold for the accent to the end of the line
Enjoy the "birth of a writer" Thanks to the Daily Times!
I predicted winning, invisible helpers I proclaimed
Saying "Come fellows, get busy, if we're to have fame!

I was a thoroughbred tomboy, if ever there was one
It sure beat housework, and lots more fun,
Playing football, baseball, or riding the mules,
After Mother said, "Don't ride" but I broke the rules.
Result a broken arm, that ride was on a Sunday,
Too bad, Guardian Angels change shifts on that day!

My family left me alone in the house one cold day,
As a small child, I decided not to play,
Choosing to sweep the hearthstone instead,
The broom afire, I hid under the bed.

Too young to realize the danger of this,
My guardian angels, I'm sure did assist,
And many times since, those escapades of mine
A job well done, they've worked overtime!

Chimney corner "switchings" were not much fun,
Until it came time for Brother Sam's turn
I'd stick out my tongue, pull back on my ears,

'Til Mother spotted my ugly jeers,
A second helping my actions did earn,
Then Sam's time to laugh, my bottom to burn!

These mountains stood so stately and tall
The height of their beauty was in the fall,
We owned the mountain top, as rich as Jay Gould,
A carefree living, mixed with a bit of school.

Gathering eggs from the old hens nest
And gathering chestnuts were the chores I liked best,
Singing round the fireside with all our might,
Was a memorable occasion on Saturday night.
But a dose of caster oil, helped cure the sick,
When liniment or poultices might well done the trick.

Around the fireside, after supper there were plenty,
Encounters and "haint" tales, in fact there were many,
Dad told them over and over to strangers with pride
My feet high off the floor, I was glad to be inside,
Armed with only a knife, It was hard to sit still,
Hearing how Granddad killed the panther, my greatest thrill!

Gladys and I sawed wheels to make our new wagon
We huffed and we puffed 'til we were worn ragged,
Harmon and Wesley snatched them quicker than a flash,
Threw them in the river with a forceful splash.
We threw down our saw and chased them away,
They laughed at their sport, sure spoiled our day,
You bet I'll remember, you brothers of mine,
I'll remind and haunt you, when next time we dine.

Candy, apples, oranges, and popcorn balls
A doll named Rose with a pretty shawl,
Handkerchiefs, firecrackers and sparklers too,
Christmas tree aglitter, the celebrations grew,
The feasts that were coming grew off the land
Lovingly prepared by my Mother's hands.

Kissin' kin, yes, relatives by the dozens
Old timers and friends that I called cusins'
Whether they were good, indifferent, or bad as sin,
I kissed them all, why they were kissin' kin!
Pallets were fashioned to make them a bed
From the middle room we borrowed a spread.

A flock of old roosters were crowing at dawn
A visiting city slicker was heard to yawn,
An observation not meant us to hear,
"It doesn't take long to spend the night around here!"

Beside the woodshed, wood was stacked,
In double rows, back to back,
Molasses made, jars and cans filled
Stored, labeled and tightly sealed,
And stored along the pantry wall
While Old Jack was safely back in his stall

Geeing' and Hawing' the old mules for plowing,
Giddup' and Whoa' the crops for sowing
Sharpened hoes and wearing wide brimmed hats,
Fresh water buckets and a curly tailed cat.

The mules were hitched to the plows very early,
We children unhappy and no doubt a bit surly,
Cows swishing flies with cuckleburred tails
Old Jerze kicked over the gallon milk pail.

Hog killings always meant a busy day,
Big kettles, boiling water, the butchering under way,
Going by the book, the boys felt was smarter,
Than Dad' old fashioned way to fill the larder.

The hog scraped clean and hung on a pole,
Hind feet in the air, and he was still whole,
Quoting from the book, how to slice his fat...

He fell in the mess below, Well, boys, what does the book say about that?'

New balloons now appeared, this special kind can't be bought...
You'll retch a bit, if you give this serious thought,
We children so soon, now were much sadder.....
Our balloon busted... it was the hogs bladder...!

At church, one man prayed at very rapid speed,
His winding down was music set by my creed,
When down to a whisper, I knew he'd soon hush,
I'd listen for that "AMEN", almost with a blush!

Awaiting the weekend a neighborly visit to trek,
Why news and gossip had to wait a whole week,
No telephone, no car 'til 24 we just used the buggy,
Transportation was at times a bit rough and muddy.

My family attended a school sponsored radio affair,
The program quite coarse, was just plain vulgar,
My Mother stood, saying aloud, "Come children let's go!
She marched us right out with me on tippy toe!
A wee tot was I, at this ghastly affair
Oh, how I wished that I'd never been there,
70 years and more, have passed as I recall that shame,
I chuckled out loud as I wrote out that scene!

I've always been a winner, won contests galore,
While I'll do most anything to avoid a household chore,
Numbered high on my list of spectacular thrills,
A voice saying, This is Alex Haley calling from Beverly Hills,
Carl Sagan says you are some gal' I must meet,
On July 10 at Airport Hilton we'll eat,
I'll bring Mia and you can bring Gladys
After pictures and press we'll go to Madison Avenue.

Since the tales I'd told Carl of my life on the farm
Glory be, Gladys already had them in handy book form,

While her version might differ a bit from mine,
I introduced her to Haley, saving his and my time.

After meeting Alex, my family tree I begun to shake
Like all family trees, crop failures, make no mistake,
I've found some real jewels, pearls and diamonds too...
Some so great, in fact, should be published if true!
One grandson wrote of Martin Trentham, of how
He helped win the war with genius and prow,
Becoming their prisoner, he pretended to be insane,
He spied 'til he learned how they played their game,
Information all gleaned, he escaped unnoticed or not...
Fashioned a cannon from a pine log, took the stronghold without
firing a shot!
He was a doctor and wealthy land owner I see
The grandson wrote a book to tell of this family
The book said that Martin was the devil raised by Lorenzo Dow,
From a pile of tow sacks, then explained how,
Lorenzo a preacher, used object lessons for fright,
But always preaching with all his might,
To scare the sinners into becoming saints
Even if he had to use some home-made "haints."

Trentham church, in England, and relics of the mansion remain to
this date,
Monk Trentham was one pastor, so tally up one Trentham saint'!
They weren't all good nor were they all bad
But my few drops of royal blood is surely looking sad
Divided and divided into infinity
I bequeath this royal line to all my family.

I still have pages and pages of words that don't rhyme,
But work as I do, I'll get them in time,
That fact that Shakespeare perhaps married a Trentham
Hasn't helped me, my writing, one whit, nor momentum!

Speaking for myself, loathing housework, I don't deny,

Dirty dishes, dirty windows, almost make me cry,
A friend who helps me with housework is here now,
Likening my meal's cooking to Harlie Rrindstaff's cow,
She could eat more hay, drink more water, give less milk, and shit
on more axe   handles.................

Climbing a pailing fence, Sister Kate found so exciting
Tearing her dress tail, I remembered while writing,
Writing prose or poetry is surely not my trade
At this first attempt, I won't ask a grade
Such a waste of good paper and ink
I already know that my writing will stink.

But it's been more fun that I had imagined,
Reading it, seeing it take shape with chagrin
I've joke about writer in the family, in fun,
Now, by golly, a poet, I aire' one!

POINT-BLANK - An expression we used to emphasize a point as being exactly on target. We'd say it was a "point-blank" lie. This meant absolutely, positively!

POISON IVY - Mix equal parts salt and apple cider vinegar. Heat as warm as can be tolerated and apply the mixture to the skin with a clean cloth. Remember, "Leaves three, let it be!" A chiropractor from Knoxville phoned asking me for my salt and vinegar cure. I have also had calls from New York and New Jersey for this remedy. You must use this however at first sign, else if you let it go and get into the blood stream a trip to the doctor will be necessary. (2) Howard Kerr tell of a miraculous treatment of his poison ivy by just rubbing on the leaves of the horehound weed and the immediate blessed relief.

POLK or Is it POKE SALLAT (SALAD)? - Mother picked wild greens, using only the very young sprouts of a polk plant when it is no more than 6- to 8- inches high. She was careful not to cut below the surface of the ground. Parboil the stalk and leaves at least three times. Boil one minute, pour off the water, cook with the fourth water until tender. Drain. Fry in bacon drippings. Serve with vinegar. I never cooked any polk. I was afraid of not getting it right as that plant, its roots, and berries are known to be highly poisonous. Lots of people I have talked with, including my mother, thoroughly enjoyed eating poke with no concern about its poison.

POLIO - During the 40's, 50's, and early 60's, we were afraid to allow our children to swim in public pools, which were suspected of spreading polio. Many children who contracted polio died or became badly crippled. Some remain in wheelchairs even today. Dr. Jonas Salk developed a vaccine believed to have stopped the spread. I recall very vividly taking that sugar cube upon which drops of the vaccine were placed. In fact, practically the entire population took this sugar cube. Some of the early victims are again experiencing some apparent additional or re-occurring problems. One of our good friends, George Carroll, with whom we play pinochle, has been in his wheelchair for 47 years due to polio. He tells that of the 25 servicemen with polio who were hospitalized with him, only three of the wives have not since divorced. One of those is his own dear Fern. How he has been able to maintain such a cheerful outlook and enjoy life while tied to that wheelchair has amazed me. My hat goes off to George and Fern. (George died 2001)

POLITICS - During the 1920's and 1930's it might safely be said that Sevier County, Tennessee, where I was born, voted 99 3/4 % Republican. It did however, have a two party system - male and female. When my parents, staunch Republicans, spoke of a Democrat, they used a tone of voice that left me, a child, not knowing if a Democrat was a man-eating monster or someone with leprosy. At that time, I only knew of one person who was a Democrat, my uncle Sam Pickel. I never allowed myself to get close to him when we visited my Aunt Nancy. I always stayed on the opposite side of the room from him, because I did not know if he was dangerous or had something contagious.

The second Democrat I ever saw, I married. My late husband's father and grandfather who were Democrats were not allowed to vote in Wears Valley, Sevier County, Tennessee for quite a numbers of years. They had to go to Sevierville to vote in the Democratic primaries.

For several years Ray and I went to the polls and canceled out each others votes. Finally, I said we should save our gasoline. We got our first television in 1952. Shortly thereafter we watched the conventions of each political party. As a result, I became extremely upset with all the derogatory things Ray said about my party. That was the only time during our marriage I ever told my husband to sleep on the couch. He began to point out the many differences of what each party was doing for the American people. I listened. I have now been registered in both parties. I guess this makes me a "Mug-Womp" my mug on one side of the fence and my "WOMP" on the other.

POLL TAX - I recall my parents discussing paying poll tax to be allowed to vote. Many of the women flatly refused to pay the one or two dollars. By the time I was eligible to vote, a tradition, perhaps a carry over from the poll tax era was still in effect. A man always stood at the entrance to the polls handing every voter a $1 bill. Like everyone else, I accepted the $1. I never questioned the why or wherefore as we were never asked to vote for a particular politician. I never knew who supplied the money. However, being in Sevier County, Tennessee, a region where Democrats are or were at that time scarce as "hen's teeth", I can now be sure that it had to come from a Republican. I have since listened to taped interviews of some of those early politicians who were laughing about how they would send someone to every house to learn just how many votes they needed to buy to be elected. They described how cloth was purchased for a new dress for some housewives. These men were never seen going to these homes. When questioned about how and when this was done, one man quoted the scripture that "men loved darkness rather than light."

POOR FARM - Blount County, Tennessee had a "Poor Farm" until approximately 1950. Indigent senior adults were housed there in a huge home. Many acres of ground were tilled in crops with every able-bodied person doing his share. Some residents had mental problems. One that I recall refused to wear any clothing. They tried strapping belts on this person, but nothing seemed to work. Finally, everyone just accepted it. The pastor's home of the Laurel Bank Baptist Church, where my husband pastored was located on the property adjoining this farm. We were close friends of the Marsh family, who supervised the home. We ate many good meals with them in their quarters. They told one story I recall regarding the farm. A man was being driven to the "poor house" as we called it. He was offered some corn by a concerned neighbor. He asked if the corn was shelled. When he learned it was not, he responded, " Drive on." (2) The pauper says if I had great wealth what great good I would do. The rich man says if I had greater wealth what great good I would do. The person who has done ALL with what he has stands highest!

POOR PATTERN - (see COURTING)

POTATOES - Never plant potatoes when the moon signs are in the bloom or bowels. I learned this through experience. I'll never forget the day that Ray T. and I had worked very hard all day planting a huge potato patch in wonderful soil. We expected to harvest at least twenty-five bushels of potatoes. Quite late in the afternoon Ray's parents dropped in and asked what we had been doing. We told them we planted potatoes in this wonderfully rich garden. "Harrumph!!" said his Father. "You won't get your seed back. The signs are all wrong." Of course, we laughed at Dad. I have never before nor since seen such beautiful plants. They were at least three feet tall and full of blooms. How carefully we cultivated those beautiful plants because we intended to show Dad a thing or two. Alas, we did not get our seed back when we dug those potatoes that fall. Unbelievable!

PRANKS - During the early 1900's, Sam Brock and Sam Jones of the Marlowe Community were best friends. They constantly played pranks on each other. When the two were crossing the Clinch River on a ferry boat, Jones threw Brock's hat in the river. When Jones was passing Brock's store driving a mule with a sled load of hay, Brock set the hay on fire. Jones unhitched the mule and led him to safety. Then he unloaded the hay so that the sled would not burn. When the fire was out, he hitched the mule to the sled and went to Brock's barn. There he loaded his sled with hay and proceeded on his way home. (2) My parents told of a man known as "Lying Bill" who was well known for his falsehoods. A group of people taunted Bill as he passed them saying, "Tell us a lie." Never hesitating one step, Bill said, "Sorry, I can't." He named a well-known member of the community and said he had just died of a heart attack. He told the group of people he was on his way to the man's house. Soon people bearing food and condolences started showing up at the man's house only to be greeted at the door by the "deceased." And so the pranks continued.

PRAYER - Prayer was a very real part of life. Sometimes the prayers at the end of a church service lasted so long we were afraid the "dinner on the ground" outside the church would be cold before anyone could eat. Old time preachers were known to stop alongside the road to pray (a sight you will never see today). One preacher was described as having one eye on a hog with the other eye on the Lord. The Reverend Tom Sexton, known as The Blacksmith preacher and a fellow minister, a Mr. Conner, were en route to Chattanooga on horseback. Rev. Sexton was said to pray as if he were speaking to his biological father. He stopped along the way to pray. His prayer was : "Lord you have promised to supply my needs while I am doing your work. Right now I need a new pair of shoes, and I'll to be looking for them. Thank you. Amen." Their first stop after reaching Chattanooga was at a grocery store. The owner called Sexton into the back room and fitted him with a new pair of shoes. (2) In a recent survey of doctors a remarkable 99% said they were convinced that religious belief can heal. This number is 20% higher than the general public. Seventy-five percent of the doctors believed the prayers of others can help a patient's recovery, while 38% said they think faith-healers can make people well! (This survey was conducted by Yankelovich Partners at a meeting of the American Academy of Family Physicians.) It is estimated that people who use self-help and other alternatives reduce their visits to doctors by 30 to 60 percent. (3) Have we missed the formula for prayer today? One can prostate himself all day on the floor in a worshipful attitude trying to persuade an electric lamp to burn. Until the person checks the bulb, the power supply, and turns on the switch, the light will not burn. It must meet all the conditions. Is it so with prayer? Jesus promised that any disciple of his would be able to do the things that he did, even greater. He gave sight to the blind, cured the sick, cleansed the lepers, exorcized demons, walked on the water, and raised the dead. The people of Jesus' day were just as skeptical as we are. In Mark 9:22, the father of a boy possessed with demons brought his son to Jesus and said, "If you can, take pity on us and help us." Jesus' response was "If you can believe, everything is possible." (4) Some churches today suggest that when we pray for the sick that we should not pray in vague terms such as "Bless all who are sick." We must be specific. If the patient has given permission, mention his name, then make an imaginary picture, seeing him well, or happy or engaging in some special event. Faith is believing what you know is not true. Conjure up happy healthy scenes, no matter how ridiculous they may sound. For example, say "Here is nurse so and so, a member of our church, a girl of only 21. She is suffering from such and such disease. Her temperature is very high; she can't sleep without drugs, and she hasn't eaten in several days." Now picture yourself going into her room, standing with Christ next to her bed. Do not pray that she may get better, because that is putting her cure in the future. See Christ touching her now so that his healing power is in her body right now! Do not let your mind wander. Let it concentrate, watching and helping Christ in his healing work. Let His healing power flow through you as if you were an electric current to light a lamp. (5) A woman awaiting surgery for cancer was visited the night before by a ball of light. She knew that she was in the presence of something holy, so she prayed for her cancer to be cured. Something in the light said that what we usually think of as prayer is actually complaining: if she really wanted to pray, she should send her love and light to her worst enemy. She did that. As she did, she felt a physical shift in her body as if her cells were coming alive. When she finished praying, she was told in spirit that she had prayed for the first time in her

life. When she went for surgery the following morning her cancer was gone. (6) A medical missionary in Africa occasionally had to travel two days by bicycle a to a nearby city for supplies. While traveling, he had to camp out over night. He once treated a seriously wounded man, with whom he witnessed about Jesus. Several weeks later he was approached by this man, who said that he and five close friends had followed him into the jungle to his camp and had intended to rob and kill him. When they arrived at the camp, he was surrounded by 26 armed guards. With only six robbers, they left him unharmed. The missionary laughed, saying, "That's impossible, I can assure you that I was alone in that campsite." "No," he said, "My friends all saw and counted them, too." Several months later this missionary was telling this story in a church in Michigan when one of the congregation jumped to his feet, interrupting the missionary, and said something that left everyone stunned. "We were with you in spirit that day," said the man. The missionary looked perplexed. The man continued, "On that night in Africa it was morning here. I stopped at the church to gather some materials for an out-of-town trip to another parish. As I put my bags into the trunk I felt the Lord leading me to pray for you. The urge was so great that I called the men who were in the church to pray for you. Then the man turned around and said, "Will all of those men who met with the Lord that morning please stand?" One by one they stood - all 26 of them! All minister's tell us to have faith but I have yet to hear them tell us "how."
My formula for having faith is: Begin by trying HIM.

PRAYER IN "UNKNOWN TONGUE." - While I am not familiar with this practice, it occurs in some area churches. Some very interesting incidents have been reported. In one case a native of a foreign country was said to be amazed to hear his language spoken when he heard a recording of church-goers "speaking in unknown tongues." The Saturday Evening Post, once reported that six men were instantly relieved of long-standing afflictions when praying in the unknown tongue.

PREACHERS - Mountain preachers preached hell-fire and damnation with a vengeance. Their chief topics were drinking alcohol, card playing, gambling, dancing, and mixed bathing. They mixed grit in their gospel. Few were formally educated in seminaries or "Bible colleges." Some could preach down a hurricane while others made a joyful noise. Many churches could not afford a full-time minister. Preachers rode a circuit. They would preach at a church one or two Sundays of the month. They often stayed in the homes of members of the congregation when they were not near their own home. It was also expected that the preacher would go to "Sunday dinner" with a member of the congregation. Fried chicken, mashed potatoes, fresh or canned green beans, and freshly baked pies were most often served. It was important to compliment the cook profusely. Invitations could become complicated. A minister could not go to one home too often, as it was a mark of social status to entertain the minister. On the other hand, some cooks were not so good. Some ministers also got reputations for "hogging" the best pieces of chicken or for " wearing out their welcome." Some seemed to show up during the week just as "dinner" or "supper" was on the table. (2) One preacher said that he had told God that he would preach if his chewing tobacco was always supplied. And, it was. (3) My half-brother, Orlie, and a group of young men and ladies went overnight camping in the mountains after he returned here following a stint in the military. A local minister got in up church the following week and called down hellfire and damnation on their souls. Since no man in these mountains in those days was more influential than the Baptist preacher an indictment of that sort was sufficient to drive a person in shame from the area. However, Orlie knowing that the group was innocent of any wrong doing, proved that he was never one to truckle to a bully, ecclesiastical or otherwise. He offered to engage in hand-to-hand combat with the man of God - something unheard of in those days. The preacher thought it over, decided that the strayed lambs were innocent and made a public apology. Orlie was never particularly impressed with the clergy after that and to my knowledge never again entered a church door. (4) Because of the life I saw for ministers, I promised myself when I was a young girl that I would not marry a minister. Ray went to seminary after we were married. I am glad to say that by the time Ray T. came on the scene, the subject matter became much more diversified and was presented with much more dignity.

PROGRESS - There is no way that I can tell you how it was in our early days compared to the technology in evidence today. When we first heard some discussion about putting a man on the moon, we thought they were nuts. Breaking the sound barrier seemed just as impossible. We never heard of a Computer, a coronary by-pass, cloning of plants or animals, or birth control pills. I hope my descendants will just remember this: whatever can to be imagined can somehow to be attained. I believe your first thought forms the nucleus for an idea to become reality. It is like planting a seed in the ground: it must have water and heat to sprout. The knowledge is out there: learn to tap into it. Some people have learned that sleeping on a problem really does help them to solve it. Others use prayer to obtain answers. Picturing and speaking the end result is extremely important. I put a miniature copy of my license plate on the picture of a car that I won in 1973. I pictured my license plate on that car at least 600 times during the three months previous to the drawing. See a picture of the end result in order to obtain it. Now, this is your grandmother telling you something very very important!

PROHIBITION - 1919 - It is said that prohibition made criminals of our innocent mountain people. European settlers to this area followed the tradition in which everyone made his own wine or alcoholic drinks. This was never considered illegal. Before Prohibition, alcohol was not taxed so that our government could get revenue from its use and sale. In 1919 the great experiment to prohibit the manufacture and sale of alcohol began. Although the Great Depression did not officially begin in the rest of the country until the late 1920's, it began in the mountains much earlier. Farmers were unable to get money for their crops. There were few other source of income unless families moved into towns. Many mountain children would have gone barefoot and hungry without family members who made homebrew. My Father never made any to my knowledge as he helped the revenuers cut down the stills in our area. One time our grist mill was burned in retaliation. And, our old mule was shot in the ear and became deaf in that ear, because he could find any still in operation. One of my half-brothers was once asked who was the best among the revenuers. He replied, "My Dad's, Dad-jimmed old mule!"

The Prohibition or Eighteenth Amendment to the Constitution was put into effect in 1920; repealed in 1933.

PSORIASIS - Make paste of Epsom salts and water. Bind on the skin or soak in a bathtub. Do not allow water temperature to fall below 98 degrees as the body heat will pull poison back into the pores of the skin.

PUBLIC ROADS- Public roads were always a problem in very early days.. Before the days of county work crews and asphalt on roads, horses or early cars drove on narrow, dusty, or muddy lanes. Gravel or rocks were put in the roads for traction and to keep down the dust. Time was when every able-bodied man had to give one day per month to work on the public roads. Work crews would level the roads and clear the ditch lines. If a man failed to work, he would pay $1 for each day he failed to work. If he furnished a team and plow to run the ditch lines, he was credited with more time. However, today Tennessee is known to have the best roads but the poorest in the educational systems.

PULLEY BONES - I am afraid my great-grandchildren will never know the fun of the pulley bone or wish-bone. It has disappeared from the chicken dinner table as no one today seems to know how to cut up the chickens. Growing up in the country and looking forward to a Sunday meal of fried chicken, we hoped to be the lucky one to get the exceptional bone we called the pulley bone. The pulley bone is a forked bone found in the chest of the chicken. After the meal, two diners each held one end of the bone and pulled it apart. The person left with the larger piece got his wish. Back then we called the noon meal dinner and the evening meal supper. Mother always fried the chicken in lard, because no one had ever heard of cholesterol back then. If we had, I am sure we would have fried it.

PUMPKIN - My Mother overheard my doctor say he would induce labor six weeks early for my first baby due to acute kidney infection, albumen poisoning. Out of earshot of the doctor, she said, "Harrumph, I'll take you home and make some punkin (pumpkin) seed tea." Bruising fresh pumpkin seeds, hull and all, she slowly brewed a pumpkin seed tea. She then made me drink this gosh-awful stuff. When I went back to the doctor the following week, the poison was all gone. The doctor did not ask what I had done. Mother used the old field pumpkin seeds as the new dark pumpkins we use for Halloween decorations do not have good seeds. They are also not good for eating. I ate lots of apples with the second and third pregnancies and had no further problems.

PURITAN - Even though some families made moonshine and a few may have stolen a horse, we lived in a time that would have been described as very Puritan. My mother was very strict. There was no fowl language in my home. She would not allow words like "gosh" or "golly" because they were too much like "God." She would say "pshaw." We could not play cards or dance. Eleanor Roosevelt, wife of the late president of the United States, told us how puritan our world once was known to be. As a young girl she was forced to sleep with her hands out from under the covers on her bed. Now the pendulum has swung so far in the opposite direction that nothing is sacred. What we are seeing on television and on the Internet shows all that goes on behind closed doors. Nothing is left to the imagination. I have no idea what it will take to start our world in the opposite direction. Perhaps flipping the poles of the earth back to the stone age..

PYORRHEA - Mix a weak solution of salt and vinegar, and rinse the mouth three times per day. Gradually strengthen the mixture. The condition should clear within three weeks.

Q

QUAIL - When we were children living on the farm, it was fun to chase the quails late in the evening. Their call, which sounded like they were saying "Bob White," led us to them. They roosted in a circle on the ground with their tails together. Their heads faced outward so that all could watch for predators. Their nest contained from ten to eighteen or more eggs. Their young could leave the nest within one hour after hatching. We never killed them as hunters do today. That made them somewhat tame, so that brother Sam and I could get close to them.

QUARE - (rhymes with square) a term used to describe a person who is unusual. i.e. "He's a might quare." This is probably a mispronunciation of queer. If a word or a name could be mispronounced, we did it.

QUILT - CRAZY QUILT - When I was a teenager, my next door neighbor, Dan Davis, showed up at our back door with what he called a Crazy Quilt he had made on the sewing machine. I had never heard of such a quilt, but I was amazed at its beauty. There was no color scheme or anything made to match. He said that he just forgot the rules and got a little crazy. He began with a piece of backing about ten to fifteen inches square. Muslin, an old bed sheet, or just any fabric was used for backing. He begun by pinning an odd-shaped scrap, having as much as five sides, in the center of the backing. Then he placed a rectangular piece of fabric right side (edge) down on top of the starting scrap and stitched. He flipped it right side up and pressed it. A second scrap was added to the adjoining straight edge of the beginning scrap, then stitched in a straight line onto the first added piece, until he had gone completely around the beginning scrap. He did not trim any of the overlapping pieces as they would just add warmth to the quilt. Once the original square was completely covered, he trimmed any overhanging pieces before sewing it to another square. The number of squares then determined the size of the quilt. Different colored thread was used for stitching. Smaller pieces were sometimes sewn together to fill in a spot. An embroidery stitch then covered the seams, but was not necessary. Crazy but gorgeous!

QUILT - FRIENDSHIP - During 1948 the good ladies of The Laurel Bank Baptist Church presented me with a "Friendship Quilt." A pattern had been chosen, with each lady making one square each, then embroidering her name on it. All those squares were then sewn together to complete the quilt. I find it so interesting even today, 53 years later, to look over the many names and the beautiful loving work that so many did just for me.

QUILTING FRAMES - In the early days a set of quilting frames could to be found in almost every home. These were suspended from the ceiling or set on wooden saw horses on the floor. There were no stores where one could buy a quilt. Making quilts was a necessity, rather than a hobby. Keeping the family warm on bitter cold nights when the fire died down in the fireplace (after being covered with ashes) made these frames a necessary part of the household furnishings.

R

RABBIT TOBACCO - Rabbit tobacco is good for people who have sinus trouble and asthma. Put the plants in the sink and run hot water over them, then inhale the fumes.

RACCOONS - Many hunters hunted raccoons for food. They had special dogs called 'coon dogs that were particularly good hunters. (2) To make a coon trap, build a very small wooden box with a hole barely large enough for the coon to put his foot through. Lay a dime just inside the hole. The coon is highly attracted to shiny objects. He will reach in to get the dime in his fist. Refusing to turn the dime loose, he is caught in your trap! (Be sure to anchor the box, or he will take it with him.) (3) If raccoons get into your house, you are in a heap of trouble. They will turn on every knob and switch. Trying to deter raccoons from his garage, one man placed a battery-operated radio in his house hoping to keep them away. They carried the radio high up in a nearby tree with the volume blasting. Two days later the battery finally died.

RAMPS - A garlic-like onion that grows wild above 2600 feet sea level in our area. When one eats the ramps, the odor is extremely obnoxious and exudes from ones pores for at least a week after eating them. As youngsters, if we wanted to be excused from school, we just ate some ramps. If a person is around others eating ramps, his only protection is to eat ramps himself. Then he can't smell them. A ramp festival is held every year in late June or early July at Cosby, Tennessee. There people eat all the ramps they want. They have to be very sure that they really want them, however. Other people will not want to be around for a week. Yes, they smell that bad!

RECKON I KNOW WHAT I'M DOING!- Ray T. enjoyed telling the story of one of his ancestors. It seems the man climbed a good-sized tree to saw off a large limb. The trouble was, he had stationed himself out on the limb and was sawing close to the trunk.

Someone on the ground called his attention to this danger. He replied, "Reckon I know what I'm doing." Very shortly he and the limb fell to the ground breaking his arm. All our married life, if someone pointed out our error but we continued on our headlong way, we would always say, "Reckon I know what I'm doing."

RED-EYE GRAVY - (see GRAVY)

REFRIGERATION - Before our first refrigerator, an ice delivery man brought 25, 50, 75, or 100 pound blocks of ice to put in our ice box. Each family had cards with those four numbers printed on opposite sides of them. If we needed 100 pounds, we hung that number at the top of the card for the iceman to see from the street so he would know which size to deliver. Ray T. delivered ice for a short time in the Waldens Creek and Wears Valley area. He made a date with seven girls on his route and then went to a movie alone that night. (2) Our first safe, quiet refrigeration came in 1933 when we purchased our first Stewart Warner refrigerator. It ran for more than 30 years without ever being serviced. It was still running when Mother sold the home.

RINGWORM - Apply the juice of black walnut hulls. (2) This remedy came from Texas where we lived for a time in the 1940's. Burn a piece of notebook paper rolled into a cone shape. Catch the residue, which is a yellow oil. Apply the oil to the ringworm. A child will dance a jig when this is applied. It cured ringworm that my son, Don, got in the barber shop.

ROCKS - Almost all the mountain farms had lots and lots of rocks - ours included. The grandparents and those before them had picked up tons and tons of these rocks and built fences with them. Rocks seemed to appear where none had been the year before, giving way to the superstition that "The devil plants a new batch every year to tempt mortal souls."

RHEUMATISM - Carry a buckeye. (2) Recent- Stretching all joints as if pulling hard on an imaginary rope in all directions. This therapy has taken patients out of wheelchairs.

S

SALT - There was no substitute for salt. Mountain women were known to walk as far as five miles to buy one pound of salt for $1 (perhaps equivalent to $15 today). However, women leached lye from wood ashes to make soda.

SALT CELLAR - Unlike today, salt was not in a box or salt shaker in early days. It was kept in what was called a salt cellar. It was usually hardened and had to be spread with the end of a knife and rubbed into food.

SALT LICKS - A log or huge rock was hewn out on the top side to make a trench into which salt was placed for animals grazing in the mountains. Cattle owners took salt to their cattle about every three weeks "to gentle them and keep them familiar with their owner."

SASSAFRAS - Tea made of red root sassafras is dee-licious. Some believe it thins the blood. Sprinkling sassafras tea on flowers makes them healthy. Chewing a twig calms you down. Sassafras poles make good chicken roosts.

SAUCERED AND BLOWED - Your coffee that is. Today's young people will have missed this. I have seen it done many times. Time was when boiling hot coffee was poured into the saucer underneath the coffee cup. The person then blew on the hot coffee to cool it before drinking. It was rumored that a gentleman once offered a young lady his coffee, saying that it was already "saucered and blowed." I also saw men with long beards (my father never wore one) who, after drinking their coffee, would lay their forefinger across their mouth, press down their mustache, and make a sucking "swishing" noise to strain any remaining coffee into their mouth. (Ugh!)

SAW-MILL GRAVY- (See **GRAVY**)

SCABIES- (see **ITCH**)

SCARECROW - By the time my great-great grandchildren arrive on the scene I doubt if anyone will know what a scarecrow is or was. In my day we did lots of gardening. When we planted corn, the crows would come. In one day's time they could take up several rows of the young plants to get that one grain of corn underneath the plants. We built a dummy person with tattered overalls, colored shirt, straw hat, and a corn cob pipe that we called a scarecrow. We attempted to make the crows think that someone was nearby so they would leave our plants to grow. I think this may have helped somewhat for a while. I once claimed to have made a scarecrow so ugly that the crows brought back the corn that they had stolen the year before.

SCHOOLING - In very early days anyone who could read, knew the blue-back speller, and could write a good hand could make an agreement with concerned parents to teach the children. This was called a subscription or "Made-Up School." However, one mountain man was heard to observe that the only schooling a girl needed was to learn how to pin a diaper on a baby. Of one such teacher, hired by the parents, one scholar wrote:
Lord of love, look from above,
And pity the poor scholars.
They hired a fool to teach this school
And paid him fifty dollars!

When there was a special school building, and before pot-bellied stoves became available for heat, a hole was cut in the center of the floor. A fire could to be built on the ground. Mother told how her heels were frost-bitten while she was a youngster at school. The seats were hewn logs, and a slate was used for writing. Pencils and paper were not yet available. Later quill pens were made from the wing feathers of a goose or turkey, with ink made from poke berries. However, in those days if you kept a child in school, you had "done a good part by him!" Can you imagine school children today seated in a crude structure, no windows, one door, puncheon seats, and a place in the center of the floor to build a fire with hardly any place for the smoke to escape? Thank God that steam heat, better buildings and much better equipment became available during my school years. Today we can hardly imagine children drinking water from a water bucket and many sharing the same drinking cups. As late as 1939 each teacher in our Sevier County was given the following school supplies for the year: one box of chalk, one eraser, one broom, one dipper and one water bucket. Later many of our country schools were a two-room building, with the first five grades in one room and sixth, seventh and eighth grades in the other. The only books were the McGuffey Reader, Webster's Blue-Back Speller, and Venable's Practical Arithmetic. All the children read together as the teacher pointed to the words. Chart packs made of large sheets of paper with words and letters on them sat in the front of the room. When each page was learned, the sheets would turn over on a wire frame to reveal the next page. Spelling bees were usually held on Friday afternoon. When a child misspelled a word, he dropped out of the contest. A dunce cap was sometimes used when a student appeared not to be using his mental faculties. The pyramid effect may have helped more than the shame. The only shame unleashed upon us was when a teacher drew a circle on the blackboard. A misbehaving student was required to stand with his nose in that ring. (With all the lawsuits, I am sure a teacher would hesitate to use this form of punishment today.)

SCOTCH WHEEL - We enjoyed using an outdoor toy we called a Scotch Wheel. We pushed a large round metal loop with a stiff wire, approximately three feet long. This wire had a hook on the end. We walked behind the wheel and pushed it along in front. of us. I became quite an expert with this craft happily rolling it up and down the trails.

SCOUTING - A term applied to anyone hiding-out in the hills rather than go into the Confederate or Union armies. Family or friends supplied food and clothing so that soldiers could hide for months to avoid the official searches. A "Rich Man's War and a Poor Man's fight" sent many men from Tennessee into war. This tradition led to the nickname of "Volunteer State." East Tennessee, however, was said to be overwhelmingly Union.

SCRATCH ANKLE - A small area located around Martin Street inside the city of Mayville where "Hoot" John Heney Gibson. well known fiddle player once lived. So named perhaps due to the mosquito bites. Formerly known as Paddle Butt because one could hardly walk down Martin Street without seeing a child getting a spanking.

SCYTHE - A long curved sharp cutting blade attached at an angle to a long curved handle or snatch. It was used to cut wheat by hand. A frame, called a cradle, was often attached so that the wheat could to be laid in a orderly pile. This process was used before mowing machines became available.

SEARS CATALOG - (see MAIL ORDER CATALOG)

SECOND SIGHT - an unexplained knowing of events. Scots-Irish people believed in signs, spells, spirits, and were thought to predict the future.

SENILE - I do not remember that older people appeared senile. Maybe I was simply not around senility. Maybe they did not live lives that were as complicated. (2) Recent: Senility may be due to a lack of zinc. Lower levels of zinc are found in senile persons. Taking 15 mg per day may be helpful. (3) 1000 mg of Vitamin E twice per day and B5 when taken with other B vitamins are also said to help.

SEVIERVILLE, TENNESSEE - When the first small jailhouse was built in Sevierville, officials built stocks outside the jail. These were wooden frames with holes for the legs, arms, and heads of prisoners. As a practical joke, the sheriff was asked if he would mind testing them to be sure that they worked. Suspecting nothing, he readily agreed to be locked up. The townsfolk were then called out to take a look. This was said to make an impression on the lawless and give the good folk a chance to see the sheriff hard at work. However, the red-faced sheriff was left locked up much longer than he anticipated before he was finally released. We were not told how he settled that score. (2) During this time court affairs were held in a stable, which was infested with fleas. The itching, scratching attorneys gave a man a bottle of whiskey to burn the stable. (3) The Sevierville "Slow and Easy," as the train was called, had a problem crossing the Boyd's Creek Bridge. Fearful that the trestle would fall, the conductor would order all the passengers out of the train to walk the distance of the bridge. Then he would send the train across the bridge. Everyone then returned to their seats and continued the trip to Knoxville or Sevierville. (4) Some of the people in Sevierville, who did not want the train, filled the tracks with a tar compound. Others dug up the filler or placed sand or oil on the tracks. Hecklers lined the streets and applauded as the train crews tried to move the train forward. Apparently the have-nots won. The tracks are now missing.

SEXTON, REV. TOM - Known as the Blacksmith Preacher. Buried under the Tellico River at the Tellico Dam was the little town of Morganton. In this town lived a man whose legacy will touch people for generations to come. He started as a drunken gambler. Tom was born in White County, Georgia, April 1, 1858. His father gave him alcohol as a child, saying a little would not hurt. For thirteen long years Tom thought only of his need for alcohol. He had no money for his children, and he exposed them to a very drunken father. In July 1886 his tired but patient wife awoke telling him that God had warned her to get him out of Loudon, Tennessee. She said it was a place where devilment and alcohol were too easy for him to find. She said God told her to use the ferry to take him and the family across the Little Tennessee River to Morganton. Since he did not have a penny in his pocket, he knew they could not pay the ferry fare. Undaunted, his wife packed everything they owned in a wagon. She knew God would provide. The ferryman knew Tom was a blacksmith. As luck or providence would have it, Morganton's only blacksmith had left town that day. The ferryman told Sexton that he would collect the fare when money from "Smithing" came in, so the family was allowed to cross. Here Tom Sexton's life would to be changed forever. In Morganton, Tom heard the first sermon in his life. He tried every method he knew to try to avoid going to the services.

He got back on his horse four times. He believed he was too great a sinner, but encouragement from his family and friends helped him to become a servant of God. The many people to whom he owed money heard the story and now expected him to pay his just debts. Since he had no money, he felt sorry for himself bought alcohol again. But he found he simply could not drink it. Soon after this triumph Tom began to preach anywhere that someone would listen- in their homes, in shops, on the road, even while standing on river rocks. His great sense of humor and the simplicity of his messages appealed to people. He preached in 26 states and saw more than 30,000 people accept Christ. His explanation of the Trinity demonstrates how he simplified ideas. He gathered some ice, snow, and water to demonstrate how three could to be one and the same. When told of his death at age 65, his good friend, Rev. Billy Sunday, said, "One of God's truest soldiers has hit the golden trail." He was buried in Knoxville's Woodlawn cemetery.

SHAKING THE FAMILY TREE - If a young person showed any interest in another for possible courtship, the parents felt duty-bound to trace the family roots. This was especially important if any "black sheep" were known to exist in the family. This was known as shaking the family tree. My Mother was quite adept at that. Fortunately, for me, she knew nothing of my wonderful husband of 35 years, Ray T. Myers's early shenanigans, else there would have been no wedding there. Later becoming a minister quickly overshadowed his and his brother Huberts having operated a "beer joint" on Waldens Creek.

SHANKS MARE - or "walker's hack" meant that a person walked.

SHARECROPPERS - A sharecropper would pile his entire crop of corn in two separate piles. The land owner had first choice as payment of rent for that growing season.

SHEEP EYES - (see COURTING)

SHINGLES - Place bark or leaves of the English walnut in boiling water and allow to simmer. Apply the liquid to the affected area. (2) Recent: Flu shots are said to help.

SHIVAREE - A very noisy mock serenade by a group of people as they pounded on the door of newlyweds or new neighbors. The serenaders used spoons, dishpans, wash tubs, plow points or anything that would make a noise. They brought cakes and other goodies, partied for an hour or two, and went on their way confident they had properly welcomed new members to the community. Before people locked their doors, these groups were known to enter homes without knocking. Sometimes they found people in bed. Occasionally, revelers went into the wrong house.

SHOES - Many mountain children got only one new pair of shoes per year. This occurred just before school started. I have read that we are all supposed to have gone barefoot, but I cannot recall ever seeing anyone come to school barefooted during cold weather. Unlike today when children try on and choose the style of shoes they want, in early days a small stick was placed in the old shoe to determine the length of the shoe needed. Then the parents took the stick to the store to assure the correct length. Early shoes where not in boxes. They were tied together by the shoe laces.

SHOUTING - Until the 1930's and early 1940's it was common for someone to shout during a worship service. They would say they were filled with the spirit. One woman shouted at almost every service. She would shout for awhile and then find a man into whose arms she would fall until she 'fully recovered.' My father once saw that he was her intended "victim." He stepped aside and let her fall to the floor. I recall seeing a woman in our Evans Chapel Church who would throw her baby into the air as she started shouting. Aware of this trait, someone was always ready to catch the baby. I recall hearing her heels tapping the floor and her eyes set on the ceiling above, as she came up the aisle. I had to conclude that her shouting was genuine. Mother told us that when she was a young girl she was mocking a woman who shouted. After quite a display, mother was struck to the ground totally paralyzed for quite some time before she recovered her ability to move. Mother assumed this was a warning that she was making sport of something genuine. A man told about being in church when he was a very young boy. His mother began to shout. He described how he caught hold of her dress tail and followed her all over the church. Later he overheard her as she gave a neighbor bean seeds from a pocket that was sewed onto her petticoat. She remarked, "What if I had dropped my bean seeds when I cut that through [shouted] at the church."

SIGNS - (see MOON, SIGNS OF THE)

SIGNS - Coming into Tennessee from Kentucky by way of Cumberland Gap years ago, a huge sign printed in box-car sized letters hung across a huge ravine. It read: "PREPARE TO MEET THY GOD." The shock it gave to unsuspecting travelers was interesting and amusing. It was proof that one was indeed entering the Bible belt, as this region is commonly known. (2) Without materials to make road signs on the trails such as we enjoy today, the Indians devised their own, using nature's supply, namely rocks and trees. Certain types of rock piles indicated the main trails while other designs indicated certain villages. Branches of trees were sometimes used when rocks were not available. Directions were marked by arrangements of piles of rocks and bent tree branches. Perhaps some of those rock piles remain today.

SINKS - A very popular swimming hole, known a the Sinks, found along Little River Gorge Road, Hwy. 321, in the Great Smoky Mountain National Park. Early mountaineers named the spot because swimmers sometimes disappeared there never to be seen again. Our parents never allowed us to swim in the Sinks. A scuba diver/football player who escaped described his ordeal as being like two big hands grabbing his ankles and pulling him into a strange whirling machine that pulled him under and banged his head repeatedly against the rocks. He said he surfaced twice but was pulled back under water. Then, he was thrown out of the water as if someone picked him up and threw him. The water flows into the river over a wedge-shaped boulder near the waterfall with such great force that a hydraulic-like process is created. The effect is like a horizontal whirlpool in the underground cavity, where a swimmer can go round and round like in a washing machine. Old-timers believed a hole sucked the body into an underground cavity never to be seen again. Two people have drowned there in recent years- one in 1982 and a 13 year old boy in 1995. The extremely cold water brings on hypothermia quickly. We local people know of this danger, but millions of visitors come here every year and receive no notice of this danger. I believe a huge warning should be placed next to this popular swimming hole. I checked with the Park's official whose policy is neither to encourage nor forbid swimming. A public affairs officer for the park service was quoted as saying "I personally wouldn't swim at the Sinks, no."

Outside the park, still on highway 321 east of Gatlinburg, my son, Glenn, and his friend, Fred Caustic, had a most terrifying experience while wading in the river. Glenn fell through a hole into a good-sized underwater cave. Fred immediately followed. One of them would climb onto the shoulder of the other trying to find something in the surface above to hold onto to pull them out. Meanwhile, Fred's nephew, who was with them observed that they both suddenly disappeared. He ran more than 150 yards up and down the river bank screaming while they frantically tried to climb out. Glenn said something told him to be calm. Glenn and Fred are both over 6 feet tall and weigh over 200 pounds each. They needed a very strong object to grab at the mouth of that hole.. Finally, Glenn climbing on Fred's shoulders, grabbed onto something that was not there, and pulled himself out. Then he helped Fred to get out. If those two did not believe in guardian angels, they do now. I have overheard the two of them discussing this amazing event. They agree they still do not know what it was that Glenn grabbed onto to pull himself out as nothing could be found at the rim of that hole.

SINUS - See allergies. Mountain doctors carried honey comb in their medical bags. They gave the comb to sinus sufferers to chew like gum. It was chewed for 20 minutes every hour for 5 or 6 hours and then discarded. This was continued for two days, and then once each day for 7 days. (2) To prevent sinus attacks or hay fever take two teaspoons of honey every day for 30 days before the pollen season begins. (3) Put two tablespoons of brandy (any flavor) in a cup of boiling water. Surround the cup with your hands and sniff the steam through the nose and out through the mouth. Then breathe through the mouth and exhale thru the nose. Continue for 15 minutes. Drink the brandy. Amazing! I have used that one. (4) One old mountaineer asked to borrow some Copenhagen. He sniffed it deep on each side of his nose several times, then he started sneezing. After he sneezed some 15 or more times, he said that his sinus's which were totally blocked, were now all clear.

SKIN- AGE SPOTS - Home remedies: Apply buttermilk, or lemon juice daily. (2) Mix egg white, apple cider vinegar, and sugar, (3) Rub with the inside of an orange peel. (4) Urine. Recent: (5) Apply Vitamin E oil. (6) Apply yogurt.

SKINNY DIPPING - Before swim suits became available, swimming in the nude was quite common. A group of girls were swimming when some boys came along. The boys sat on the river bank refusing to go away. The girls were forced to stay underwater much too long. Finally, one of the girls found a dishpan in the river bed. Holding it up in front, she proceeded to tell the boys exactly what she thought of them. They countered with, "Yes, yes. We know what you think. You think that dishpan has a bottom in it." (2) My nephew, Olin Watson, and a friend were swimming when a water spout caused the river to rise suddenly. They were left on the opposite side of the river from their clothing. Perched on a big rock, they waited a very long time for the waters to recede. They were later found naked, chilled, and hungry.

SLEEP - Can't sleep? Mix 3 teaspoons of apple cider vinegar in one cup of honey. Keep refrigerated. Take 1 teaspoon 30 minutes before bedtime. This one may be a believe it or not to induce sleep, that being to press gently for three minutes with the index and middle finger of the left hand on the inside of your right wrist three finger widths below the crease of your wrist. Release, switch hands, repeat for another three minutes and get a good nights sleep.

SLIPPERY ELM POWDER - I can not say enough good things about slippery elm bark powder. Sometimes pharmacies must special order it. For sores under dentures, there is nothing better. Dampen a small amount of the powder and put it in dentures to fit over a sore spot. To eat steak, put heaping dry powders on dentures to fit on each side of a sore spot. The powder acts as a cushion. Since it is also good for the stomach, there is no problem with swallowing it. (2) Used as a poultice, the powder will draw out infection of boils, carbuncles, or other infections. Mix with Vaseline for longer lasting poultices or with water for short term. The water soon dries out. (3) When our second son, Glenn, was 10 months old, he fell while standing in his highchair. He stuck his hand into a boiling hot bowl of gravy I had just set on the table. Washing his hand quickly in cold water, I applied a very thick coating of slippery elm powder mixed with Vaseline. I left the salve on overnight. The next day I could find no sign of this terrible burn. (4) At age 60, I asked a pharmacist for slippery elm powder. He curiously questioned what I intended to do with it. Explaining its use for dentures, I asked him why he needed to know. He explained that the powder is sometimes used for abortions, and he was not allowed to sell it for that purpose. I do not know how it was applied. (5) In very early days food or gruel was made for infants using one teaspoon of slippery elm powder mixed with powdered sugar and one pint of boiling water. It was mixed slowly and flavored with cinnamon or nutmeg to make a very wholesome food for infants. Some think that is as nutritive as oatmeal.

SMOKEHOUSE - A necessary out-building where meats were smoked and stored. Potatoes, apples, and canned goods were also stored for safekeeping. Our smoke house in Wears Valley had two rooms- one outside door and an inside door leading into a second room so that different types of items could be stored..

SMOKING - While out behind the barn, many youngsters smoked rabbit tobacco or corn silks wrapped in pieces of brown paper bag. (2) To stop smoking mountain style: For a three week period take one-third teaspoon baking soda in water three times per day. My theory behind this mountain cure is that high levels of acid in the body create a craving, while baking soda neutralizes the body acids, reducing the desire for more tobacco. One must eat alkaline foods during this time, such as almonds, apples, berries, carrots, celery, grapefruit, lima beans, milk, mushrooms, onions, peas, raisins, sweet potatoes, squash, tomatoes, and sunflower seed. These foods are said to calm one down as does the tobacco. No alcoholic beverages or smoking is allowed during this time or one will get a double dose hangover. Note also that drinking coffee and smoking at the same time causes blood pressure to shoot to higher levels for more than two hours.

SNAKES - I once read an entire book which set out to prove that there are no such things as "hoop" snakes. I beg to differ, because I have seen two, one alive and one dead. After the police and school children had helped to find my missing son, Glenn, a six year old, I went to the site to survey the danger had a train passed while he was on the narrow railroad tressle. Hearing a loud whrrrrring noise, I stood paralyzed as a hoop snake came rolling straight at me, rolled on by just inches away, and went on down the Emory River bank at perhaps perhaps 10 to 25 miles per hour. Sitting on the back porch while visiting Ida and Bruce Myers in Wears Valley we spied a black snake crawling across the lawn. Bruce shot and killed it, being 8 foot 4 inch long with an unusual tail bone, approximately one inch long ,which fastened perpendicular to the spine. The area surrounding this cross-piece bone was well worn which explains how he was able to hold onto his tail. I put him in a gallon glass jar, stopped numerous times enroute to Maryville at Service Stations etc., showing him but no one had ever seen anything like that cross-piece bone growing onto the end of his tail. My husband had such a fear and hatred of snakes that he was furious that I had driven from Wears Valley with that snake in the car. I explained that the snake was "good and dead" but that didn't help my case.(2) Once I watched a black snake charming a bird. Both were up in an apple tree. The snake started movements in a counter clock wise manner approximately four feet from the bird. The snake moved from limb to limb circling the bird, keeping his eye on the bird at all times. There was no reason that I could see why the bird could not have flown away at any time. Instead it was just hopping up and down, up and down, twittering. Each circle brought the snake closer until he was just ready to pounce on the bird. That is when I interceded, by hitting the snake to bring him down from the tree. I found it strange that the bird appeared to be too dazed to fly away for quite sometime. (3) Copperheads were so numerous we fought with them en route home for lunch from the cornfields. They hid under the plantain leaves and chased us, so that we had to carry a hoe with us for protection. Every time my husband left his house when he was a child, his mother said, "Now, watch out for snakes." This adversely affected him so much that he spent the rest of his life dreadfully afraid of any kind of snake. (4) I leaned to detect the presence of an unseen snake. They have an odor like a horse. If you smell a horse but do not see one, better look behind you because a snake is pretty close. My late husband, Ray T., and I stepped out on our back porch to look at the full moon, when I smelled a horse. There underneath the small step-down at the screen door lay a copperhead that we had both stepped over. We did not have a hoe handy so he got away. (4) One morning Grandmother Susan Myers went to the smokehouse to get ham for breakfast. The ham was in the second room of the smokehouse. As she went into that room, she pushed the door wide open. The door happened to fasten the tail of a copperhead to the floor. With his tail fastened under the door, the snake would strike at her. She had no way out since this was the only door to the room she was in. She feared that at any moment he might to be released. All other members of the household were still fast asleep. Granny screamed "bloody murder" for quite some time before being rescued. (5) I recall fishing late one evening with my sister and brother. I squatted down to put another worm on my hook. When I chanced to look directly underneath my skirt to find a snake that we called a spread-head or blowing adder which was coiled, ready to strike. Just as I looked underneath my skirt, he blew in my face. All I can recall now, these 70 or more years later is that I fell backward. Beyond that I do not know my condition nor his. A childhood memory of looking a snake right in the eye, just inches away, while he blows in your face is traumatic enough to recall!

SNIPE HUNTING - Older boys sometimes took younger boys or unsuspecting youth on a snipe hunt. The victim was often told to hold a bag while the conspirators went into the woods saying they would scare a snipe in the direction of the victim. The victim was left "holding the bag" until he realized no snipes would be coming in his direction and that he had been had..

SNOWS - Our mountain weather prophets counted the number of heavy fogs in August to determine the number of measurable snows in the winter time. The number of snows was supposed to be the same as the number of fogs. (2) When birds ate on the ground, it was another sign of snow. (3) If the fire made popping sounds similar to someone walking on snow, old-timers said that the fire was popping snow. They said to watch out- it was coming. (4) Sounds can to be heard much greater distances during very cold weather. We could hear the train whistles at Townsend during very cold weather.

SORE THROAT - see GARGLE: Tie a red ribbon or scarf around the left wrist and neck, otherwise wear nothing but white for three days. (2) Massage the second toe for sore throat. I once burned my second toe very badly and instantly it set my throat on fire.

SOURWOOD - A walking stick cut from a sourwood tree will dry out and not season crack as do other woods. (2) The honey that the bees make from the bloom of the sourwood tree is my favorite flavor of honey.

SOUTHERN OATH - After the Civil War many Southerners repeated an oath which follows: "Of my own free will and choice, I do hereby in the presence of these witnesses swear to be loyal to the South. And when speaking of Yankees, I will refer to them as

Scalawags or Carpetbaggers. And I promise to whistle or hum Dixie as a sign of my loyalty and token of my new outlook on life."

SPIDERS - When I was growing up, we always watched for the deadly poisonous black widow spider. It is shiny black with a red hour glass on its abdomen. Its silk web is said to be stronger than Kevlar, the polyfiber used in bullet proof vests. Fortunately, only one of my brothers was ever bitten by a black widow spider. I can recall hearing him cry out in pain. My parents beat egg whites, put them in a small mouth bottle, then held it on the bite to pull the poison out. He survived the ordeal. Little was ever said about the brown recluse spider, which I understand is also poisonous. The writing spider was given some attention perhaps in jest. We were told that if he wrote our name in his web, it was a very bad omen. Spider webs were said to have been used extensively to stop the blood from puncture wounds, but I do not recall my parents ever using them in this manner. To discourage spiders, one can add cedar chips or spray with rubbing alcohol around a room.

SPINNING WHEEL - We only used a spinning wheel to wind bobbins of thread for weaving linens and rugs on the loom. I understand that earlier a spinning wheel was used to spin thread from cotton. We never raised cotton . I only heard of one man of our area who tried to raise some. He reported that he only grew enough to make a shirt tail.

SPITBALLS - The deep dark secret of throwing those deceptive spitballs was our very own slippery elm bark. This powder placed in one's mouth increased the saliva used in their construction.

SPRING TONIC - Every spring we children were given sulfur mixed with molasses as a spring tonic to rev up our tired blood after the long cold winter months. Take one teaspoon every day for five days. It did not taste bad. In fact I liked it. I never hear of its use today.

SPRINGING - When it became obvious that one of our cows was expecting a calf, my family would comment that "the cow is springing." As our family and boarders were sitting around the fireside one night, one of my brothers noticed that the midsection of one of our boarders was considerably larger than normal. Today we would call it a beer belly. My brother remarked, "Charlie, you look like you're springing."

STINGY - Being stingy was considered to be one of the worst things to be said about a mountaineer. A few months ago I talked with a man who described his family's plight during the depression years. His father deserted his family, leaving his mother with six children. She had only fifty cents in the house, so she sent him to a neighbor who had killed a hog that day. The child asked to buy just fifty cents worth of meat. The neighbor refused to sell him any meat. Next morning a second hog belonging to that stingy neighbor was found dead. You did not eat meat unless you knew the cause of death. Those starving children concluded that God had killed that second hog because the man was too stingy to sell them just fifty cents worth of meat. That child, now a man of my age, said that they survived on mush and water. He also said that when his wayward father returned after many years, the family took him in. He also said it left many scars.

STOMACH TROUBLE - My choice is golden seal, also called yellow root. This shrub grows near water. I have dug many roots for my mother, who cleaned and put them in water. She let the mixture set overnight and then drank it for stomach distress. It can be purchased in capsules as golden seal or yellow root. Today I buy the capsules, open them, and put them in water for a very refreshing drink for digestive problems. Golden seal has also been suggested as a remedy for Crohn's disease. (2) For ulcers, eat servings of raw and cooked cabbage every day for three weeks. It is believed there is an enzyme in cabbage not yet identified. (3) Drink sauerkraut juice for upset stomach. It tastes terrible, but it works. (4) Tea made by boiling peach tree leaves is great for upset stomach and diarrhea. I can several quarts of peach tea every year. I also put the leaves in the freezer. (5) Blackberry juice or slippery elm capsules are also great for the stomach. (6) Suck on a piece of ginger.

STORES - ROLLING STORES - Old school busses were converted into rolling stores. Shelves were built along each side after the seats were removed. The shelves were stocked with available canned goods. A chicken coop was fastened to the rear of the bus so that chickens could to be traded in for groceries. Eggs, corn, and potatoes were also used as barter items. The rolling stores were very convenient when they stopped at the front door of those who lived in the country. Fred Atchley and Burt Whaley owned the ones I can recall patronizing in Sevier County.

STOVE - COOK STOVE - The first known cookstove arrived in this area in 1782. People were said to have traveled from miles around to see it. Since we did not get electricity until 1933, I recall well our wood cookstove. Home Comfort was the brand name, I believe. Our stove was the top of the line at that time. Three meals per day were cooked on it. It had what we called a warming closet that hung above the stove eyes. Four of the round metal stove eyes, approximately eight inches in diameter, could be removed so that the cook could set pots inside the opening to place the food closer to the fire. This afforded much quicker heating. Left over food was stored in the warming closet until the next meal. On the right side of the stove was a reservoir that held perhaps ten gallons of water. This supply of hot water was most helpful. The stove also heated the room well. This was especially helpful in the winter when it was bath time. We had a wonderful warm spot behind the stove in that number two washtub. I shall never forget the time my little brother had taken his bath and donned his long-handled underwear. Arriving back in the living room, where all the family was gathered around the fireside, his head protruded from the trap door of the long Johns. His feet and legs were where his arms should have been. His arms were where his legs should have been. That incident happened more than seventy years ago, and I can almost hear my father laughing yet at that sight.

STRANGER ROOM - An enclosed room on the front porch of the George Tipton's home in Cades Cove was widely known as the "Stranger Room." The room had a private entrance and contained only a bed, a table, a chair, and an old oil lamp. It was free to people who were passing by to spend the night. It was often used by cattle drivers passing to and fro.

STRANGERS - Until it was absolutely determined WHO you were and WHAT you wanted to know, you got little, if any, information from many of our mountain people. This incident happened among my own Trentham family. One of the sons, who lived near a country store, had invited one of his friends for a visit. Finding the store but unable to locate his friend's house, the visitor found an old man standing on the store porch. He inquired of the old man where this friend's house was located. He did not identify himself as a friend who had been invited. The old man replied, "Never heard of him. No one lives here by that name." After the two friends met somewhat later, this conversation with the old man was repeated. The friend replied, "So, it was YOU that my father was talking to." Sly, secretive, suspicious folk could dodge leading questions and appear to be as dumb as a wooden horse. All the time they were laughing up their sleeves. During my father's youth, strangers were closely scrutinized. During the reign of terror of the White Caps this was particularly important. If strange human footprints or tracks were found on the mountain trails, they were closely studied to possibly identify their owners. Noting how fast a person was walking, the type of shoe, or the size of the foot could suggest or eliminate lots of people. Afterwards local people were asked if they had seen someone in the area. In fact, my father traced the person who burned his grist mill by his footprint. Today, it is hard to imagine people recognizing a footprint. However, none of the roads or trails during early days were blacktop or concrete.

STUMPED TOES - Stumped toes and stone bruises were part of everyday life for most of us mountain children. We could hardly wait for the first day of May to arrive. On that day no matter how cold it might to be we had our parents' permission to discard our shoes and pull off our Long Johns (winter underwear.) We had this saying: "On the first day of May, pull your shoes off and throw them away!"

SUGAR TIT - If a newborn baby cried for food before the mother's milk became available, a lump of sugar was tied into a clean white cloth. The cloth was then dipped into water and given to the infant. Being a "sweetaholic" all of my life, that must to be the way I got my start.

SUGARLANDS - The area on Hwy. 441 two miles south of Gatlinburg and east of The Great Smoky Mountain National Park headquarters. Settlers were said to have moved into this area during the 1800's bringing an axe, a plow, and a gun. The Indians hunted and farmed this land before that time. The area received its name because of the maple trees that grew there. Indians taught the settlers how to collect "sweet water" gathered from auger holes bored into the trees. (See **MAPLE SYRUP.**)

SUNBURN - Apply apple cider vinegar to the skin. (2) Apply baking soda dissolved in water. (3) Oatmeal in an old sock in cool bath is great for sunburn. (4) Recent- Take aspirin immediately.

SUN POISON - Apply vinegar and soda. (2) Use Palmolive soap then pure Vaseline. (3) Recent: For acute sun poison, dab spirits of camphor, then take a cool bath and apply peanut oil.

SUN SCREEN - We simply wore big hats. We did not know that it was necessary to protect out skin from anything other than sunburn. Recent: One doctor said that Mary Kay cosmetics has the best sunscreen. (I do not know if he owned stock.)

SUPERSTITIONS - Regardless of religion or education many superstitions are still with us. Luckily for those of us who never heard some of them, we survived. If a spider lowered himself from the ceiling into the room or a rooster came to the door and crowed, it was said to be a sign that someone was coming. Dropping silverware or itching noses were also an announcement of guests. When your ears are burning, someone is talking about you. This one was brought home to me when I was a member of a prayer group that took time once a week at a specific time to say a special prayer for one member of the group. It was my week to have them remember me. At eight o'clock, the designated time, my ears started burning unlike anything I had ever experienced. It suddenly dawned on me that was the exact time that the group was to say that special prayer for me and I had forgotten it.

Bad luck comes from returning home by the same route taken to work or having a black cat cross your path. If a black cat crosses your path, you can reverse your luck by turning your hat around or returning home. My grandfather, Ephraim Ogle, started from home one day when a black cat got in front of him and kept moving back and forth for quite some distance as if to stop him. He continued his trip. One of his children was badly injured while he was away, and he felt the cat had tried to stop him. We were told not to allow a baby to look into a mirror before age 6 months, or that breaking a mirror brought 7 years of bad luck. Do not walk with one shoe off and one shoe on. It is bad luck. If there is one funeral in the community, there will to be two more. If you take the last piece of food on the plate, you will to be an old maid. You must exit a house or other building through the same door that you entered or you will have bad luck. I always wondered if one really believes a certain superstition if it give power to that particular one as regards you?

Carrying a four-leaf clover, patting a redhead's head, or carrying a rabbit's foot can bring good luck. Eat chicken gizzards and you will get the spouse of your choice. If you plant a lilac tree close to the house it will keep away lightning. When a stone, called a madstone, was found in the stomach of a slain animal such as a sheep or deer, it was carefully preserved and passed down from generation to generation. If rubbed on a dog bite wound the madstone was believed to ward off rabies. A meal of black-eyed peas and hog jowls on New Year's Day is supposed to bring good luck for the year. One of the worst years of my life was the one in which we followed that tradition.

My father-in-law firmly believed that a woman should never visit others on New Years Day. He always visited all his family on that day for good luck. To say that he was furious with me for visiting his home on New Years Day is putting it mildly. He let me know in no uncertain terms how upset he was. It so happened that I became pregnant with my beautiful daughter during that year. Still seething over my New Years visit to his home, he said, "See, I told you you'd have bad luck!" To which I replied, "That was not what caused it!" Enough of superstitions, better you do not know them!!!!!!!!

SUPPER TABLE - "Supper is ready" was a most welcome announcement in early days. Every member of the family had to be present. This family tradition has long since been lost, cheating today's children of the fellowship and very precious family ties. It was either a funfest or a free for all. You laughed or complained.

SURGERY - Early surgery was done under screams. Whiskey was often the best way to dull the pain. (2) Never have elective surgery during full moon or when the sign is in the body part. According to beliefs about moon cycles, there is a much greater risk of excessive bleeding. (3) Ether was available in my early days. In fact, ether was used during the birth of my third child. When not properly monitored ether can prove disastrous. As in my case, I was dead for a short time. This was confirmed by the attending Dr. Lester Olin. See full details in my book entitled: "During My Near-Death Experience, I Saw God."

SWEETS - Stop craving sweets: Drink 4 oz grape juice at 10:00 AM and 3:00 PM. (2) Place a clove in the mouth and suck on it for one hour. Do not swallow it. (3) Recent: Drink juice of two lemons in 8 oz. water at 10:00 AM daily.

SWIMMERS - When we played in the river (ice cold to me today) our parents warned us to listen for a "roar" in the water. Many times water spouts would hit high up in the mountains while the sun might be shining at our place. This caused the water to rise rapidly and dangerously for us. (2) To prevent ear infections, put olive oil (we called it sweet oil) in ears before swimming. Oil coats the canal enabling water to run out more freely.

T

TAILHOLDER - Cow's tail, that is. While this was never a problem on our farm, some mountain children really hated the chore of holding the cow's tail while grandma milked the cow. In the summertime when the cow's tail was full of cockle burrs and flies were extremely bad, a cow swished its tail vigorously from one side to the other. Getting hit over the head or trying to duck (avoid) that tail was some chore, especially if perched on a three-legged milk stool. A tail-holder was most welcome. (Imagine a kid today holding the cow's tail. Never!) Those cockle burrs, known as beggar's button, had hundreds of shreds or hairs growing from a center. Each shred had a hook on the end of it that caused great entanglement. We can thank the cockle burr for suggesting the idea for making the Velcro whose use we greatly enjoy today. And such an honor for all the little "Tail Holders" of yesteryear to at last be recognized for the lowly job that you did we salute you!

TATER HOLE - (Potato) Due to lack of storage facilities, some early settlers dug a deep hole in the ground, lined it with straw, and covered it so that rain water would drain off. They stored potatoes, cabbage, and turnips for the winter. Keeping food items below the frost line kept them from freezing. One would uncover, scratch away the straw, get enough for a meal, and then cover again. These underground conveniences were used until the 1940's but my family never used them because we had a "Smokehouse" with an underground room where all those vegetable could safely be stored. That very primitive means of preserving food was sufficient for that day and time but would hardly fit in our well manicured lawns of today and beside that would be rather unhandy, rather than being able to reach into the refrigerator for a potato. Our apples were individually wrapped in newspapers so they kept well until after Christmas.

TAYLOR - BOB AND ALF - My Father really enjoyed telling stories about Bob and Alf Taylor, brothers who opposed each other for the office of governor of Tennessee. Their mother insisted that each brother sign an oath that if they ever became angry with each other, they would quit the race. However, they agreed they could argue party platforms. They held 41 debates.

At the first debate Bob said, "I have a high regard for the Republican candidate. He is a perfect gentleman, because he is my brother. I've told him to come with me, and I will furnish him with crowds and introduce him to society. We are two roses from the same garden." Bob wore a white rose in his lapel; Alf wore a red rose. Many people had to check the color of the rose to know which was Bob or Alf.

Bob had a great sense of humor. One of his typical stories went like this:

"I was at a celebrity dance. The fiddles were playing, and we were swinging corners. The boys got to slapping each other on the back. Finally one fellow slapped too hard and knocked another fellow down. His brother shot that fellow. That fellow's brother cut the other fellow's throat. The fellow who was originally knocked down drew his knife and cut the fellows liver out. The old man of the house got mad, ran upstairs, grabbed his shotgun and turned it loose on the crowd. I saw there was going to be trouble, so I left.."

Stories such at that drew great crowds. Bob was elected by 13,000 votes, but Alf set a record for the largest Republican vote in Tennessee up to that time. Both went on to serve as governor for three terms. Alf was elected in 1921 at age 72.

After Bob had served two terms, he left office pennyless. He wrote Alf for advice. Alf responded that if Bob had served two terms as governor and came out of office broke, his hands were clean. Alf said he would take care of Bob until he could get on his feet financially. He gave him money and told him to pay his debts and move into his home.

Bob moved in with Alf where he wrote his lecture, "The Fiddle and The Bow," which brought him $75,000. Alf wrote, "Yankee Doodle" and "Dixie." They entertained the voters and left a political legacy still remembered as "HONESTY!" With politics being what it is today, Oh, for another refreshing Alf and Bob Tayler.

TELEPHONES - The earliest telephones were eight-party lines. We twisted a crank located on the right side of a large black telephone that hung on the wall. Twisting the crank connected us with "central" or the operator. She inserted phone cables into the correct line to connect us to the other party. (And she could listen to our conversation.) Subscribers had three numbers assigned as their telephone number such as 780R. On the eight-party lines, we heard the rings of four different parties, one of which was our own. Those rings consisted of two longs and a short ring, or two shorts and a long ring, or two shorts or two long rings. Many experienced considerable difficulty when others listened to private conversations during the eight-party line days. What a happy milestone when we moved to a two-party line, especially if the other party was someone who respected our privacy. At that time the phone subscriber heard only his or her own ring. Only by chance did one pick up on the other conversation. We thought that we were right up town when we finally moved to private lines. It felt like a real milestone of progress, never before experienced! (How insignificant it is today, comparatively speaking.) With the private lines came seven-digit numbers with area codes designating certain sections of the country. Now we are driven to distraction with all the options when we phone any business location. If none of the options fit your problem, it makes one wish for the "good-ole-days" when one could talk with a live person.

TEMPER - One mountain man, known especially for his hot temper, would start a fight before asking questions. One day getting the worst of an encounter, he vowed never to roll down his shirt sleeves until he gave his opponent a licking. Never getting the chance to do this, he lived the rest of his life wearing his sleeves rolled up!

TETANUS - (see NAILS) Tetanus shots were not available so that blackberry leaves mixed with lard or peach leaves beaten into a pulp were applied to sores or puncture wounds. We most often used the peach leaves. For a rusty nail stuck in the foot, we always bruised peach tree leaves and bound on the site.

TIMER - Parents lit a candle as a very early "timer" for dating. The visiting beau and the farmer's daughter could "spark" until the candle burned down and went out. Then it was time for him to go home. No ifs, ands, or buts! I wonder if they ever "snuffed" it out and lit it again to gain time. Just trying to imagine such an incident in today's society stretches our imagination.

TIN TYPES - Very early pictures were printed on tin or called "tin types.' I once had one, in good condition, of my Father who was born in 1867. Interestingly enough it may have disappeared at one of our family reunions.

TOBACCO - Known as Indian Weed was the money crop for many local farmers. From planting the seeds to getting the harvested crops to market takes thirteen months. My brother gave his two very young sons tobacco to chew and smoke, urging more and more, until they both became very sick of it. As a result neither smokes or chews today.. Some farmers packed a "chaw" (chew) of the leaf tobacco in their jaw before tamping some into and lighting their pipe. The nicotine habit was passed on to children at an early age. The tobacco patch was in many cases planted close to the cabins and tended with even greater care than the food stuff. Fortunately, my father did not grow, chew, nor smoke it. While I was working in the Kaiser Ship Yard, in Portland, Oregon, during WWII, helping to build Liberty Ships, I tried smoking a cigarette as it was definitely the "IN" thing to do in those days. Fortunately it made me "sick as a dog" and I never tried it again. In fact, I cannot stay in the room today where others are smoking. In 1964 the U. S. Surgeon General warned that cigarette smoke was causing cancer and other diseases. Today some three million people a year die of tobacco-related illnesses. With millions dying, the addiction appears to be very difficult to overcome

TOMATO BEER - If a family had only one cow for milk and she went dry, they either got milk from a neighbor or made tomato beer. Ripe tomatoes were washed and then mashed. Three pounds of brown sugar was added to one gallon of mashed tomatoes and left standing for nine days. The pulp settled to the bottom so that the liquid could be poured from the top. The concoction was bottled, sealed, and aged. The longer it aged, the better it tasted. One or more cups was added to a gallon of sweetened cold water. Some lemon juice or lemon extract was sometimes added.

TOMATOES - Always store tomatoes stem side up to ripen. Put them in a brown bag with a banana or in a sunny window helps to ripen them. Punch holes in the bag. Pinching the top of a plant will cause it to bear fruit earlier. Stir one tablespoon Epsom Salts into the soil underneath the plant when planting. And in case you are wondering - we hillbillies do not water our tomatoes with "Moonshine" or "White Lightning" that good old mountain dew, in order to have "stewed" tomatoes. Once believed to be poisonous and to have caused the death of an unfortunate lover, tomatoes were named "Love Apples." George Washington was said to have been one of the first who dared eat a tomato. Good old George, I'm so glad that he did. I grow them and eat lots of tomatoes, sometimes drying them in a dehydrator. Anyone who smokes should never handle young tomato plants, as it tends to inhibit their growth. Tobacco mosaic virus may to be on their hands. Dipping hands in milk before handling should help.

TOOTHACHE - Place two cloves in the jaw. Chew a bit to release the juice. (2) Split a raisin in half; cover with black pepper; and place on the tooth.

TOOTH BRUSHES - Very early tooth brushes were made from a tender birch stick. It was cut approximately five inches long with about one inch of the bark removed from one end of the wood. The stick was chewed until the fiber broke apart and was then flattened into a circle. The circular fiber was used to brush the teeth.

TOOTHPASTE - Packaged toothpaste was not available to us early on.. We brushed with a mixture of baking soda and salt. The taste is really very pleasant once you get used to it. It also acts as an abrasive to remove tartar.

TOOTH PULLERS - (see DENTISTRY)

TONGUE -BURN - Apply granulated sugar.

TOYS- We made toys from whatever was available. Balls were made from a variety of sources including hog bladders. Dolls might be made from spools of thread tied together. The only toy I ever saw in our general store was a monkey that climbed a string. I was disappointed because my mother did not buy it for me. I don't recall seeing any dolls in the stores when I was very young.. Rose Skelly of Houston, Texas, made my first nice big doll. She sewed its beautiful dress and cap and sent it to me for Christmas. Since we had no motels, she and her family had asked to spend one or more nights at our house. Mother and Dad never charged anyone for spending the night that I can recall. The Skelly's sent us a big box of gifts at Christmas time following their visit. I was a multimillionaire when I got that doll, which I named Rose. My son, Don, played with it. My sister, Kate, flew to Houston years later and visited with the Skelly's. Louis Skelly was the son's name.

TRAGEDIES - Life was often hard for family members. Without medical care or basic health information, tragedy was part of many lives. Two men were known to have been caught in bear traps and died in these mountains. One of the men lived in the Gatlinburg area. He left home in the fall to cross the mountain into North Carolina to buy salt for his family. His wife and children expected him every day throughout the winter. When spring came, hunters found his body caught in one of his own bear traps located just a few miles from his home. (2) Perhaps one of the most heart-wrenching stories was of a family we knew whose father was sent to prison for a very minor offense. During this time his small son got a blister on his heel from a new pair of school shoes. He got dew in the sore, and blood poisoning set in, which caused his death. This father wrote the child a letter telling him how very sorry he was that he had to be away while "the child was in the throws of death." This letter was placed in a glass jar on the child's grave. His grave was located at the foot of Levi Trentham's wife's grave in the Elkmont cemetery. A good friend of mine, who lived near The Trentham Cemetery, told me how she and her siblings often went to that cemetery after school. They would take out that letter, read it aloud, while all of them cried. (3) A tragedy of another kind happened while Mother was in school. Students were allowed to go outside in pairs to study spelling. One pronounced the words while the other young student spelled. One day one of the young girls had a very bad case of diarrhea and was on her way to the outside toilet when the call of nature became so great that she had to stop en route. Unfortunately, she chose to stop at a spot on the river bank directly over where two boys were sitting several feet below. A direct hit on one of the boys sent him to the river, where he would wash awhile then exclaim "Damn the shit!" The other boy rolled on the ground in laughter to such extent that it disturbed the entire school body. They all came out to check the problem. Mother felt so sorry for this poor girl, who quit school due to this embarrassment. (4) The late Bob Hicks related the story of how George Walker hunted coons by day and followed them to the tree where they made their den at night. He had a heart attack and died while cutting one of those trees. Accompanied by his dogs, his body lay there all night in the rain. His blue tick hound named "Will" slept on his coat beside the body, so that the coat was still dry. These dogs were so protective the people had to find someone who knew the dogs before anyone could come near his body. (5) While researching my Father's family tree, I found an extremely sad story. While en route to Missouri by wagon, one of the Trentham families buried two small daughters on the way. One can hardly imagine the horror and heartbreak of such an event.

TRAILS - (see SIGNS)

TRANTHAM - While researching my Trentham family tree, I encountered many who spelled the name with an "A" instead of an "E." One , Leona, who was taking at least 15 children per year, entirely at her expense, on a trip to England and elsewhere. I inquired as to her reason for this unusual act of charity and the time she was spending with these underprivileged children and found her story quite interesting.

As a small child her family was very poor such that fellow school children taunted her to such unbearable extent that one day she ran away from school and went up into the hills alone. During her climb to the top of a mountain she chanced to pick a wild flower that attracted her attention.

Very late in the afternoon, still carrying this flower she chanced to meet a botanist who was searching that area for that exact very rare flower. By showing him where she found it he gave her the sum of five hundred dollars, a very very substantial sum in those days.

This incident not only turned her life around at school, but changed her entire life. She later married a well known politician whose financial status provided her with the means to do something special for underprivileged children, because she herself had been there. And a beautiful story worth repeating!

TRANTHAM, JOSEPH'S WILL -WILL DOCKET TO JULY TERM 1850

NORTH CAROLINA
BUNCOMBE COUNTY   THE LAST WILL AND
TESTAMENT OF JOSEPH   TRANTHAM

IN THE NAME OF GOD, AMEN. I, Joseph Trantham being far advanced in life and realizing under sore and heavy afflictions but thanks be to God of perfect mind and memory and knowing the mortality of my body and that it is appointed for all men once to die, do hereby make and ordain this my last will and testament.

FIRST: I give and recommend my soul unto the hands of Almighty God who gave it, secondly, I give and recommend my body to the earth to be buried in a decent Christian-like burial at the discretion of my surviving friends.

SECONDLY: As touching my worldly estate where with it hath pleased God to bless me in this life, I give and bequeath in the following manner and form: First I give and bequeath to my dearly beloved wife, Mary, all that tract or part of land on which I now live, during the time of her natural life as far up as the fork of the creek bounded on the north by an east and west line crossing the creek at the fork. I further give and bequeath unto her my sorrel mare, and two milk cows, my entire stock of sheep together will all my hogs, also all my farm utensils of every description with all my household and kitchen furniture of every description. Secondly I will that all my just debts be paid.

I give further and bequeath to my daughter, Elizabeth Edwards, and the heirs of her body fifty acres of land laying to the head of the flat branch, it being fifty acres of the north end of my mountain tract to be laid off an equal width clear across the survey.

To my daughter, Belinda Scuttles, I give and bequeath the heirs of her body the remaining fifty acres of my mountain tract and joining the lands I bequeathed to Elizabeth and to be laid off in the same manner.

I further give and bequeath to my daughter, Minerva Wallace, and the heirs of her body the remaining fifty acres of my mountain tract and to join the lands bequeathed to Belinda on the south side.

I further give and bequeath to my son, Joshua, a certain piece or parcel of land lying and bounded a follows: Beginning on William Whitaker sons line near the salt log, beginning thence north with said line to a stake in the said line east of the neck of the Medel Mountain, thence west to the neck of the mountain of said middle mountain, thence to the beginning, containing fifty acres to be the same more or less.

I also give and bequeath unto my three youngest sons, James, Thomas and David all the remaining portion of my mountain land to be equally divided amongst them according to valuation, also the place where I live after the death of my wife, Mary, also my small bored rifle gun. Unto my son Jeptha I give the young mare he took away with him. I also give and bequeath to my son, Riley, and daughter Margaret the sum of thirty dollars each, and to my grandchildren Joshua and Amy Grant I give each the sum of fifteen dollars, said sum to be paid in two years from the time of my decease.

The sums above mentioned to be raised by the sale of my young brown mare and two cows and my rifle gun, and if any further remains on hand at the time of my death it is to belong to my wife, Mary.

I further nominate constitute and appoint Ed Reed and Joshua Grant as my sole executors of this my last will and testament, hereby revoking all other or former will or wills, by me at any time made and declaring this and no other to be my last will and testament. In testimony whereof I have hereunto set my hand and seal in the presence of Jacob Reed, John Wright, and Andrew Grant. February 10, 1850.

Jacob Reed, Jurat
John Wright, Jurat
Andrew Grant   Joseph Trantham

State of North Carolina
Buncombe County
July term AD 1850
The foregoing will was duly proven in open court by the oaths of Jacob Reed and John Wright, subscribing witnesses thereto and is ordered to be recorded. R. B. Vance.

TREES - In Sevier County, where I was born, there are approximately 100 species of trees, 1200 flowering plants, 50 types of ferns, and some 2000 fungi. It is said that no other Temperate Zone can boast a larger variety of trees than this region of white, red, black and chestnut oak, hickories, beech, maple, basswood, black gum, sycamore, birch, willow, cedar, pine, hemlock, chestnut, and poplar, the most prominent. Cross-cut saws and long handled axes were first used to cut down these trees, which were "snaked" down the sides of the mountain using "cant hooks and hand spikes."

TRENTHAM, BETSY - Born in 1686 in Germany, died in 1835 at age 149. As incredible as this may seem, there is too much evidence for it to be dismissed as legend. Indisputable documents exist for 132 of those 149 years -1702 to 1834. According to The American Academy of Arts and Sciences she headed the list as having been the oldest person to have lived in The United States. Drake's Dictionary of American Biography which may be found in the State Library and Archives lists her age as 154. Also, during a nationwide debate during the 1930's Betsy won hands-down as being the oldest person to have lived in the United State. Her grandson or great grandson, Lewis Peach, wrote a two page letter describing her life, saying that she was 149, while refuting the publication which said she was 154 years of age. He said she saw Queen Ann crowned April 23, 1702 when she was age 16 and was en route to the U.S.

She is supposed to have made medical history when her son, Martin Trentham, was born when she was age 65. This Martin was a spy during the American Revolution and fought under General Francis Marion in the Carolina Swamps. He allowed himself to be captured by the British where he feigned insanity to such good purpose that no restraint was put on his movements. When he gained all the information he needed, he escaped and the American troops fashioned what looked like a cannon from a pine log and took the strong-hold without firing a shot.

Betsy lost her eyesight at age 120. She later regained it as good as when she was a young girl. During her last years she had to be kept between two featherbeds to maintain her body heat. She could not distinguish between the tastes of vinegar and sugar.

Peach described her as being tall and slim, with deep set eyes, masculine features. She was never known to fret or worry. She very rarely shed a tear and always had a merry twinkle in her eye. Her intellect was clear and strong to the very last.

According to family tradition, she was been buried in an unmarked grave at the Goshen Methodist Church Cemetery near Santa Fe, Tennessee in Maury County, a short distance southwest of

Nashville. At one time there was an inscription, now illegible, which identified a Mrs. Blackburn as a descendant of the aged Mrs. Trentham. Among the stones at Goshen will be found one for Emarintha Blackburn 1838-1915 which may lend some credibility to this claim.

After learning about Martin, Jr's pretending to be insane and taking the stronghold without firing a shot, I decided with forbearers with ingenuity like that, I must be pretty special. This set me off on the long and arduous task of researching my roots.

TRENTHAM, CALEB - (1844-1937) Caleb, my grandfather's brother, fought with the Union forces during the Civil War. He and other prisoners were marched to Meanness Junction and loaded into cattle cars destined to Belle Isle prison. As the train was crossing Virginia going toward Richmond, the prisoners started singing "Pop Goes The Weasel" while kicking loose a sideboard of the cattle car with each "Pop." When they had removed enough boards they jumped board, hit the cinders, and ran into the forest as they dodged bullets. Caleb then made his way across Virginia and North Carolina on foot.

He was captured by the Cherokee Indians near New Found Gap, where they stripped him of all his clothing. Completely naked, he managed to make his way home during the deep snow. He lived to age 93.

One history of local Huskey families suggested that Caleb's mother may have been a sister to Radford Gatlin's wife.

TRENTHAM CEMETERY - In the Great Smoky Mountain National Park two miles south of Gatlinburg along highway 441 approximately one fourth mile before the Sugarlands Visitors Center is the Trentham Family Cemetery. It is located approximately 300 yards south of the Two Mile Branch The horseback riding stables are presently located some 50 yards north of the cemetery. In addition to other close family members, my grandfather and grandmother, Robert L. and Mary (Polly) Fancher Trentham, my great grandfather, William Thomas, and great grandmother, Easter Trentham, are buried there.

TRENTHAMS OF ENGLAND - Among the Trentham Nobility were Sirs, Counts, Viscounts, Knights, even a Monk. Una Kate Trentham (1877-1940) was descended from Edward III, King of England (1327-1377) As for the Trentham's in the United States, research has shown that we are less than one one-thousandth of one percent of the people of America. I have traced the Trentham name back to the 6th century and found the above listed royalty. But I suppose that royal blood is mighty thin by now.

The Trenthams take their surname from Trentham, a hamlet on the River, Trent, near Stoke, in Staffordshine, England. The surname frequently appears in the early records of the county from the 12th century.

Members of the family migrated to Shrewsbury in Shropshire, and represented that town in Parliament from about 1220. In the next century the Trenthams increased their influence, and Richard Trentham, of Shrewsbury, secured from King Henry VIII a long tenure of the Priory of Trentham, and was afterwards granted the abbey of Rochester and its lands in Staffordshire and Derbyshire. His only son, Thomas Trentham, was Lieutenant and High Sheriff of Staffordshire, and was a trusted and influential supporter of Sir Francis Walsingham. He was one of those who conducted Mary Queen of Scots to her trial. His daughter, Elizabeth, was a god-child of Queen Elizabeth, and one of her Maids of Honor, when she married Edward de Vere, the Earl of Oxford, Lord Great Chamberlain of England. (Some believe he was the true Shakespeare. See Scientific American Magazine's infrared photography research.) He gave Oxford University its library.

This alliance was important, because, after the death of the only child of the union, Henry, 18th Earl of Oxford, the greater portion of the ancient de Vere estates passed by entail to the Trenthams. Upon the deaths of Sir Francis, Sir Christopher and William Trentham, another Elizabeth Trentham, wife of Brian Cokayne, 2nd Viscount Cullen, inherited the great estates of the Trenthams, and the de Veres.

Today the Trentham Gardens, rose capital of England, along with the park and pleasure grounds are located just south of Stoke-on-

Trent. Trentham Hall, the mansion, now in ruins was described by Benjamin Disraeli in his novel, Lothair (1870) as "Brentham" the ducal home of the hero's college friend, where the stables had the best riding horses in England and the guests played croquet on the velvet lawn, watched by the duchess from a Turkish tent.

Lothair, Disraeli's book is out of print, but I fortunately was able to obtain a copy. It has been a real joy to read how the family lived in the mansion, known as Trentham hall, especially how they used their beautiful voices to sing in the evenings., (see picture of Trentham Hall)

I have in my possession a letter from the late Graham Trentham of Calgary, Canada. He says, "The Trenthams (of England) were Roman Catholics and did not support the Kings break with the church of Rome when he divorced Catherine of Aragon, married Ann Boelyn and founded the church of England. The Trenthams lost their wealth and property and never regained it - The estate eventually passing to the Duke of Suffolk in 1539. There is no explanation of how the estate came into Royal hands but it was likely seized."

I have since learned that charges were many times "trumped-up" against someone, and their property seized or they were deported to another country after being unfairly charged with a crime.

TRENTHAM, ISAAC - (1836-1931) My Grandfather's brother was appointed postmaster of the Trentville Post Office located at Forks Of The River community in the 1890's. He was said to have sold the TRENTVILLE name to a community located north of Knoxville on Hwy 11-E for a shotgun. He lived to age 96 and fathered 24 children, many of whom died in infancy. The 24 included three sets of twins.

I recall visiting in his home and seeing his very long flowing white beard and the walking stick that he kept by his chair. No matter how cold the weather, the front door to his home was always open. I thought it was so strange to have a huge fire with the door open. And at times, I can recall our front door standing open in the winter time while a huge fire roared in the chimney.

TRENTHAM, JEPTHA - We find record of more than one Jeptha. One of which we are told would marry a wife, have several children, then move on to marry another, then another, such that we have record of one of the Jeptha's having fathered 28 children. Among those 28 we have the following names: India, Lee, Frank, Larkin, Tom, Dave, Elisha, Lawson, Newton, Robert, Cindia, Kate, Leona, Delia, Sarah, two Johns, two Joes, two Shermans and Merritt. (That Cinda and Robert might be our Lucinda and Robert William.)

Also, the Jeptha, who was the son of Joseph, was not given any land as were the some of the other children, rather he was given only the mare that he took away. Sounds as if he may have been the black-sheep of the family.

TRENTHAM, JOHN - Was recorded as having been deported from England as a bonded passenger to America during Lent, 1722, for stealing a sheep. With history showing that so many charges were trumped up against people to seize their property, we will never know if that was the case with John.

In fact, we had been led to believe that no Trenthams still lived in England until my daughter, Lynda, landed at Gatwick Airport in London and spied the name Trentham at a construction site at the Airport. It took some three or four years longer to find Peter and Christine Trentham, of Roman Way, Stanford Dingley, Reading, Berkshire RG7 6LT, England. It has been a real joy to hear from them, receive a picture of the family there and to get further data of the Trentham's of England.

That family's resemblance to our clan is very interesting. At one of our Trentham reunions, that came from six or more states, Some of them, complete strangers, could have passed for identical twins. The Trentham genes seem to strongly carry many of the same characteristics.

TRENTHAM, LEVI - 1852-1936 - My father's oldest brother was in a class all by himself. I hardly know where to begin with his story. He claimed to have killed 200 bears in one year. He had the distinguished honor of driving his team of oxen [neutered bulls], named Dock and Cooly, across the Henley Street bridge in Knoxville, Tennessee, for its grand opening ceremonies. The oxen had wooden yolks across their necks.

Levi had a grocery store at Elkmont, Tennessee in which he did a credit business. He used a form of shorthand known only to him. While trying to collect for a hoop of cheese, the customer stated that he had never bought cheese but that he had bought a mill-rock. Levi then replied, "Oh, I forgot to put the hole in it.' (A picture, no less.)

Any mention of Old Glory, The U.S. Flag, reminds members of the Trentham family of Uncle Levi's incident that set a legal precedent. Many stories abound regarding this incident, but this one is straight from the horses' mouth, well, almost. Eppie Shelton Phipps, daughter of Jim and Caroline Walker Shelton, whose parents were leaders of the group who hung out at the grocery store, played a joke on Levi.

Levi, well known for his high temperament, was extremely upset that the group cut the top out of one of the pine trees located near the grocery. They said they planned to mount the United States flag in the top of the tree. Eppie said her father completely ruined his tennis shoes while climbing up and down that pine tree so many times in preparation for mounting the flag.

Andrew (Drew) Shelton, a well know photographer at the time, set up his tripod for a picture, while Caroline, his wife, was stationed to snap a picture when the flag was to be unfurled. She not being familiar with the
 equipment failed to put her head underneath the black canvass. Therefore she failed to get the picture.

Due to Levi's well known temperament, the group had a deputy stationed near him. When the flag was unfurled, Sam Henry, the postmaster, said to Levi, "Doesn't Old Glory look good waving in the breeze?" Levi replied, "To Hell with YOU, and Old Glory!" As was prearranged, the deputy stepped up and arrested Levi.

Since this was a duly appointed deputy, somehow this turned out not to be such a good joke after all. Levi was sent to Birmingham, Alabama and fined $500, a very sizeable sum in those days. He was also placed on probation for a year.

Many times Eppie heard her parents tell how they planned and executed this incident. She said they did NOT tell that they and other members of the group were later able to convince the judge that this was all a well-planned joke. They convinced him that the remark was made intentionally to provoke Levi's response and it should not be considered a crime. The $500 was eventually returned to him.

Apparently my father never knew that the money was returned, as he remarked that "Maybe Levi will learn to keep his mouth 'shet.' Eppie stated that Drew Shelton organized a Sunday School which Levi's wife, Emmaline, attended-- much to Levi's displeasure. Such was Levi's disgust that he threw her best Sunday-go-to-meeting shoes on top of the house to prevent her attending those services. He appeared to be somewhat jealous of Shelton.

Emmaline once laid out clean clothes for Levi, which needed a button. Levi asked her to sew a button on his shirt. She told him to sew it on himself. Levi countered with, "If it were Old Drew's shirt you would sew it on." But Emmaline was said to have the last word when Levi got upset. She could always stop him by saying: "Now, Levi, you have said enough!"

When Emmaline died, Levi had her grave dug near the river on their property. Their son's did not approve of the location, so they spent the night carrying water from the river to fill the grave. That proved that it was an undesirable location which made it necessary to move her grave to where the cemetery is located today. Emmaline's was the first burial at the present Elkmont cemetery.

TRENTHAMS OF TENNESSEE - If we had paid a genealogist a sizeable sum to research our Trentham family tree, we might have to pay a much larger amount of hush money. Since I approach all subjects with an open mouth instead of an open mind, you can expect some scatterbrain accounts in no particular order. After meeting a number of times with Alex Haley, author of *Roots*, I remarked one day that since Alex had such great success tracing his family, I might try tracing mine. A family member said, "Never mind, I have all there is to know."

With that challenge I began writing many letters to the North Carolina cousins asking for information about my great-great grandparents, Lucinda Bugg and Robert William Trentham. But, everyone disclaimed any knowledge of them. We knew that Lucinda Bugg had left North Carolina under cover of darkness with her young son, William Thomas Trentham (1793-1848) because her family, the aristocratic Trenthams', were planning to take her baby from her.

In North Carolina at that time a child could not be taken from a mother until it was three years old. During that three-year period, she apparently married a Mr. Bugg. Lucinda told the family in Tennessee that Robert William Trentham was the father of William Thomas, but she apparently failed to elaborate further. The family in Tennessee assumed that she had perhaps been married to a Robert William Trentham and because she was only 13 years old, the marriage had been annulled.

Because she would not elaborate further, as to *who* Robert William Trentham was left a question that was unresolved for many years. The family here always believed that something was amiss in our family tree. Apparently because she was now Lucinda Bugg, no one ever suspected that Robert William was her brother. (My uncle Caleb Trentham said that he was glad the father was a Trentham-- else we would all be bugs.) In fact, Professor Otis Trentha
m, of Mars Hill College questioned my father about this state of affairs. After Otis left, Dad said that when he got back to Robert William Trentham, he would always "hit a stump."

Finally on October 20, 1985 I got a five page letter from Evelyn Trantham Alexander (Mrs. Ben C.) of 12813 Old Dayton Pike, Soddy Daisy Tennessee. She said she did not know the story but that she could tell me of someone who could. She also said this person might tell me more than I wanted to know. (I have her letter in file.) She gave me the name and address of Victor Trantham, Sr. of Ashville, North Carolina as the source of this information. (Yes, they spell it Trantham)

For two years Victor refused to tell me the story because the families there had agreed never to tell the Tennessee Trenthams the truth. He believed he would be breaking a sacred family trust to do so. Finally, a second pig valve in his heart was leaking, and he said he did not plan to undergo further surgery. At that time I began pleading in earnest with him, because he was my last and only hope of ever learning the truth. I insisted that we already knew something was amiss and at this juncture it would not change anything. It would not affect our self esteem or our lives in any manner. Finally, the truth came out. And, as bad as it was, I shall be forever grateful to Victor Trantham, Sr. for settling this question once and for all.

After Victor related the story, I had him repeat it in front of my sister so that the families would not think that I was fabricating this story. He said the truth as he knew it was that Lucinda at perhaps age 13 had been made pregnant by either her brother, her father, or her grandfather. We find in one list of Jeptha's 28 children there was listed a Cindy, a Robert, and a David (there was more than one Jeptha) . Victor thought that Lucinda's father might have been named David. Victor elaborated further that the Trentham's did not like Mr. Bugg and "they threw him out and he came to Gatlinburg." This explains why Lucinda came here with a young child, as she surely would have had to know someone here. Don Trentham of Hugoton, Kansas went to NC and was told that he did not want to know about the Bugg family. Their reputation must have been pretty bad.

Mrs. Sadie Smathers Patton, official court reporter and state historian for the state of North Carolina, before her death at age 90, stated that Robert William was the father of William Thomas. She said that he was known as "Big Bill", and that due to some "trouble" he had to leave North Carolina. He went to Mississippi where he died on April 10, 1809. Court house records of Wilkinson County, Mississippi show he owned 425 acres of land on the River Amite. Claim # 627. File #189 showed inventory was made on 5-13-1809, naming the appraisers and Registrar who showed he had 20 head of cattle @ $20. 16 head of hogs @ $5. Plus farm and household equipment. He paid $32.50 for schooling for his children. Page 256 showed his estate on May 13, 1809 to be valued at $1,148.25. His heirs as listed on June 18, 1812 were Margaret and Martin under age 14 with Elizabeth Trentham as guardian.

Elizabeth's name became Elizabeth Trentham Perry. Her "last will and testament" was recorded April 11, 1836. It listed Margaret Roundtree as her daughter. Pamela Sussanah Trentham and Martinetta Trentham were listed as granddaughters, children of Martin. Martinetta's married name was Mrs. Seaborn Gardner who died May 5, 1852, age 16. She was buried in Terrell Cemetery. Matilda, wife of Martin, born Feb. 13, 1799 died Sept. 16, 1869. Their names were also spelled Trantham.

According to the Huskey family data it was believed that Radford Gatlin's wife, Elizabeth, was a sister to Mr. Bugg. This would then explain why Bugg came to Gatlinburg. Isaac and Caleb Trentham did lots of work for Radford Gatlin. This bit of data would also explain that close relationship.

On Christmas Day, 1996, it suddenly dawned on me that we had no idea where Lucinda was buried or whatever happened to her. I phoned Victor again and asked "Whatever happened to Lucinda?" Without a moments hesitation, he replied, "She and Bugg went to Mississippi." I failed to ask if she went to where Robert William lived in Mississippi. We need further research there. She must have stayed in Tennessee until William Thomas was of some age, or he would not have stayed alone here to have become a school teacher, postmaster, and community leader. Records show that William Thomas Trentham was appointed postmaster of White Oak Flats, now known as Gatlinburg, Tennessee, on November 11, 1840.

The tragic story of how William Thomas arrived at home after an extended trip in the woodlands with a ruptured appendix resulting in his untimely death at age 55 has distressed me considerably. Also the fact that he left a pregnant wife, Easter, and 6 children to care for is tragic. My grandfather, Robert L. at age 12, was the oldest son. Easter appears to have survived the ordeal and lived another 35 years.

Whatever the case, Lucinda's stock went up for me when I realized that she fled undercover of darkness, facing bears, panthers, rattlesnakes, and copperheads to keep her baby. I would like to have known her. For me, this finally puts a closure to the question that so long has plagued my family.

TRENTHAMS- MY FAMILY- My parents and grandparents were simple mountain folk who lived close to the soil. They were rich in good ole common horse sense when it came to knowing what to do when emergencies arose. My father was Noah H. Trentham. My Mother was Mary Jane Ogle Carr Trentham. Dad's first wife, Sophie, died of tuberculosis leaving him with five children: Orlie, Lillie, Mack, Munsey and Willie. Mother's first husband, Amos Carr, died of a possible ruptured appendix, leaving her with three children: Ollie, Mayme and Wesley Carr. Mother moved back to her parents home in the Sugarlands after her husband's death. It seems my Dad's excuse to go to Ephraim Ogle's home to see Mary Jane was to buy timber. Since my Mother was tall and skinny, her brothers said that Dad went looking for timber and found a sapling.

At any rate, Dad had five children, Mother had three children, and then there was five of us: his, hers, and our children. I am one of "ours." We are: Johnny Kate, Gladys Janet, Noah Harmon, Bonnie Lynn and Samuel Ephraim Trentham. We thirteen Trentham children were never all together at one time, because the older ones were married and some were living in distant states when we were born. Just the five of us made up our family as we were growing up.

The Depression had no major impact on our lives, as we had everything we needed on the farm. Dad lost some money in the bank, but he only mentioned it one time. My parents got little formal education, but they proved that one could gain a liberal education outside the classroom. My Father was born in 1867, 45 years before the first school was established in Gatlinburg, However, he helped me work second year algebra and geometry. He could not put math in XYZ equations, but he could explain to me the principle and I could put it in the proper form. He helped me to be the valedictorian of my high school graduating class. Dad learned to read using the Knoxville Journal every night by the light of a kerosene lamp. My daughter has the little brass lamp my father bought in 1890 for fifteen cents at the Charles A. Ogle Store in Gatlinburg. The lamp was priced at twenty-five cents but because the handle was loose, he got it for fifteen cents.

He was an engineer or surveyor who helped abstract titles to the properties of what is now The Great Smoky Mountain National Park. Park officials told me after his death that Dad's photographic memory was put to great use when the little hillside farms needed deeds quickly in the race between North Carolina and Tennessee to acquire land as quickly as possible.

I have fond memories of my Father. Most memorable were the many tales told around the fireside at nighttime, and his mellow bass voice singing the old hymns. My father gave us a home that I wish every child could share...the safety, the love, the contentment and well being. My father was a deacon in the Baptist church and taught the first Sunday school class I can recall attending. I can't recall anything that he taught, but I do remember the smile that he always gave us wee folk.

Dad lived to age 82 and mother to 79. Those eggs, ham, sausage or bacon, gravy and hot biscuits every morning in no way seemed to affect their health. Even at that advanced age both were mentally alert, with never a mention of failing memory as we are hearing almost daily among today's seniors.

Mother was born in the what is now The Great Smoky Mountain National Park in Wears Valley, Sevier County, Tennessee near where the famous Walker sisters lived. In fact she spent many night's at the Walker sister's home.

She took a midwife course and later delivered approximately 195 babies without losing either a mother or baby. Charging only $5 for her services, many times she came home to return with sheets, clothing or other needs for families with newborn babies. My two older sisters always hated to hear that midnight knock on the door for what we called her "Rabbit Catching." This meant they would have to cook breakfast the following morning.

The story was told many times that when I was approximately two years old one such knock came, and I raised such a ruckus that the man whose wife was soon to be delivered had to carry me on his hip around the mountainside by lantern light so my mother could go in peace. In fact, he teased me many times during the past few years regarding that caper of mine. Having two older sisters, I never had to help with cooking breakfast when Mother needed to be away. In fact I was never allowed to cook but one meal before

I was married. I burned and ruined more food the first year of married life than we were able to eat.

I believe my Mother was one of the most saintly, God-fearing mothers ever. She lived her religion. She taught us not to steal a pin. We were never allowed to use just one slang word such as "gosh" or "darn." But she said "pshaw" which I believe was just a corruption of another not-so-nice word. I was always proud to hear her pray in public as her thoughts were so beautiful. Mother told me that before I was born she prayed that I would be a boy and would become a minister. I often wondered if my husband of 35 years, Rev. Ray T. Myers, was the answer to her prayer. In fact, my sister Kate's husband, Hulett Stogner, also became a minister, so that Mother had two ministers in her family.

I can never forget the lectures from Mother that always preceded any public function I attended. She told me among other things that she would rather see me in my grave than to see me have a baby out of wedlock. That coming from your Mother will certainly get your attention. But I did not disappoint her in that regard. With a heart of gold I will have to say that she was the BEST.

I have led an interesting and very very busy life. Would hardly know where to begin trying to recall a few of the more interesting highlights. Was valedictorian of my high school graduating class. Was Co-Editor-In Chief of our High School Newspaper. Was chosen by Pi Beta Phi High School officials to demonstrate math skills of our school for the Tennessee State Board of Education in order for the school to get state accreditation. Math problem after problem was given me while at the blackboard and I never made one error. Found a three carat diamond stick tie pin, was given $1 reward for returning it to its owner. Won the Tennessee Homecoming '86 grand prize for best best essay. Was Nielsen rating person for five years. Chances was one in 60,000 of being chosen. Represented 200,000 people each time I watched a program. Was business manager for the summer time Grand Ole Opry Show in Gatlinburg including Archie Campbell, and sons, Sat in on the very first ever session of Hee Haw, a TV series that ran for eight years. Archie Campbell gathered a group of us and acted out a production of the show, to ask our opinion of the show that he was helping to plan for TV. We performed so poorly, I hardly gave it a chance to make the show that it later proved to be. Chet Atkins, Porter Waggoner, Joy King, Ocie Ownby among others. Made every motion to organize The Madison Avenue Baptist Church, Maryville, TN and named it. It now has over 2000 members. Had twenty-nine years flying time with Delta Air Lines, visited the beautiful cathedral of Notre Dame in Montreal, Canada, two trips to Hawaii, saw the Magnificient Christmas Spectacular at Radio City Music Hall in NY. Two trips to Las Vegas where I hit a jackpot where money rolled in the floor. Won hulu dance award in Hawaii. Won my first beauty contest after age 65. Got Charles Barkley's autograph while in Los Angeles Airport. The late Carl Sagan, World renowned Scientist introduced me to Alex Haley. Alex and wife Myron later flew from their California home to meet me regarding my Smoky mountain stories.. Won a new 1973 Mustang car in a drawing. Won many spelling contests, some with only college professors competing. Published one book entitled "During a Near Death Experience, I Saw God.". Due to my persistence and ingenuity made legal history when suing The United States Automobile Club. Our case then studied in The University of Tennessee Law School. The late Governor Frank Clement introduced me the then Vice President of The United States, the late Hubert H. Humphrey. Attended Governor Ned McWherter's inaugural ball, danced with the governor. Then vice president, Dan Quayle was guest speaker at grandson's graduation. My three children got scholarships to the University of Tennessee. Accompanied actor Rock Hudson and Al Gore, Sr in Oak Ridge parade, and was married this past 14 years to Polish Baron Roy G. Ruszkowski who passed away in 2001. Am retired from Blount Memorial Hospital and at age 81,staying as busy as a bee in a tar-bucket

TRENTHAM, ROBERT-The result of researching his family's involvement in the American Civil War is the creation of his production *In Thinking of America* which he has toured to 120 cities across the United States. He has sung with regional theater and opera companies throughout the country and has sung solo at the finest American concert halls including Carnegie Hall and the Kennedy Center. Many songs from his Compact Disc recording

Epitaph - A Collection of Civil War Songs are heard on the Civil War Preservation Trust's multimedia exhibit The Civil War Explorer at National and State Parks throughout the country and on The Civil War Experience™, a reference CD-ROM developed by SouthPeak Interactive™ in conjunction with The History Channel® and the Civil War Preservation Trust®. In Thinking of America debuted at the Gettysburg Civil War Heritage Days Festival. For further information on In Thinking of America or Epitaph, write Spring River Music, 848 Woodland Avenue, #25, Ojai, CA 93023 or e-mail rdtrentham@aol.com.

TROUSER WORM - If a group of men were out somewhere together, and a pregnant woman walked by, rather than say she was pregnant, they would say that she had been stung by a "trouser worm." In the very early days many pregnant women would not allow themselves to be seen. I've read where they would come to their front door and only allow their head to be seen.

TRUNDLE BEDS - were laced with sinew ropes on which a corn shuck or straw tick mattress was placed. Due to its smaller size the trundle bed very easily slipped underneath the regular-sized bed to which it was attached. This space-saving piece of furniture was a great space saver in early days and is not a bad idea today when hordes of relatives come visiting.

TUBERCULOSIS - Eat watercress and get lots of sunshine.

TUMBLEBUGS - We had great fun harassing those little guys which we found only in the barn yard. Unless you live where there are farm animals you may never have the pleasure of meeting Mr. or Mrs. Tumblebug. Also known as dung beetles, they laid their eggs in animal waste. They rolled the eggs into a perfectly round ball, then set out rolling it to bury it in some soft dirt. It was a very interesting to see a large bug, perhaps one and one-half inches long, trying to roll a ball at least four times his size. The ball was perhaps just a bit smaller than a golf ball. Sometimes the bug flipped a-- over teakettle while trying to push this ball. The ball's huge size in comparison, showed their strength and determination, no matter what we children did to them. We did not deter them. What we did not know at the time was that their babies were in those balls. But we never saw them bury one. The larva eats all the waste of the ball in its early stages before emerging to the outside world.

TURKEY GEORGE - George built a log enclosure in Wears Valley and trapped ten wild turkeys one night. When he stepped in among them the next morning, they gave him such a beating that he was always know thereafter as "Turkey George."

TURKEY SPURLING - Law enforcement officers long suspected Mr. Spurling of having a moonshine still somewhere on his property. Each time they made a search he was said to go outside and gobble like a turkey. As a result, he became known as Turkey Spurling. If he had a still, it was so well concealed they were never able to find it. Someone asked him about the product. He said it was not made to drink; it was made to sell.

TURPENTINE - (See also **DIARRHEA**) Used for birth control in the mountains. I do not know the amount taken, but they had to take lots of castor oil along with it. Two or three drops of turpentine will usually immediately stop a bad case of diarrhea, so that enough to cause an abortion must have been a sizeable dose. (2) When someone took what was called "painter's colic", I understand that turpentine was held to the navel, but I would not recommend it. (3) When our cows had what was called "hollow-tail" or "Hollow-head", they held turpentine to their navel as a remedy. (4) When mischievous boys decided to send a stray dog on the fast track out of town they "turpentined him" on the rear end section.

TURTLES - We were told that if a turtle got hold of us, it would not turn us loose until it thundered. When wading the streams, we steered clear of the turtles. The mischievous boys would build a fire on the back of a dry land terrapin just to see him move along very fast. Ray T. fed one so much buck-shot that it could not move. A friend, who had a construction company, dissected the shell of a turtle and found it to be of such unique design that he used the design in his construction business.

TYPHOID - It is said typhoid could be cured by tea of boneset (a wild plant found in the Smokies.)

U

ULCERS - (See **STOMACH TROUBLE**)

UPPING BLOCK - Many early home had an "upping block" used especially by women to mount their horses or mules. It was usually located in the front yard near the home. Side saddles and very long dresses with lots of petticoats made the upping blocks a necessity.

URINARY TRACT INFECTION - Cinnamon tea. (2) Cranberry juice. (3) Eat pumpkin seeds or bruise and simmer the seeds in the hulls to make a tea.

V

VINSANT, BERT- One of my favorite mountain people for many years wrote a special column called "Strolling" for the Knoxville-News Sentinel. And stroll he did. He strolled up all these hills and hollers looking for something interesting. He especially enjoyed the "haint tales" of mountain people. This and our interest in parapsychology was a subject he could not discuss freely with everyone. He and others spent the night in so-called haunted houses with no spectacular results. One of his columns I really enjoyed told of a young man who went far back into the hills and got a job at a logging camp where a man had been killed late that afternoon. Hired on the spot, he was told that he would have to share his room with another worker. When he arrived at his assigned room, he found his roommate already in bed apparently soundly asleep. So as not to disturb his roommate, he very quietly put away his few belonging and got into bed. Very shortly the door opened and two men tiptoed into the room. They sat quietly and reverently whispering in low toes about someone being killed that afternoon. Realizing that his bedfellow had not moved, he eased his hand over to find a very cold clammy hand. With that revelation he came out over the foot of the bed with the sheet totally up in front of him and went straight out the window and to the ground below with the two visitors right behind him. He was caught three-fourths of a mile away. He was still carrying the sheet. Three changes of clothing were necessary before work time the next morning. Perhaps the moral of that story was "If they don't snore, go out the door"

When I read this one, Ray T. had asked me to turn out the light so that he could go to sleep. I promised to do so as soon as I had read the above article. I did not know then that if I really get tickled while lying down, I could not stop laughing. I was totally unable to stop laughing until it became serious. After much effort on my part without success, Ray had to resort to some rather very stern advice to help me to stop. I told Bert what happened to me, so that he repeated the article in the following Sunday's newspaper. It seems that my sister, Kate, chanced to read his column and ruined her make-up on her way to church.

One day I got a special request to go to Bert's desk at the newspaper office in Knoxville.. With absolutely no clue as to why he wanted to see me, he looked me straight in the eye and asked how much longer he had to live. Dumbfounded by such a question, I calmly stated the first thought that came to mind, "If you have any big projects you want to finish, I'd get to work on them!" He went straight to work on another book that he finished or almost finished at the time of his death. I was caught so off-guard with that question that I was unable to come up with something less provocative. I really hope my comment did not hasten his demise.

VOICE (TO RESTORE)- Beat the white of one egg. Add the juice of one lemon and a small amount of sugar. Take a teaspoon every half-hour.

VOMITING - Peach tea. Recent: Syrup of ipecac will induce vomiting. Check first with the poison control center.

VARICOSE VEINS - Soak a piece of cheesecloth in witch hazel and wrap around the affected areas.

W_____

WALKER, CAS - Cas Walker was a very colorful character from Sevier County. His family was so poor that he never owned a pair of shoes until he was 8 years old. He walked five miles to school across the hillsides. At age 8 he started trapping raccoons and bought his first pair of shoes. He was one of 12 children who were raised on a $200-a-year peach crop. At age 14 he went to Kentucky and worked for 7 years. He slaved 12 hours a day for $2.50 each day. By 1924 he had saved enough money to open his first grocery store in Knoxville. Three prosperous nearby groceries dwarfed "Walker's Cut-rate Grocery." At age 21 he used his ingenuity to attract customers. A sign at his entrance read: "Don't Laugh at Me - You were once Small!" His approach appealed to the underdog. He lived all his life in a house that cost $8000. He drove a small car. Every Saturday he advertised that 10 chickens would be thrown off the roof of his store into the hands of anyone who could catch them. Delaying this event for an hour, he served free popcorn so salty that customers were required to buy soft drinks. Sometimes 1000 people would wait for those free chickens. Cas became a multimillionaire. He owned a chain of 22 supermarkets in three states, 19 other profitable businesses, and 73 parcels of valuable real estate in Knoxville. He sponsored radio and television shows that featured local country and bluegrass musicians. I recall hearing Dolly Parton, perhaps 10-years-old at the time, sing on his radio programs. I said then that she would someday make her mark in the world. He never lost sight of the drive that helped him become rich. He said, "You must have a lot of determination, because a man determined to make a million dollars is too stingy to lose it." So that is the formula!

WALKER SISTERS - The locally famous Walker Sisters were the daughters of "Hairy John" N. Walker, a Civil War veteran, and his wife, Margaret Jane King Walker. "Hairy John" grew a beard to distinguish himself from all the other John Walkers. He, along with my grandfather, Ephraim Ogle and my great grandfather, William "Buck Ogle" helped to build the present Little Greenbrier School preserved by the park service today. Nine of the Walker children attended this school. Their mother, a typical mountain woman, bore 11 children in a 24-year period. She doctored the family with herbs. To emphasize the family's medical self-reliance, John once stated that he had only spent fifty cents for the services of a doctor - when one of his sons had measles. Mrs. Walker faced danger with great courage. She showed great ingenuity when a weasel latched onto her thumb. She simply walked to a nearby washtub, thrust the weasel into the water. She knew that it would soon have to turn her loose or drown. Needless to say, the weasel did not drown.

The sisters were Margaret Ann, Mary Elizabeth "Polly", Martha Ann, Louisa Susan, Hettie Rebecca, Nancy Melinda, and Sarah Caroline. I first visited in their home during the early 1940's. My mother was born a short distance from their home and spent many nights with them. Except for Sarah Caroline, who married Jim Shelton, and Nancy Melinda, who died in 1931, these sisters remained on their rocky farm all of their lives.. They resisted selling their property, bucking the United States Government while The Great Smoky Mountain National Park developed around them. On January 22, 1941, however, the sisters sold their 122.8 acres for $4,750. While it was appraised for more, they had asked $15,000. They were allowed to live, farm, and cut firewood the remainder of their lives. (Except for Lem Ownby, no other person, including my family was allowed to break a twig of any tree after we sold.) In 1956 the Saturday Evening Post carried an article that caused tourists to beat a path to their door. At first they put up a sign saying "Keep Out." They soon changed the sign to read "Visitors Welcome" when they began to sell apples, coverlets, and the poems that Louisa wrote.

Their life style, the same as our great great-grandfather's, was an example of the old ways passing from generation to generation. While most of us chose to adopt modern life styles, they chose to stay with the old ways. This made them unique in that time. Great tragedy befell both Polly and Martha when they planned to wed. Their intended grooms each met with accidental deaths somewhere in the woodlands.. Polly was so devastated emotionally that her grief was an overriding factor for the remainder of her life.

Margaret Ann, the oldest daughter, was considered to be the boss. This was the norm back then. For some reason she chose to be a spinster, or old-maid, as we described them. She made every effort to influence all the sisters to accept her way of thinking. She apparently had little influence on the brothers, James Thomas, William Wiley, and John Henry, all of whom married. Giles Daniel left home at an early age and joined a branch of the military service and we have no further record of him. Both young men whom her sisters had planned to marry met with accidental death in the woodlands.

Living off the land required much ingenuity and hard, hard work. Forest fires seemed to be the only fearsome thing in those hills that could not be dispelled by relying on dogs and guns. Women spent their lives digging in the earth with a mattock, planting, and cultivating all the food they ate. Throughout their lives the Walker sisters continued to wear long-sleeved ankle-length dresses, high top shoes, and sunbonnets. For many years five spinning wheels were running at the same time, weaving the cloth for their dresses, suits, bed clothing, and saddle blankets for their mules. Wool was produced from the herd of sheep they kept. In latter years their dresses were made from fabrics bought in the stores for summer wear. They returned to their home-woven linsey-woolsey for winter wear. Washday found clothes boiling in a big black iron washpot in the yard. When sending a nephew some socks, Hettie remarked, "Guess it ain't every soldier in Germany that can say that his old-maid aunts raised his socks on a rocky mountain-side for him." The sheep were said to refuse to come in to be sheared if anyone wearing pants was there. A visitor once asked the sisters if they would mind if he smoked. Margaret replied, "It'll only make two people sick, you and me."

Their father, "Hairy John", built most of their furniture, including their five spinning wheels. He also built all of the outbuildings including: a barn, corn crib, smoke house, applehouse, spring house, and blacksmith shop. In addition to the poultry yard, there was an ash hopper, a tar kiln, drying rack, a charcoal-making pit, and the palings enclosing the garden. Their apple orchard was said to contain twenty-three varieties of apples, while the yard contained more than thirty varieties of roses. The one building that was missing was a privy or "Out-House." The women used the woodland below the house while the men used the woods above the house. I recall when the WPA (Work Projects Administration) built "free" outhouses on all our properties. At this time and when family members offered to build an outhouse for the sisters, they refused. They said it would have an odor. They also said that people would see it thereby causing them embarrassment.

Even though early cooking was done in the six-foot wide fireplace, their meals were always elaborate and of greater variety than was found in most early homes. Corn bread, baked in a Dutch-oven, was covered with fresh churned butter. Life was made easier when the they acquired two wood-burning cook-stoves, two chests of drawers, a sewing machine, tables, and chairs. The sisters purchased a hand-held grist mill to grind corn for their cornbread rather than having to carry it a great distance to a water-powered mill. This grist mill was also used to grind corn for their old mule whose teeth were bad. This mule grew so cantankerous or bull-headed in his old days that the sisters could not use him to plow the garden or drag in firewood. They had to have a relative come to work for them, saying that "a Tennessee Mule" had to be handled special, because none of them could cuss!"

The housefly is not a modern pest. It was a problem for the Walker Sisters before the invention of screen wire and air conditioning. To stay cool in summer, doors and windows had to be open. Of course, flies gathered around the dinner table. A "fly-sweep" made of thin strips of newspaper fastened to a pole and mounted on a contraption that sat on the floor underneath the table was pedaled by foot, shooing the flies away.

The living room was also the bedroom. Five three-quarter size beds and a trundle bed underneath one of them provided places to sleep. My mother mentioned sleeping on the trundle bed while spending the night there when she was a child. Once each year the walls of the house were "scalded" and fresh newspapers covered with brightly-colored pictures cut from catalogs and calendars were applied. Nails were driven into the logs holding every item imaginable. Even though it was mass confusion, the sisters seemed to know exactly where every item was located. Slats were nailed to the rafters holding shoeboxes and baskets filled with old letters and records. Nothing, absolutely nothing was ever allowed to go to waste.

Most of the Walker sisters' furnishings and personal belongings were purchased from their heirs and are presently in storage in The Great Smoky Mountain National Park. Someday the artifacts are to be displayed in a museum located at Occonaluftee Visitors Center. My last visit to this homesite was in 1997. The park service has kept the home, barn, and spring house in excellent repair. Tourists are welcome to visit the site. To reach the site, drive U. S. Highway 321 (Little River Gorge Road) to the historic Little Greenbrier School House near Metcalf Bottoms picnic area. From the school house, one can walk the old road approximately one mile to the Walker home.

The father, John Walker died at age 79 in 1921
The mother, Margaret Jane King Walker died at age 62 in 1909
Nancy died at age 51 in 1931
Polly died at age 70 in 1945
Hettie died at age 58 in 1947
Martha died at age 74 in 1950
Margaret died at age 92 in 1962
Louisa died at age 81 in 1964
Caroline Walker Shelton died in 1966

WARTS - Charming warts was a great pastime in the mountains. Children who had warts would seek out a wart charmer at church gatherings, family reunions, and other events. Adults occasionally had their warts charmed as well. Charmers were usually older people, who kept the process secret. Wart charmers insisted the secret could be passed only to a member of the opposite sex. I suppose it has something to do with the positive-negative poles. I could not stand to be left out in the cold regarding how this was done, so I found a man who was willing to tell me. The charmer used his or her finger to draw a circle around the wart. He or she started in a clockwise direction seven times and then counterclockwise seven times. As the charmer went around the wart with the finger, he or she moved his lips counting. If the wart did not come off in two or three weeks, the "patient" was to return for a second treatment. I think it is the power of suggestion and the patients mind that does the work. We had many more remedies for removing warts. (2) Apply castor oil nine nights. (3) Mix soda and castor oil and apply. (4) Steal your mother's dishrag and bury it. When the rag rots, the warts will be gone. (5) Rub the wart with a sliced onion. Bury the onion. (6) While I've never had a plantar wart on the bottom of my foot, I understand they can be quite painful. Old-timers used a single application of linseed oil and Podophyllum in lanolin. They kept it on seven days. This was said to take it off. (7) Recent: Rub the inside of a pineapple peel on the wart. (8) Apply juice of aloe plant. (9) Wet an aspirin and bind it on the wart for three days. (10) Rub the inside of a banana peel.

WATER-CLOSET - Better known in early days as "W. C." Many years from now young people seeing the letters "W C" posted on a door would have to be informed that it meant "water-closet" or restroom. The first W C model came with a wooden seat with a cistern and a valve for flushing. Before this everyone could go behind the barn, behind a tree or to the outhouse.

WATER PURITY TEST - MOUNTAIN STYLE - Put one cup of water in a clean jar. Add 2 tablespoons of sugar. Tighten the lid, and place in a warm lighted room. If the water remained clear after 9 days, it was declared safe to use. (I doubt this would meet today's standards.) We children had a better one than that. If the water flowed over seven rocks, we declared that it was safe to drink. (I am sure the good Lord was watching over us!)

WATER WITCHING- (see DOWSING)

WEANER CABINS - Very early on a small cabin was built close to the main house to wean the bride from their families. The newly married couple lived there the first year of their married life, until they built a home of their own, or until another sibling married and needed the cabin. When a covered roof area connected the two buildings, this area was called a dog-trot.

WEASEL - A blood-thirsty little critter about the size of a cat that killed poultry, mice, rabbits, and birds. I do not think ours was the type that gave ermine fur. If so, I never heard of anyone using their furs. They seemed to kill just for the fun of it. Many times they left dead bodies without eating them. If a weasel bit a person, the best way to get him loose was to hold him under water until he drowned.

WEATHER - Sights and sounds were significant factors in predicting the weather. If the fire made popping sounds, we knew it was going to snow.

COLD WEATHER: Large groups of birds eating lots of food on the ground also usually meant snow. When we could hear the train whistle at our home in the park - the train being at Townsend - we knew much colder weather was on the way. When first you hear a katydid, mark the date on your calendar. Frost is just six weeks away. He beats his two hind legs together to make his tune, so we children were told. Others claim that the tip of his front wings are used to make this tune. Many local people make much of the fogs in August. They are said to indicate the number and severity of upcoming winter snows. If snow does not stick to the trees, it indicates the snow will stay longer on the ground. This reasoning being that the temperature has fallen below freezing and the cold spell is more likely to stay. If the snow sticks to the trees, it indicates that the cold front may have moved on somewhat. This will allow the snow to melt a bit and will stick to the trees. As outlined above, this phenomenon was: "No sticky, stick. Sticky, no stick snows."

Find a wooly worm. If it is totally black, expect a very cold snowy winter. If black on each end and yellow in the center, expect a warm period during the middle of the winter. If yellow on each end and black in the center, expect warm then cold and warm winter again. The weather can change quickly, as hikers in our Smoky Mountain have found. Without adequate protection a thunderstorm can reduce the body temperature sufficiently to induce hypothermia and death. Almost unknown is the bizarre behavior that mountaineers say sometimes results from freezing to death. In later stages as the skin freezes, it burns so much that it causes the victim to strip off nearly nude.

STORMS: If the old wizard owl began to make different kinds of noises, a storm was on the way. Old timers believed if thunder occurred in January, it would likely frost in May. They were careful about putting out young plants too early. The "Weather Swan" (a glass barometer - a bulb- shaped body with an open-ended spout) was filled with water. In a low-pressure system the water is pushed down in the main body and up in the spout. If a high-pressure system is approaching, the water returns to the main body of the swan indicating good weather. Nearby tornadoes have been known to force the water to overflow the spout, so that more water must to be added.

My grandfather, Ephraim Ogle, and some friends were setting up camp near the Chimney Camp ground location in what is now The Great Smoky Mountain National Park. While lean-to's were being built, someone built a camp fire. Grandpa noted that the smoke from the campfire went down on the ground moving in zigzag fashion like a snake. Realizing that they were located in a dangerous spot he persuaded them to leave just before a water spout hit that area in such force that they could not have survived. Sometimes it pays to listen to old-timers.

RAIN- If the new moon is tilted so that it would hold water, the next two weeks will to be wet. If the new moon is tilted so that it appears the water has already poured out, the next two weeks will to be dry, no rain. Cows lying down in the pasture field meant rain. If half are up and half down, it means 50/50 chance. A halo around the moon indicated approaching rain or snow. The number of stars within that circle indicated the number of days until it arrives. A croaking frog is a good sign of rain. They croak louder if a storm approaches. Tulips and dandelions close their petals when rain is imminent while pitcher plants open their petals. When you see the underside of the tree leaves, expect rain. If the sun goes down behind a cloud on Sunday evening expect rain by Wednesday. If smoke rises-fair weather. If smoke stays near the ground, it is a sign of rain. If rain falls while the sun is shining, it is a sign that rain will fall again at the same time tomorrow. Surely everyone knows the "Evening red and morning gray, sets the traveler on the way, Evening gray and morning red brings down rain upon his head."

Early morning fog and heavy dew, expect a fair day. The chirping of a cricket can help you discern the temperature. Count the number of chirps in 15 seconds, then add 37 to that number and you have the Fahrenheit temperature. (An Example 40 chirp in 15 seconds plus 37 equals 77 degrees Fahrenheit. Crickets do not chirp if it is below 40 degrees. Nature's early warning signs are considered accurate within approximately 10 to 20 hours. These signs may not always to be accurate, but you'd to be surprised at how often they come close.

And now for my weather forecast, for the upcoming winter: "Colder than a well-digger's wallet."

WEATHER ROCK - I once built a "Weather-Rock" that is 100% accurate for weather predictions. It is never known to fail. It surpasses modern technology. The secret lies in the line and the weight of the rock. To build a weather rock, find 3 strong poles about 4 feet long. Set them up outside, arranged in tepee fashion, tying the tops together with the bottom ends firmly planted in the ground. Find a rock weighing at least one pound and a stout rawhide cord. Tie the cord to the center top of the teepee, allowing it to come about three-fourths way toward the ground. Then fasten the cord to the rock. Print the following instructions on a large flat stone:

If you see:
1. Shadow underneath the rock: Clearing and sunny.
2. No shadow underneath the rock: Cloudy, overcast.
3. Rock wet and dripping: Rain
4. Rock swinging to and fro: Heavy wind.
5. White stuff on rock: Snow.
6. Rock jumping up and down: Earthquake
7. Rock missing: Flood.

WEAVING - The rhythmic beating of a loom was heard in many of the mountain homes, including our own. We wove rugs, place-mats, scarves, etc. I never learned how to put on a warp, but wove lots of the beautiful pieces.

WEBS, SPIDER - (see INDIANS)

WEDDINGS - Weddings were usually simple affairs held in the home with a small group of friends and immediate family in attendance. Bridal showers were very rare. Family members provided flowers, decorations, and food for the guests. Either a minister or justice of the peace officiated. Alcohol was rarely served. If it was, there was definitely a punchbowl "with" and one "without." My wedding took place on September 27,1941. My sister, decorated the beautiful altar and arranged the flowers. The Rev. Edd Watson performed our evening ceremony. Rev. Watson had known me since childhood and took advantage of the situation to give us some words of wisdom that ran several minutes. I recall how badly Ray's hand's were shaking from fright during the ceremony.

Sometimes friends and relatives played practical jokes on newly married couples. Some of Ray's friends took him into the mountains the day of our wedding. They brought him back so late that some of the guests had gone home before he arrived. I decided the wedding might not take place. Our two-week honeymoon was spent at The New Gatlinburg Inn (the same hotel where Rocky Top was later written.)

Even though we registered under an assumed name, our bed was short-sheeted, then filled with salt. The bathroom door was removed and a speaker was put in the air duct. Music was played to us until 3:00 a.m., at which time other guests complained that the music was carrying throughout the ventilating system of the entire hotel. When I discovered the music was coming from the front office, I gave the manager just thirty minutes to remove the speaker before I pushed it down the three-story heating and ventilation shaft. Only then did the guilty parties, Rex Parton and Wendell Moore, beg for mercy. They said they did not want to pay for the speaker if it fell. Otherwise, we received royal treatment with breakfast in bed and all the other amenities. When we checked out two weeks later, the hotel owner, Rellie Maples, made us a wedding gift of the two-weeks of charges. This was perhaps due to all the fun they had at our expense.

Those pranks were simple compared to what had been originally planned for us. We escaped this plot by a whisker. Some friends planned to kidnap us for rides down the street. I was to ride in a wash tub and Ray was to ride on a rail. From there we were to be separated for a period of time. My brother, Harmon, was part of that plan. I was able to escape from him. Some of our wedding guests, who were not aware of this plan, did not understand our quick get-a-way. One very pious guest remarked that "we sure were in a hurry..........!"

Regarding the tradition of riding the bride in a tub and the groom on a rail, one unhappy groom, who was a victim of this cruel hoax, told his captors, "If it weren't for the honor of the thing, I would just as soon walk."

Very few African-American weddings today use the traditional ceremony of "Jumping the Broom." It symbolizes leaving all the past behind and starting anew, a clean slate. While none of our folk ever used this ceremony, we nearly always used that expression. Rather than saying "getting married," we would say they are "jumping the broom."

WELLS - Before city water became available, people had to dig wells. They were hard to come by, however. Many times they were dug by hand. Gutters were attached to outbuildings funneling rain water into barrels or tanks, called cisterns. Pennies and silver were tossed into the water to help keep it clear. This could well to be the basis for today's "Wishing Wells" in which tourists are encouraged to toss in coins. It may be why the wishing wells are crystal clear. Before the merits of dowsing for wells became known for accuracy, well diggers often just tossed their hat in the air and dug wherever it fell.

WHITE CAPS - From 1892 to 1899 Sevier County, Tennessee, where my parents lived, experienced a reign of terror perhaps unequaled anywhere else in the United States. Lewd women were brought to court with someone always swearing them to be the "prayingest" woman in the church, so that the judge declared his court to be "hamstrung!" What to do? What to do? So, a group agreed to band together to "beat hell out of them!" They wore white sheets over their heads with holes cut out for eyes, nose, and mouth. They also wore overcoats turned wrong side out to prevent identification. At first driving these immoral women from the community met with approval. Soon anyone at all might to be the next victim of attack of these hooded characters. Soon unmerciful whippings or home burnings became routine. The entire populace was "between the devil and the deep blue sea." No true bill could ever to be returned in the court against these perpetrators since they always made sure some of their group was on the jury. Some people left the state rather than testify against them. The situation became so bad that something had to be done. A group calling themselves the "blue-bills" organized to try to stop them. For one year there were murders among these two groups. Finally when two men named Wynn and Tipton were convicted and sentenced "to be hung by the neck until dead," it put a stop to this bloodshed. My father, age 32 at that time, witnessed this hanging. The two men confessed, explaining details, so there was no doubt as to their guilt. My father said that there was such a mob of people at the courthouse for the hanging that he had to climb a tree to see the execution. But he said he would never climb another tree for such a purpose. I am surprised that no movie has been made of this terrible ordeal. I am glad that someone put a stop to this state of affairs before I made my appearance. Any way, my father's family escaped any confrontation during that time.

WHITE-EYED - If mountain folk became faint from field work in the sun such that they became pale around the eyes and mouth, they were described as being "white-eyed." This is an expression we never hear today. Then again, perhaps we do not work that hard anymore.

WHITE WASH - Many farmers whitewashed their trees to reflect the sunlight away from the bark. This was supposed to hold back the budding and blooms until all frost had passed. We always used buttermilk with lime. Other people mixed skim milk with lime.

WIDOW - In early days if a widow was left with small children, the neighbors helped, feeling it was a disgrace to let anyone go to the poor house. They built houses, raised barns, and cleared fields. Unlike today, the entire community worked together to help her.

WILDERNESS TRAIL - Of the many lovely motor tours that lead from Gatlinburg into The Great Smoky Mountain National Park, one of the least known is the Wilderness Trail. This beautiful drive begins on Airport Road, and proceeds through the Cherokee Orchard. Traveling one-way on a winding road through some spectacular views of the valley below, the trail provides magnificent views of age old trees that give the feeling of being entirely away from civilization. The trail ends on Roaring Fork Road. So impressed with the beauty of this drive one four-year-old granddaughter was moved to say, "This is so beautiful, it must be the driveway to God's house." However, after spending the day at Dollywood with granddaughters, Andrea and Jennifer, I told them there was one more thing that I wanted them to enjoy. That was the Wilderness Trail. The last leg of this trail is two very narrow car tracks hanging on the side of a very steep mountain side overlooking the deep ravine below. When we finally reached level ground below on Roaring Fork Road, Andrea exclaimed, "Whew, I thought we'd never see dry land again!" Only then did I realize just how frightening that last segment of the trail had been for them.

WILLOW TREES - Many old-timers truly believed that if a person set out a willow tree, he or she would die when the tree grew to the height of the person who planted the tree. I set out a willow tree at our new home in Gatlinburg. My father-in-law was furious with me for doing such a stupid thing, reminding me of my fate. We sold that property and moved back to Maryville because of the heavy traffic in that area. The dear lady who purchased our home, apparently healthy at that time, died a few months later.

WILLS - Many early "Last Will and Testaments" were hand written expressing the likes and dislikes of the deceased. One man's will read that he did not want his brother, Oscar, to have a d---thing. He said he had buried $600 dollars, but his relatives could count it when it comes up. He also said he did not want any dumb-headed preacher to put a roof on the meeting house, in fact to watch him like a buzzard.

WITCH - BELL WITCH OF TENNESSEE - Adams, Tennessee, located north of Nashville in Robertson County, is the site of the most authentic documentation of any witch or supernatural events in all of American history. It all began in 1804 when the John Bell family moved to Robertson County from North Carolina. By 1817 John was an influential member of the community and shared his nice home with his wife and nine children. At first skeptical neighbors' curiosity led them to spend the night in the Bell home. They heard gnawing, scratching, knocking, and gulping sounds. Soon covers flew off the beds. If they held on to them they were left holding just the corners. The Bell children's hair was pulled. Betsy's face was slapped until it was red. Then the spirit began to talk. (It often called itself: Kate.) It could quote entire sermons of two preachers, in their voice, which were given at the same time in different churches. The spirit said that she was at each of the churches during the same time. It could tell what people were doing, saying, and thinking in England. It gave accurate weather predictions as to when it would rain, snow, or frost. It quoted the Bible chapter by chapter and attended church regularly. It knew if a person went to sleep in church. It sang beautiful songs in church-songs never heard before. It told if a man came home drunk and beat his children, or scolded his wife, such that the entire community became a model community. It called a man who prayed in church, "Old Sugar-Mouth." It brought apples, oranges, and rare delicacies from the West Indies. Speaking of itself, it said that it was from everywhere: heaven, hell, the earth, the air, in houses, any place at any time, that it had been created millions of years ago. This spirit appeared to hate black people. Upon entering a house where a black person was hidden, it immediately told him or her to leave. But it would send help to needy neighbors. General Jackson, camped 12 miles away, came with a group to see this for himself. The spirit beat up one of his men and said it would whip another the next night. The men did not tarry very long. This witch swore that she would kill John Bell. He died on December 20, 1820 from a mysterious illness. She sang drunkenly at his funeral. She announced that she would to be leaving in 1821 but would return in seven years. Documented accounts indicate she returned in 1828. A cave remains on the old Bell farm today. Visitors have reported being touched, seeing and hearing sounds, etc. One boy had a cap snatched from his head and deposited on a ledge 30 feet above. The cave is privately owned and at last report, it was open seven days a week from May to November until 6:00 p.m. Phone for information was 615-696-3055. (Area code may have changed.)

WOLVES - It was believed that the noise from the huge forge hammers in Cades Cove frightened the wolves never to be seen again. This was a very sad day for the Indians who revered the wolf as a watch dog. They would never kill one if they could avoid it.

WOOD - During very early days a cord of wood sold for 35 to 65 cents each.

WORKHOUSE - Early jails were called "workhouses" because the prisoners had to do road maintenance. Later when the inmates did little or no outside work they became known as jails or prisons.

WOUND - Open wounds, disinfect with propolis, sugar or kerosene.

WRINKLES - (see face lifts and facials.) Today we have laser, facelifts, and lots of great devices to try to eliminate wrinkles. In the good-old-days women once ironed their wrinkles. They took big spoons and little spoons and very hot and very cold mugs of water. Heating a spoon in the hot water, they held it against the crease or wrinkle. This treatment was followed by holding a cold spoon against the same wrinkle. Don't say we didn't try! (2) Apply beaten egg whites or oatmeal paste to the wrinkles.

X

X - HIS MARK - I am age 81 and have seen only one person who signed his name with an "X." He touched the pen while someone else wrote the "X" and his name, saying that it was his mark. I understand that two people must sign as witnesses to this.

Y

YARN BALLS - Every string was saved, no matter how small. It was wound into a ball. The balls were given to the children at Christmas time.

Z

Well, I do declare, it was so good of you to stop, sit a spell, and share my reminiscing of the early life and times of Smoky Mountain people. The history we learn in school is a record of great deeds by great men and women. Often it is embellished, sometimes far from the truth, just to make the stories sound good. The story of a people who quietly sacrificed to build a country has been neglected. The story of my family and Smoky Mountain people is a story which goes far beyond the walls of my home, family, and ancestors. From the very crude beginning we find the heroes, the villains, the saints, and the sinners. Putting these stories and observations in some kind of order has made me realize how much Smoky Mountain people deserve more recognition. Rather than the stereotypes and misconceptions which have for decades influenced unfavorable opinions of our people, they deserve recognition as a proud and industrious people.

I have been greatly blessed to live in a time and an environment that allowed me to witness the pioneer spirit and life style, yet live long enough to enjoy the very modern conveniences that make life and work so much easier. I have witnessed the evolution from horse and buggy to the computer age. This a quantum leap from so very primitive to so very advanced. All the years of my life have been full, good years filled with generous, warm-hearted friends. We have shared laughter and tears in one of nature's most beautiful spots. Into our hands has been placed a priceless heritage. We do not belong to the past; the past belongs to us. Like a valued possession, this is my bequest to each of you, each of my descendants. I hope you have enjoyed this journey back in time. Never again will we crank the old telephone, ask the operator for 431-J to call home or take our living room rug outside to whack it with a carpet beater. I am now in the twilight of my life, the great adventure of my death cannot be too far off. I am looking forward with great curiosity and anticipation to seeing all the loved ones gone before. I expect that reunion to be an unspeakably happy reunion. I will look in on you from time to time. I promise!

I hope I've made you laugh, brought a tear, prompted a prayer, warmed your heart, kindled a childhood memory, or in some way touched your soul. My reward is knowing that I'm leaving you with a ray of hope and a sprinkle of joy.

This project began with the desire to communicate with my friends and family. It has grown into a desire to compile a comprehensive study of Smoky Mountain life. If readers have comments or additions, please mail them to me at: Bonnie Trentham Myers, 301 Broadway Towers, Maryville, Tennessee, 37801 or E-mail them to me at   or to my daughter at

GENEALOGY AND BRIEF TRENTHAM HISTORY

IDENTIFICATION OF FAMILY MEMBERS
Compiled by Bonnie Trentham Myers
E-mail: bltrentham@AOL.com

Abbreviations: b=born, d=died, s=son, dtr=daughter, w=wife, m=married, ch=children. Birth/death date=(0000-0000) wd=wedding date.

WILLIAM THOMAS TRENTHAM - (1793-1848) My great-grandfather, son of Robert William Trentham and Lucinda Trentham Bugg.

ROBERT LEE TRENTHAM - (1833-1908) My grandfather, son of William Thomas and Easter Ogle Bohanan Trentham.

NOAH TRENTHAM - Born 11-2-1867, died Sept. 30, 1949. My father. m. 1st. - Sophie Ogle. Their ch: (1) Orlie, (2) Lillie, (3) Mack, (4) Willie and (5) Munsey.
   (1) ORLIE born 1-29-92, died 6-26-1976. m. Bessie McCarter, Their children: (A) Eugene and (B) Ralph.
      (A) Eugene b._____ died_____ m._Dorothy_____
      (B) Ralph b.6-14-18, died 1968. m. LaVerna Rose Chismar b: 1-27- 20 wd 1-20-40.   Their children: Janet and Brian
      Janet b 1-21-61_____   Brian b. 3-4-44_ m_ Maria Milena Elizdndo b 10-24-69   wd 9-10-89 Dtr: Emila La Verna b 4-1-92
      Orlie m2nd - Verna Tennent. Orlie m3rd - Katherine Caudel.b.4-25-02,d 3- 26-73 wd 7-10-37 Their Ch: (A) Bruce and (B) Robert. (Bob)
      (A) Bruce b 12-05-39_m_Charlotte Starkey b 11-15-39 wd_9-23-61
      Ch: (1) Alan (2) Brent
         (1) Alan b 3-4-63 m Cameron Cooke b 4-19-? wd8-29-86

Ch: Teresa Nichole b 10-27-94   Tyson Alexander b2-23-99
(2) Brent b 9-17-66 m Barbara Layne b 8-17-
66 Wd 10-27-90
Ch: Sydney b 12-29-93 Allison b 2-10-97

(B) Bob b. 4-25-44 m Brenda King b_____wd_____
Ch: Scott b:4-24-?? m Lisa b_____wd_____
Ch:Jordon, Scarlet, & Noah
Jordon b_____m_____b_____wd____
Scarlet b_____m_____b_____wd____
Noah b_____m_____b_____wd____

Orlie m. 4th Inez Eades on Jan. 30, 1974 the day after his 82nd birthday.
Orlie & Katherine are buried in Smoky Mountain Memorial Gardens Pigeon Forge, Tennessee.

Mack, Munsey and Dowe Trentham are buried in Highland South, Memorial Gardens located along side Chapman Highway at entrance to Valley Grove Baptist Church. At entrance to cemetery keep extreme left, count to the number 5 lamppost. Starting at the 5th lamppost, going straight toward Chapmans highway, count to approximately 27 yards.
Lillie and Willie buried in White Oak Flats Cemetery, downtown Gatlinburg,

LILLIE (3-4-1894 - 1-5-1954) m. Ellis Watson, b 11-9-1888 died 1970. wd 3-24-1910
Lillie's children:
(1) Olin, (2) Clell (3) Charles (4) Hugh.
(1) OLIN (4-27-12 - 1-14-88) m.Mayme Stogner b12-30-10 wd 11-29-31
ch:(A)Mary Elizabeth (B) Christine. (A)Mary Elizabeth b.7-18-35 m_____Fox b___ Adopted dtr: Susan Fox b 4-28-67
(B) Christene_b_6-27-40_m Charles Franklin Perry, Jr. b 8-14-37 wd_____

Ch:1.Candice Sue 2.Chas Franklin,III   3.Casandra Ann,4. Christopher Olin

   1. Candice b 10-3-61 m Gary McCarter b___wd____

   Ch: A. Briana Leigh, B. Heather Lindsey

         A. Briana b 4-9-79 m___ b____ wd___

         B.Heather b 12-8-83 m_____ b____ wd_

   Candice m2 James Dale b_____ wd___

   Ch: 1. Casandra Ann,Twins:2.Victoria Elizabeth,3.Angelina Christine

        1.Casandra b 2-13-88 mStephen Reuben

         Ch: David Allen b_____

        2. Victoria b 6-17-89m_____ b___ wd___

        3. Angelena b 6-17-89 m_____ b___ wd___

 2. Charles Franklin,IIIb_____ m_____ b___ wd

        3. Casandra b____ m_____ b____ wd_____

        4. Christopher Olin b___ m_____ b___ wd____

 (2) CLELL DAVID b12-24-17 m Beulah Betty Ogle b 5-5-16 wd   8-7-36

   Ch: (A) Jack Ellis, (B) Dorothy Lee (C) Brenda Sue.

   (A) Jack b 5-15-37 m Annette Beck b_____ wd_____

   Ch: 1. Anthony Lee 2. Jeanie Lynn

   1.Anthony Lee b 10-13-57   2. Jeanie b 10-17-60 m Dwight Johnson Burnett b_____ Wd 10-20-84

       Ch: Audrey Liane b 5-10-88

   (A)Jack m2nd Martha Davis Smith b_____wd_____

   (B)Dorothy b5-14-39 m Lloyd M. Middleton b 7-3-31

     Wd 4-3-65

  Ch: Michael Lloyd b 4-3-67 Curtis Lee b 9-17-68

 (C) Brenda b 5-3-41 n Jack Stanley McGaha b____ wd 6-13-58

    Ch: 1. Sherry Leigh, 2. Kirk Randall

      1. Sherry b 9-5-60 m Mark Andrew Shine b 12-3-60 Wd 10-21-89 Ch: Joshua Mark b 7-12-81

        Codi Marie b 8-30-91

     2. Kirk b 11-15-61 m Ronda Neely b_____wd____

      Ch: Brittany Lin b 12-8-87

Kirk m2nd Melissa Jackson b_____wd 1-29-93
Ch: Megan Deanna b 9-3-93
Brenda m2nd Roy Clarence Whaley b 5-9-40 wd 2-   23-80

(3) CHARLES (11-5-1919 - 6-2-1921)

(4)NOAH HUGH - b5-10-32 m1 Iva Kear 12-31-35 - 9-1998.
Ch: 1. Diane, 2.Michael. ch:(1)Diane b 5-3-1950 mDanny
Oakley b2-4-48   wd 7-22-70   Ch: (A) Alysia (B) Jason
       (A) Alysia b 1-22-72 ml _____Smith,
       Ch: Colby Smith b. 2-3-93   Alysia
       m2 Hank Brackens
     (B)Jason b 6-21-73   No children
     (2)Michael b 3-6-52 ml Vivian Evora b__wd 5-6-72
     Ch: Brandon
     Michael m2 Lisa b_____wd 4-97
Noah Hugh m2nd Janet Whaley b7-10-35 died 6-_-78   Wd
5-2-54
 Ch: 1.Pamela 2. David 3. Nathan 4. Mark
  1, Pamela b9-26-56 m Donald Parz b 6-4-2_, wd 5-8-73
    Ch: A. Jeremiah Jo b 11-25-73
      B. Joshua b 12-13-77
  2. David b 5-31-58 ml Frances b_____d_____wd_____
David m2 Joan Worsham b_____wd 11-22-87
  3. Nathan b 1-28-60 ml Constance Miles b____wd 4-80
    Ch:A.Zebulon Hugh B. Benjamin Nathan
    A. Zebulon Hugh b 10-19-84
    B. Benjamin Nathan b 10-1-87
    Nathan m2 Teresa Dillingham b 4-5-60 wd 11-23-96
  4,Mark b 5-19-65 ml Terri Lambert b____ wd 3-4-87
    Ch:(A) Kain Ellis (B) Sarah Jeanette
    (A) Kain Ellis b 9-3-87
    (B) Sarah Jeanette b 10-5-88
Noah Hugh m3rd Evelyn Marie Lewelling b 4-22-37   wd 1-20-79

MACK (1-2-1899 - 9-07-76) m Bess Ownby, deceased. Their son: Dowe Wesley (4-20-22 - 3-12-92)

WILLIE b 6-30-01 d 7-31-41 buried *White Oak Flats Cemetery m LENORA Oakley b 9-18-08, d 1-07-94. Ch:(A) Hazel Evelean (B) Mary Evelyn (C) Ralph
(A) Hazel Evelean b 4-19-24, d 4-19-24 buried Trentham Cemetery Great Smoky Mt. National Park
(B) Mary b 2-21-28, m James Albert Christopher b 6-7-23
    m 12-28-42 Ch (1) Darrell Dennis (2) Linda Gail.
    (1) Dennis b 10-14-44, m 1st Linda Faye Perkins, b 11-11-44. wd 12-24-63
ch: Darrell Dennis,Jr b 2-25-65, Kenneth Anthony   b 1-23-70
    2nd m Charlotte Robins, b June 25, ??
    (2) Linda Gail b ll-24-51 m. Bill Carroll, b 12-11-_
        Linda's son:_Brian Christopher b 7-01-70.
    (2) Ralph b 5-6-25 d 11-21-50
*White Oaks Flats cemetery is located on the hillside overlooking mid-down-town Gatlinburg, Tennessee. Where baskins creek joins the main road,(Hwy 441) near Ogle mall.

MUNSEY (10-12-1905 - 10-5-75) m 1st Minnie Cross. Their son: Donald Dodson b_?_____died_Young child.
m2nd Cleo Ogle. m3rd Iva Minge, m4th Glenna Farmer.

MARY JANE OGLE CARR (10-5-1886 - 6-7-66) m1st Amos Carr (1884-1912) ch: (A) Ollie, (B) Mayme and (C) Wesley. (Mary Jane and all three children married Trenthams)
    (A) Ollie (7-11-05 - 11-24-74) m Wilson Trentham
        (5-7-1901 - 2-13-70) wd 10-21-20
    Ch: A. Dott, B. Blanche C. Charles
        (A) Dott (1-20-22 - 11-17-42) Buried National Cemetery, Knoxville, Tennessee.
    (B) Blanche b 1-7-25 m Sam Harbin b 3-21-??
        Ch: 1. Eddie 2. Dawn
        1. Eddie b 7-25-57 m Bobbie maples b___wd___
    CH: Charles b 8-16-88

2. Dawn b 1-22-64 m Tommy Brackens b____wd___
   Ch: Misty b 8-14-80 m_____wd_____
C. Charles (9-3-27 - 2-24-63) m Mary Ogle
  b 5-14-28 Wd 8-14-47
ch: 1.Clell 2.Ella 3.Barbara 4.Charles Eben 5.Rosemary
   1. Clell b 4-5-49 m. Dr.Shirley Throop b 7-20-50
    wd 11-28-68
  Ch: A.Jonathan Stewart B. Matthew Ryan
  A. Jonathan b 4-5-74 m_____b_____wd___
  B. Matthew b 3-5-79 m_____b_____wd___
2. Ella b5-4-53 m Orwin Campbell b____wd 4-21-90
  Ch: Cynthia Dawn b 6-23-70 m Ervin Ogle b___wd___
   (3) Barbara b 12-1-56 m Wallace Wallin b2-22-54 wd___
Ch:1.Todd Keith 2. Angie Sue 3.Rodney Curtis
  4.Melissa Jane 5. Jeannie Marie
  1. Todd b 9-12-73 mTara Samantha Dubberly b__wd_
2. Angie (2-6-75 - 2-6-75)
  3. Rodney b 4-2-76
  4. Melissa b 2-21-78 m David Johnson b____wd__
  5. Jeannie b 7-31-82 m Christopher Black b__wd__
(4) Charles Eben b 2-13-60 m Monica Rushing b 5-8-62
   Wd 10-1-85
  Ch: 1. Caleb Edward b6-18-89
   2. Mary Lindsey b 2-7-92
(5) Rosemary b 1-30-63 m Steve Radd b_____wd____
  Ch: Tosha Rose b 6-18-80 m_____b_____wd___

MAYME (6-14-07 - 7-12-2000)
  m Carl Ray Trentham (5-6-07 - 3-30-65) wd 9-2-22
Ch: (1) Anna Gene (2) Rosa Nell (3) Carl Clarence (4) Betty
Ruth,(5) Mary Jane (6) Hugh Ellis (7) Don Wesley (8) Danny
Joe (9) Eva Mae (10) David Ray (11) Bonnie Lynn (12) Stella
Marie (13) Peggy Ann.
  (1) Anna Gene b & d 12-30-24. Buried Trentham Cemetery -
Park
  (2) Rosa Nell (1-26-26 - 2-13-2000) Dtr Drucilla b 8-9-49
   m John Woodby b 10-31-47 wd 11-22-68
  (3) Carl Clarence (Buck) (5-9-28 - 12-11-64)

m 1st   Leva Moore b 5-21-52.
Ch: (A) Helen Marie
    (B) Thelma Jean
(A) Helen Marie b 5-5-53
Ch: Eric b_____m_____b_____wd____
    Nathan b_____m_____b_____wd_____
(B) Thelma Jean b 1-10-55 m____b_____wd_____
    Ch: 1. Belinda b_____m Richard_b_____wd
    2. Richard Mason b_____
(4) Betty Ruth (8-3-30 - 5-3-43)
(5) Mary Jane (10-19-32 - 4-6-95)m Henry Neely
    b 4-26-32 wd 10-29-49
Ch:(A) Kenneth (B) Patsy Lynn (C) Tony (D)Larry
(A)Kenneth b 9-21-53m Patricia Kimbrough
    (10-8-42 - 1-18-88)
    Ch:Patrick b7-9-74 mKristin Ch:Keegan b 4-8-99
    (A) m2nd Tracey Maro Womac b9-10-64 wd_6-21-88
    Ch:1.Derrick Lee, 2. Dylan Lynn,
        3. Devan Lawrence
    1. Derrick b 1-21-89 m_____b_____wd_____
    2. Dylan b 11-11-90 m____b_____wd_____
    3. Devon b 4-22-94 m____b_____wd_____
    (B) Patsy Lynn b 2-26-51 m____b_____wd_____
    Ch: Tanner b 3-21-84_m_____wd____
(C) Tony b 7-13-60 m Pam Tinsley b____wd_____
    Ch:1.Courtney Tashina b 5-14-86
    2.Sommer Cheyenne b 7-22-91
    Tony m2nd Kim Davis b 5-2-66 wd 8-7-93
    (D) Larry b 9-10-62_m Diane Dodson b_____wd____
    Ch:__None_____
(6) Hugh Ellis (3-15-34 - 8-30- 57)
(7) Don Wesley (4-14-36 - 7-27-36)
(8) Danny Joe b3-21-38 m1st Arlene Kellog
    b12-12-80 wd6-11-57.
    Ch:(A) Billy Joe, (B) Debbie, (C) Linda,
    (D)Curtis
    (A)Billy Joe b8-12-58 mLori Steleb 4-22-62
    wd 12-12-80

Ch: Tate b 2-4-98
(B) Debbie b 11-5-62 mBilly Case b_____
   wd6-20-87
Ch: 1.Chelsie b 3-16-91m 2. Dallas b 12-2-93
(C) Linda b5-26-64 mRalph Whitted b___wd 6-2-88
   Ch:1. Courtney b 5-8-92 2. Brandy b_____
(D) Curtis b8-27-66
       mTrisha Neaderour b4-24-73 wd6-1-93
   Ch: Bryan Alexnder b 3-11-99
Danny
   m2nd Barbara Farmer b 12-03-43 wd 10-06-76
   (9) Eva Mae b 3-15-40
        m   Gordon Wayne Dyer b___wd 5-6-62
   Ch: (A) Lisa Michelle (B) Eddy DeWayne
   (A) Lisa Michelle b 12-11-65
        m Tom Tortomas b_____wd_____
   (B) Eddy Dwayne b 12-28-69
        m_____b_____wd_____
10) David Ray b 11-20-41
   m Martha Black b_____wd____
   Ch: 1. Sherry 2.Arthur
      1. Sherry b 3-17-69 m Doug Wilson b_____wd____
         Ch: Cassie 5-5-92, Matthew b 5-14-95
      2. Arthur b4-3-76 m Miranda Nelms
      b 12-28-80 wd10-22-94
         Ch:(1) Laray b 5-18-95 (2) Mason b 9-16-98
11) Bonnie Lynn (11-15-43 - 4-27-58)
12) Stella Marie b 9-1-45
   m Bobby Dean Vaughn b_____wd____
   Ch: (A) Robbie Dean (B) Karen
   (A) Robbie Dean b 4-18-66
        m Tammy Dodson b_____wd___
      ch: 1.Brittney b_____ 2.Steve_____
      1. Brittney b_____m_____wd
      2, Steve b_____m_____wd_____
   (B) Karen b 10-1-69
      m Mark Hamilton b_____wd____

Ch: Heather
    b_____m_____wd_____ _
13) Peggy Ann (11-20-48 - 6-17-77)

3. WESLEY CARR b 12-7-09
    m Reba Sophia Trentham b 5-01-ll   wd 6-29-29.
        Ch: (A) Betty June (B) James Wesley, Jr
        (C) Carol Ann
    (A) Betty June b 10-17-32
        m Joseph L. Howell b 8-15-30 wd 11-14-53.
        ch: (1) Martha Ann, (2) Mark Joseph
        (1) Martha Ann b 4-26-57
            m Marc Kevin Runyan b 4-02-55 wd 11-28-81.
            Ch: Marc Kevin, Jr, b 11-7-84
            Matthew Joseph b 11-19-89
        (2) Mark Joseph b 6-14-60
            m1st Rebecca N.Biggs b 12-12-58 wd 11-24-84.
            Ch: Brittney Nicole b 10-6-1986
                Steven Lawrence b 2-4-90
                Nathan David b 3-22-81 to Rebecca Biggs and Paul
                Bowers was adopted by Mark after his marriage to
        (2) Mark
            m2nd Pamela Woods (2-20-68 - ll-7-99), wd 2-14-92
            Ch: Eric Joseph b 10-23-1996
                Rebecca. Mark and Rebecca divorced in Feb. 1991.
    (B) James Wesley Carr, Jr., b 10-09-39
        m Norma Jean Lewis b 12-14-39, wd 8-03-57
        Ch: 1. James Kenneth, 2. Deborah Kay, 3. Michael Lee
        (1) James Kenneth b:6-17-58 m Imojean Paxton b:11-7-52
            wd: 10-21-77. Ch: James Kevin b: 8-17-81
        (2) Deborah Kay b:6-15-65
        (3) Michael Lee b:9-13-68
            m April Marie Foster b 6-16-68
            Ch: Kerstin Taylor Carr b 6-9-92
                Kendall Elizabeth Carr b 5-3-2000
    (C) Carol Ann b: 6-10-50
        m1st Joe Wesley Stofel. Died 1-3-78
        m2nd Rodger A.Bolling b 1-9-45 wd 10-26-78 Ch: none

wd: 10-26-78

MARY JANE OGLE CARR TRENTHAM (10-05-86 - 6-7-66)
    m Noah Trentham   (11-02-67 - 9-30-49) wd 2-5-1914.
  Ch: (A) Johnnie Kate (B) Gladys Janet (C) Noah Harmon
  (D) Bonnie Lynn (me) (E) Samuel Ephraim.
(A) KATE b. 10-15-14 m James Hulett Stogner b 12-17-14
  wd 6-26-37. Ch: (1) James Noah, (2)Dorothy Jean, (3) Doris
  Ann (4) Ronald (5) Esta Ruth.
  (1) James b 12-02-38 m Wanda Price b_wd_____
    Ch:_Alan Douglas b 6-30-70   (2)
Dorothy b 8-5-43 m Sidney Lawson b10-27-43 wd5-31-63
    Ch: Sharon Denise b_4-14-64 m James Martin Collier III
b_____wd 4-10-84
Stacy Gwen b 1-28-67 mEric Clifton Brewer b___wd5-21-94
(3(Doris b 8-16-47 m Roger WM.Bryant b 11-2-43 wd 7-10-
71
(4) Ronald b_8-16-44_m Darlene Shultz b 5-19-46 wd 5-27-66
Ch:Dwyne Patrick b_3-5-67 m_____b_____wd___
    Dawn Bryan b 9-22-72
m_____b_____wd____
  (5) Esta Ruth b 4-8-50 m Ben Walker Franklin(5-26-43 -)
    Wd 1-1-70 Ch: Michelle Lea b. 7-17-72
    m2nd Larry Campbell b 11-29-46 wd 10-25-97

(B) GLADYS b 1-08-17 m Samuel Haskew Russell (2-26-20 -
2-10-96)   wd_10-11-41
  Ch: (1) Sandra Sue   (2) Terry Michael
  (1) Sandra Sue b 1-07-48
    m Benny P'Pool b11-20-45 wd5-17-80
  (2) Terry Michael b 3-03-50
    m Linda Eileen Flynn b 3-11-51 wd 6-11-71
    Ch: Amy Nichole b 4-23-74, Kevin Michael b 6-17-77
    Brent Matthew b 7-9-89
C) HARMON b 3-4-19 d 7-14-90 m Lena Whaley b 9-22-18 d
11-20-80   wd 7-22-39. Ch: (A) Shirley Ann (B) David
Harmon

(A) Shirley Ann b 4-28-42 m Vance Horne b10-16-37 wd 1-20-60   Their son: Ray Vance b4-27-62
(B) David Harmon b 8-23-44 m Frances Hardiman b 3-4-45

(D) BONNIE b. 12-01-21 m Ray T. Myers (6-13-20 - 7-27-76)
        wd 9-27-41
    Ch: (A) Donald Trent (B) Lynda Raye (C) Glenn Leland
    (A) Donald Trent (11-5-42 - 5-28-98)   m 1st Billie Martin b
7-29-46 wd__
        Ch: (1) Andrea Lynn (2) Jennifer Lea (3) Diana Lorraine
        Ch: (1) Andrea Lynn b 2-1-68 m Stan Hill b 1-1-66 wd
11-24-93. Ch: Chynna Mykel Knight b 10-20-2000
            (2) Jennifer Lea b 10-1-69 m Gregory Qualls
                b 12-9-61 wd 5-1-93 Ch: Gabriel Orion b 7-12-96,
Jacob Landon b 3-27-98.
            (3) Diana Lorrine b: 11-05-79 m Jonathan Thompson
b Jan 19, 1976, wd 6-1-2002
        Donald Trent m 2nd Donna Barringer b:10-27-____
    (B) Lynda Raye b 1-05-49 m Edwin Maynard Boyer b 4-8-43
        wd 7-21-73, Son: Andrew Ray Boyer b 8-13-80
    (C) Glenn Leland b 10-26-50 m Sharon Ann Angel 9-10-56
wd 9-18-76   Ch: (1) Amanda Raye (2 & 3)
Twins: Aaron Trent & Eric Glenn, (4) Emily Angel.
        (1) Amanda Raye b 4-3-79
        (2) Aaron Trent b 11-5-81
        (3) Eric Glenn b 11-5-81
        (4) Emily Angel b 10-24-86

E.. Samuel Ephraim Trentham b.9-24-23
    m 1 Edith Mae Bradley b 4-14-25 wd –
Ch 1. Jack Dale Trentham Overstreet b 2-25-44
    m Kathleen Runyan b 3-06-48 wd 1-15-72
        Ch: 1.Ryan Matthew
            2. Anna Mae
            1. Ryan Matthew Overstreet b 8-20-72
             m Cindy Anderson
        Ch: 2, Anna Mae b 4-28-75

m Joseph Lee Harrison b 8-18-74 wd 5-27-95

Ch Josie Mae b 1-21-98

Sam m2: Sarah Ruby Stogner (b.12-10-17 wd 1 Sep 1946)

Ch: 1.Lillian Lenora

2. Michael Samuel

3. Patricia

1. Lillian Lenora Trentham b.6-9-47

m Howard Earl Lancaster b 10-9-42, wd 6-25-76

Ch:. Lara Liana Lancaster b.10-29-85

2. Michael Samuel Trentham b 4-26-50

m1 Wanda Kay Davis b.6-16-51 wd 1-14-69

m2 Nancy June Smith b.4-2-53 wd 5-.5-84

m3 Cynthia Ann Arnott b.10-9-57; wd 1-.8 -94)

3. Patricia Elaine Trentham b 5-31-53

m1 Leonard Alan Dalton b.9-22-52 wd 4-21-72

m2 Tom Henry Carver b 7-2-50; wd.6-8-84 Ch Stacie
Michelle b.9-28-84

Tom's Ch: 1. Tina Marie 2. Cindy Ann

. Tina Marie b 9-9-69 m
Christopher Allen Collins b 1-20-70 wd-1-8-91

Ch 1. Kaitlyn Christina Rose 2. Olivia Grace

1, Kaitlyn b 5-27-96

2, Olivia b 4-28-2000

2. Cindy Ann b 4-20-72 m Brett Anthony L,

Norrod b 1-9-71   wd 4-28-95

Ch: 1. Brittany Rhea b 3-20-97

2. Fletcher Thomas b 2-23-99